Vocabulary for the College-Bound Student

Books by Harold Levine

English Alive
English: A Comprehensive Course
Comprehensive English Review Text
The Joy of Vocabulary
Vocabulary for the College-Bound Student
Vocabulary for Enjoyment, Books 1, 2, and 3
Vocabulary for the High School Student, Books A and B
Vocabulary for the High School Student
Vocabulary and Composition Through Pleasurable Reading,
    Books I, II, III, IV, V, and VI

second edition

Vocabulary for the College-Bound Student

HAROLD LEVINE

Dedicated to serving

AMSCO

our nation's youth

When ordering this book, please specify:
either **R 262 P** or
VOCABULARY FOR THE COLLEGE-BOUND STUDENT, PAPERBACK

AMSCO SCHOOL PUBLICATIONS, INC.
315 Hudson Street / New York, N.Y. 10013

ISBN 0-87720-446-2

Printed in the United States of America

PREFACE

The primary aim of this book is to provide help—but help with understanding—for high school students seeking to enlarge their vocabularies, whether their goal is college admission, or a responsible position, or overall self-improvement.

A companion aim is to assist busy teachers of English interested in enriching instruction through direct teaching of vocabulary. The book provides vocabulary materials and learning procedures that have proved successful in the classroom.

Teachers know that as their students read more, they gradually expand their vocabularies. But they also know that such expansion is incidental or, more appropriately, accidental, unless teachers deliberately provide for the learning of specific words. There is therefore strong reason for teachers to supplement reading as a means of vocabulary growth by mounting direct attacks upon vocabulary. This volume provides many of the necessary resources and procedures.

Learning New Words From the Context (Chapter II) presents numerous short passages in which a possibly unfamiliar word can be defined with the help of clues in the context. By teaching students how to interpret such clues, this chapter provides them with a lifelong tool for vocabulary growth, *and at the same time it makes them better readers.*

In this chapter and generally throughout the book, the pronunciation, part of speech, and definition of lesson words are clearly indicated, and a helpful illustrative sentence is furnished to reinforce the definition.

Building Vocabulary Through Central Ideas (Chapter III) involves students in the study of twenty-five groups of related words. In the "joy" group they will learn words like *convivial, elated,* and *gala;* and in the "sadness" group *chagrin, lamentable, pathos,* etc.

Words Derived From Greek (Chapter IV) teaches twenty-five groups of words, each derived from an ancient Greek root like PHIL, meaning "love," and MIS, meaning "hate"; or an ancient Greek prefix such as HYPER, meaning "over," and HYPO, meaning "under."

Words Derived From Latin (Chapter V) does the same with Latin-derived words, but on a much larger scale because of Latin's greater influence on English.

Words From Classical Mythology and History (Chapter VI) teaches words like *amazon, jovial,* and *mentor* from the myths of the Ancient Greeks and Romans, and *laconic, Lucullan,* and *thespian* from the history of these peoples.

French Words in English (Chapter VII) teaches groups of useful words adopted from French. The "arts" group presents words like *avant-garde, encore,* and *repertoire,* and the "dress" group *chemise, corsage, toupee,* etc.

Italian Words in English (Chapter VIII) and *Spanish Words in English* (Chapter IX) do the same with loanwords from Italian and Spanish.

Sample Vocabulary Questions in Pre-College Tests (Chapter X) discusses and analyzes the officially released sample vocabulary questions for two widely administered pre-college examinations:

1. The Preliminary Scholastic Aptitude Test/National Merit Scholarship Qualifying Test (PSAT/NMSQT)
2. The Scholastic Aptitude Test (SAT)

Dictionary of Words Taught in This Text (Chapter XI) is provided for ease of reference and review.

Abundant illustrative sentences, varied exercises and drills, and cumulative reviews have been provided throughout this volume to enhance learning. Many of the exercises are patterned after the types of vocabulary questions encountered in college-admission tests.

Teachers may start with whatever chapter they wish, if they choose not to follow the author's organization. The directions have been kept simple so that, after motivation in class, students may proceed on their own. Periodic discussion of one or more groups of words from this text will provide enrichment in any grade of high school English. Since vocabulary growth is a gradual process, it is urged that this text be introduced as early as possible in the high school course. Teachers may also want to recommend this book to college-bound students studying by themselves to prepare for scholarship and college-admission tests.

Students should be encouraged to use their newly learned words whenever appropriate in their writing and classroom discussions. Only by actual use can they make them a part of their active vocabularies. They should also be helped in acquiring a good dictionary and in developing the habit of consulting that dictionary whenever they cannot define an unfamiliar word from the context.

Harold Levine

Acknowledgments

The author wishes to thank Anne M. Villalon (Mt. Greylock Regional High School, Williamstown, Massachusetts) for suggesting the idea for an additional vocabulary exercise, and both Norman Levine (City College of the City University of New York) and Robert T. Levine (North Carolina A&T State University) for their contributions as consultants and critics in the preparation of the revised edition.

CONTENTS

cHApTeR iii **BuildiNG VocAbulARy**
ThRouGh CeNTRAl IdEas

CHApter iv **Words Derived From Greek**

CHApter v **Words Derived From Latin**

chapter vi **Words From**
Classical Mythology and History

CHAPTER vii FRENCH WORDS IN ENGLISH

CHAPTER viii ITALIAN WORDS IN ENGLISH

CHAPTER ix Spanish Words in English

CHAPTER x Sample Vocabulary Questions in Pre-College Tests

CHAPTER xi Dictionary of Words Taught in This Text

Pronunciation Symbols

chapter i The Importance of Vocabulary to You

Vocabulary and thinking

Words stand for ideas. Words are the tools of thought. If your word power is limited, you are necessarily a limited thinker, since you can neither receive ideas nor communicate with others except within the confines of your inadequate vocabulary. Unless you broaden your vocabulary, you will find it difficult to do the thinking that success in life often demands.

Vocabulary and college admission

Quite properly, college admissions officers will be interested in the extent of your vocabulary. Research has established a close correlation between vocabulary and intelligence. A good vocabulary, therefore, will identify you as a student of superior mental ability. It will suggest, too, that you have done wide reading, since reading is the principal way of developing a good vocabulary. In the college entrance and scholarship tests you are likely to take, you will find vocabulary a major ingredient.

Vocabulary growth through reading

Persons who read widely gradually build up extensive vocabularies, especially if they have a curiosity about words. This curiosity, compelling them to regard every unfamiliar word as a breakdown in communication between author and reader, sends them thumbing through the dictionary. Should you, too, develop such word curiosity, you will be assured a lifetime of vocabulary growth.

Though reading is the basic means of vocabulary growth, it is a relatively slow means. For the college-bound student who has not yet achieved a superior vocabulary, reading needs to be supplemented by a direct attack that will yield comparatively rapid growth—and that is the purpose of this book.

Vocabulary growth through this book

This book will involve you in a five-pronged attack on vocabulary.

Attack #1: Learning New Words From the Context

Often, we can discover the meaning of an unfamiliar word from its *context*—the other words with which it is used. Note, for example, how we can determine the meaning of *parsimonious* in the following sentence:

> People vary in their tipping habits from the very generous to the very *parsimonious*.

Obviously, from the above context, *parsimonious* is the opposite of *generous; parsimonious* means "stingy."

Chapter II will teach you the various clues for learning the meaning of a possibly unfamiliar word, like *parsimonious*, from its context. As you learn to use these clues, you will be broadening your vocabulary and—what is even more important—becoming a more skillful reader.

Attack #2: Learning Vocabulary in Groups of Related Words

Vocabulary growth that evolves from a day's reading has one serious disadvantage: it is poorly organized. The new words you encounter as you read usually bear little relationship to one another. This, of course, does not mean that you should think any the less of reading as a means of vocabulary building. It does, however, suggest that you may achieve relatively rapid vocabulary growth by studying *groups of related words*.

In the "central-ideas" chapter you will find twenty-five groups of related words. Each group presents words revolving about one idea—*joy, sadness, flattery, age, relatives, reasoning,* etc. The new words are further explained in hundreds of illustrative sentences that have one feature in common: they present new vocabulary in such context as will make the meaning obvious and easy to remember.

Attack #3: Learning Vocabulary Derived From Greek and Latin

The principle of the lever has enabled humans, using relatively little effort, to do a great amount of work. You can apply the same principle to learning vocabulary. If you study certain productive Greek and Latin prefixes and roots, you can gain word leverage. Each prefix or root adequately understood will help you learn the meanings of the many English words it has produced. In the Greek and Latin chapters, you will meet important prefixes and roots, each with numerous English offspring.

Rounding out the attack on Greek and Latin is a briefer chapter which will teach you useful English words derived from classical (Latin and Greek) mythology and history.

Attack #4: Learning Vocabulary Borrowed From French, Italian, and Spanish

Since English has borrowed heavily from French, you are sure to encounter adopted French words in books, newspapers, and magazines. Such words are considered a part of our English vocabulary and are often key words in the passages in which they occur. Not to know the meanings of common French borrowings is therefore a serious vocabulary deficiency.

The French chapter presents more than one hundred twenty commonly used loanwords, divided into small, easy-to-learn groups. To give you confidence in your understanding of each word, care has been taken to make the definitions and illustrative sentences as helpful as possible. You will find similar treatment in the briefer chapters on important Italian and Spanish loanwords.

Attack #5: Learning to Form Derivatives

Suppose you have just learned a new word—*fallible*, meaning "liable to be mistaken." If you do not know how to form derivatives, all you have added to your vocabulary is *fallible*—just one word.

But if you know how to form derivatives, you have learned not one but several new words. You have learned *fallible* and *infallible; fallibly* and *infallibly; fallibility* and *infallibility*, etc.

Chapter X will teach you how to form and spell derivatives so that you may know how to add many new words to your vocabulary whenever you learn one new word.

"Exercising" new vocabulary

Muscular exercise is essential during your years of physical growth. Vocabulary exercise, too, is essential in your periods of word growth.

To learn new words effectively, you must put them to use early and often. The challenging drills and tests in this book will give you abundant opportunities for varied vocabulary exercise. But you should do more on your own.

In your reading and listening experiences, be conscious of vocabulary. In your speaking and writing, take the initiative on suitable occasions to use new vocabulary. Such follow-up is a *must* if you are to make new words securely yours.

CHAPTER ii LEARNING NEW Words FROM THE CONTEXT

What is the context?

Most of the time, a word is used not by itself but with other words. These other words are its **context.** The meaning of a word is often found in its context—the other words with which it is used.

Suppose, for example, we were asked for the meaning of *strike.* We would not be able to give a definite answer because *strike*, as presented to us, is all by itself; it has no context.

But if we were asked to define *strike* in one of the following sentences, we would have no trouble:

1. *Strike* three! You're out!

    (*Strike* means "a ball pitched over the plate between a batter's knees and shoulders.")

2. There were no milk deliveries because of a *strike.*

    (*Strike* means "a labor dispute.")

3. He made a fist as if to *strike* me.

    (*Strike* means "hit.")

In each of the three sentences above, we are able to tell the meaning of *strike* from its **context**—the other words with which it is used.

How can the context help you expand your vocabulary?

Here is an amazing fact: the context can often give you the meaning not only of common words like *strike*, **but also of unfamiliar words, including words you have never before seen or heard!**

"What," asks a friend, "is *xenophobic?*"
"How should I know?" you say. "I never heard of it."
"It's in today's paper," says the friend. "Here it is."

You take the newspaper and read the sentence with the strange word: The new ruler is *xenophobic;* he has ordered all foreigners to leave the country.

"Aha!" you say. "Now I know: *xenophobic* means '*afraid or distrustful of foreigners.*' The context gives us the meaning."

Of course, you are right.

What can this chapter do for you?

This chapter will teach you how to use the context to get the meaning of unfamiliar words. Once you learn this skill, it will serve you for the rest of your life in two important ways: (1) it will keep enlarging your vocabulary; and (2) it will make you an ever-better reader.

1. Contexts With Contrasting Words

Pretest 1

Each passage below contains a word in italics. If you read the passage carefully, you will find a clue to the meaning of this word in an opposite word (**antonym**) or a contrasting idea.

For each passage, enter on your paper (*a*) the clue that led you to the meaning, and (*b*) the meaning itself. The answers for the first two passages have been given for you as examples.

Do not write in this book. Enter all answers on separate paper.

---

1. "That you, Joe?" he asked. . .
   "Who else could it be?" I *retorted*.
                                   —William R. Scott
   a. CLUE: *Retorted* is the opposite of "asked."
   b. MEANING: *Retorted* means "answered."

2. Some substances that cause cancer were once regarded as *non-carcinogenic*.
   a. CLUE: *Noncarcinogenic* is in contrast with "that cause cancer."
   b. MEANING: *Noncarcinogenic* means "not cancer-causing."

3. At this stage we cannot tell whether the new regulations will be to our advantage or *detriment*.

4. If his health *ameliorates*, he will stay on the job; if it becomes worse, he will have to resign.

5. In this firm the industrious are promoted and the *indolent* are encouraged to leave.

6. Parents, I suppose, were as much a problem *formerly* as they are today.—Gretchen Finletter

7. If you are going to get up before dawn tomorrow, you had better *retire* by 11 P.M.

8. Evidence presented at the trials of the two public officials showed that they had *subverted* the laws they were supposed to uphold.

9. Many who used to waste fuel are *conserving* it, now that it has become so much more expensive.

10. Only one lower wing and the landing gear had been completely demolished. The rest of the machine was virtually *intact*.—Edwin Way Teale

11. Those who volunteered to help turned out to be more of an *impediment* than an aid.

12. The Sullivan home, which used to stand on this corner, was erected in 1929 and *razed* in 1981.

13. Time has proved that Seward's purchase of Alaska from Russia in 1867 for $7,200,000 was wisdom, not *folly*.

14. People vary in their tipping habits from very generous to very *parsimonious*.

15. . . . a wave of rebelliousness ran through the countryside. Bulls which had always been *tractable* suddenly turned savage, sheep broke down hedges and devoured clover, cows kicked the pail over. . .—George Orwell

16. Children will readily tell how old they are, but older people are inclined to be *reticent* about their age.
17. The organization is trying to put on a show of *harmony*, though there is deep conflict within its ranks.
18. Those who heeded our advice did well; those who *ignored* it did not.
19. Her learner's permit is still in effect but mine is *invalid*.
20. There once was a society in Hawaii for the special purpose of introducing *exotic* birds. Today when you go to the islands, you see, instead of the exquisite native birds that greeted Captain Cook, mynas from India, cardinals from the United States or Brazil, doves from Asia. . .—Rachel Carson

Study Your New Words

You have just defined twenty new words simply by contrasting them with other words or expressions in the context. Now, to reinforce your grasp of these words and make them a part of your active vocabulary, study the following:

ameliorate /ə-'mēl-yə-ˌrāt/ *v:* become better; make better; improve—ANT **worsen**

We expected business conditions to *ameliorate*, but they grew worse.

conserve /kən-'sərv/ *v:* keep from waste, loss, or decay; save—ANT **waste**

One way to *conserve* water is to repair leaking faucets.

detriment /'de-trə-mənt/ *n:* injury, damage, or something that causes it; disadvantage—ANT **advantage**

Skipping meals can be a *detriment* to your health.

exotic /ig-'zät-ik/ *adj:* introduced from another country; foreign—ANT **native**

The chrysanthemum is an *exotic* plant; it was introduced from the Orient.

folly /'fäl-ē/ *n:* lack of good sense; foolish action or undertaking—ANT **wisdom**

It is *folly* to go on a long drive with a nearly empty gas tank.

formerly /'fȯr-mər-lē/ *adv:* in an earlier period; previously—ANT **now**

Our physics instructor was *formerly* an engineer.

harmony /'här-mə-nē/ *n:* peaceable or friendly relations; accord; agreement; tranquillity—ANT **conflict**

A boundary dispute is making it impossible for the neighbors to live in *harmony*.

ignore /ig-'nȯ(ə)r/ *v:* refuse to take notice of; disregard—ANT **heed**

You may get into a serious accident if you *ignore* a full-stop sign.

impediment /im-'ped-ə-mənt/ *n:* something that hinders or obstructs; hindrance; obstacle—ANT **aid**

A person's lack of education is often an *impediment* to advancement.

indolent /'in-də-lənt/ *adj:* disposed to avoid exertion; lazy; idle—ANT **industrious**

I was so comfortable in the reclining chair that I became *indolent* and did not feel like studying.

intact /in-'takt/ *adj:* untouched by anything that damages or diminishes; left complete or entire; uninjured—ANT **imperfect**

The tornado demolished the barn but left the farmhouse *intact*.

invalid /in-'val-əd/ *adj:* not valid (binding in law); having no force or effect; void—ANT **valid**

The courts have ruled that a forced confession is *invalid* and cannot be introduced as evidence.

noncarcinogenic /'nän-ˌkär-sə-nō-'jen-ik/ *adj:* not producing, or tending to produce, cancer—ANT **carcinogenic**

Cancer-causing ingredients must be replaced by others that are *noncarcinogenic*.

parsimonious /ˌpär-sə-'mō-nē-əs/ *adj:* unduly sparing in the spending of money; stingy—ANT **generous**

Some accuse the government of being too *generous* in funding road improvement and too *parsimonious* in financing education.

raze /'rāz/ *v:* destroy utterly by tearing down; demolish; level to the ground—ANT **erect**

The building was so badly damaged in the fire that it had to be *razed*.

reticent /ˈret-ə-sənt/ *adj:* inclined to be silent or secretive; uncommunicative—ANT **frank**

Have you noticed that people who boast about their successes are *reticent* about their failures?

retire /ri-ˈtī(ə)r/ *v*

(1) withdraw from active duty or business

Does your grandfather plan to *retire* at 65 or continue to work?

(2) go to bed—ANT **rise**

Please do not phone after 10 P.M. because my folks *retire* early.

retort /ri-ˈtȯrt/ *v:* answer; reply sharply or angrily—ANT **ask**

"Giving up?" she asked.
"Absolutely not!" I *retorted.*

subvert /səb-ˈvərt/ *v:* overturn or overthrow from the foundation; undermine—ANT **uphold**

We are *subverting* our fuel-conservation efforts when we heat rooms that are not occupied.

tractable /ˈtrak-tə-bəl/ *adj:* easily led, taught, or controlled; yielding; docile—ANT **unruly**

A child who misbehaves may be more *tractable* in a small group than in a large one.

Do not write in this book. Enter all answers on separate paper.

Apply What You Have Learned

EXERCISE 1.   Which choice, A or B, makes the sentence correct? Enter the *letter* of your answer on your paper.

1. When I heard the noise, I ignored it. I went __?__.
   (A) on with my work   (B) to investigate

2. The more we conserve heat, the __?__ fuel we have to use.
   (A) more   (B) less

3. It is folly to __?__.

(A) apply your brakes suddenly on an icy road
(B) reduce your speed drastically in a thick fog

4. The reticent witness provided __?__ details.

(A) few   (B) abundant

5. I like __?__ food, but I also have a craving for exotic dishes.

(A) foreign   (B) American

6. You would not expect parsimonious persons to __?__.

(A) collect bits of string   (B) spend freely

7. Because of __?__, we are doing our utmost to ameliorate service.

(A) a shortage of raw materials   (B) customer complaints

8. The jewels were found intact; __?__ was missing.

(A) nothing   (B) a diamond ring

9. Most of the listeners were tractable; they __?__ the speaker's instructions.

(A) readily followed   (B) totally disregarded

10. Noncarcinogenic materials __?__ to our health.

(A) are a threat   (B) pose no danger

EXERCISE 2. Rewrite each sentence on your paper, replacing the italicized expression with a single word from the vocabulary list on the next page.

1. "Wait outside!" he *replied sharply.*

2. Can I drop a course without *injury or damage* to my record?

3. If you are *disposed to avoid exertion*, you are not dependable.

4. The structure was *leveled to the ground.*

5. We have established *peaceable, friendly relations.*

6. Our plans for the surprise party were *overturned from the foundation* by one loose-tongued individual.

7. *At an earlier period*, Zimbabwe was known as Rhodesia.

8. I could not fall asleep because I *went to bed* too early.

9. An unsigned will is *not binding in law.*

10. Remove the *object acting as a hindrance or obstruction.*

razed	retorted	subverted
invalid	impediment	indolent
detriment	formerly	retired
	harmony	

EXERCISE 3. You are to complete each sentence by supplying the ANTONYM (opposite) of the italicized word. Select your antonyms from the vocabulary list at the end of the exercise, and enter them on your paper.

1. Truly, I do not care whether you *heed* my suggestion or __?__ it.
2. Now that the *conflict* is over, __?__ may soon be restored.
3. As an officer of the club, you should *uphold* the constitution, not __?__ it.
4. I cannot see the *wisdom* of your actions; they are pure __?__.
5. Usually I *rise* at 6:45 A.M. and __?__ by 11 P.M.
6. The newcomer, *unruly* at first, is becoming more __?__.
7. Not all the trees on the school grounds are *native* to our soil. Some are __?__.
8. An early start, we thought, would be an *advantage*, but it turned out to be a (an) __?__.
9. __?__, she worked as a cook. *Now* she is studying for a law degree.
10. Did the medicine __?__ your condition or *worsen* it?

VOCABULARY LIST

folly	tractable	harmony
exotic	subvert	formerly
ignore	ameliorate	retire
	detriment	

EXERCISE 4. *Identify the Situation.* Each sentence describes a situation that can be summed up in a word. Choose that word from the following list and enter it on your paper.

indolence	parsimoniousness	conservation
amelioration	impediment	unruliness
reticence	harmony	subversion
	folly	

1. A fallen tree is blocking traffic on Bainbridge Road.
2. So far, Russ has said very little about what happened.
3. "My motto," says Angela, "is '*Take it easy.*' I could do much more if I wanted, but why kill myself?"
4. The new storm door and storm windows are reducing our heat loss.
5. There has not been a strike in Dad's firm for many years.
6. While the rest of us are trying to sell tickets, one member of the cast is privately telling people the play is not worth seeing.
7. Despite a fine income, Farrell spends very little on food and has not bought any new clothes since we've known him.
8. The child refused to stay in her seat, but ran up and down the aisle during the performance, despite the pleas of her parents.
9. More than $25,000 is now being spent to redecorate a building scheduled to be razed in six months.
10. The company, after a disastrous year, is making a slow but steady recovery.

EXERCISE 5.   Answer each of the following questions in a sentence or two.

1. What is one way to conserve energy that many people ignore?
2. Why is it folly to raze a sound, recently constructed building?
3. Are exotic fashions a detriment to America's clothing workers?
4. Why can a reticent witness subvert the process of justice?
5. Neither a parsimonious person nor an indolent one makes a good friend, but which of the two would you prefer? Why?

2. Contexts With Similar Words

Often you can learn the meaning of an unfamiliar word from a *similar* word or expression in the context.

Do you know what *castigated* means? If not, you should be able to find out from the following:

> The candidate denounced his opponent for her views on foreign policy, and she *castigated* him for his attitude toward labor.

Here, the meaning of *castigated* is given to us by a similar word in the context, *denounced*.

Do you know what *remote* means? If not, you can learn it from the following passage:

> There lay a young man, fast asleep—sleeping so soundly, so deeply, that he was far, far away from them both. Oh, so *remote*. . .—Katherine Mansfield

The context teaches us that *remote* means "far."

Let's try one more. Find the meaning of *reluctantly* in the next passage.

> My mother scolded me for my thoughtlessness and bade me say good-bye to them. *Reluctantly* I obeyed her, wishing that I did not have to do so.—Richard Wright

The clue here is in the words *wishing that I did not have to do so.* They suggest that *reluctantly* means "unwillingly."

Pretest 2

On your paper enter the meaning of the italicized word. (Hint: Look for a *similar* word or expression in the context.)

Do not write in this book. Enter all answers on separate paper.

---

1. Mr. Smith had already become acquainted with British *cinemas* in small towns. Also, he was a Southern Californian and had that familiarity with movies that belongs to all Southern Californians.
   —Eric Knight
2. Burke tossed the circular into the wastebasket without *perusing* it. He never reads junk mail.
3. The dealer asked for $1200. He *spurned* my offer of $1100, and when I went to $1150, he refused that too.
4. Your whistling *galls* me. In fact, your entire behavior irritates me.
5. I said the water was *tepid*. She didn't believe me. She tested it herself to see if it was lukewarm.
6. Eileen and I hated the book [*Bird Life for Children*], so we were quite prepared to *despise* birds when we started off that morning on our first bird walk.—Ruth McKenney

7. Everyone brimmed with enthusiasm. Carl was particularly *ebullient*.

8. She was eager to bet me she would win the match, but I told her I do not *wager*.

9. A fight started between two of the opposing athletes. Several of their teammates joined in. It was quite a *scuffle*.

10. . . . the picture changed and sport began to *wane*.
    A good many factors contributed to the decline of sport.

    —E. B. White

11. Later I realized I had made some *inane* remarks, and I was ashamed of myself for having been so silly.

12. She was supposed to be *indemnified*—the repair bill came to $180— but she has not yet been repaid.

13. Dorene is quite *finicky* about her penmanship. I am much less fussy.

14. The fact is, we have all been a good deal puzzled because the affair is so simple, and yet *baffles* us altogether.—Edgar Allan Poe

15. Though the starting salary is only $200 a week, I have been promised an early promotion and a higher *stipend*.

16. They *exhorted* us to join them for dinner, but we resisted their urging and thanked them very much.

17. When an Englishman has anything surprising to tell he never *exaggerates* it, never overstates it. . .—Stephen B. Leacock

18. I know how to change a tire, but tuning an engine is beyond my *expertise*.

19. Asians who have never been to the *Occident* learn much about Western culture from films and television.

20. Gerald suspected we were being watched. "Really?" I asked. "What makes you think we are under *surveillance?*"

Study Your New Words

You have just tried to define twenty new words with the help of similar words or expressions in the context. To strengthen your grasp of these new words, study the following.

baffle /'baf-əl/ *v*: bewilder; perplex; fill with confusion; puzzle; frustrate

At last we have found a solution to a problem that has been *baffling* us.

cinema /ˈsin-ə-mə/ *n:* motion picture; movie; film

Moviegoers are flocking to see the new *cinema* at the Bijou.

despise /di-ˈspīz/ *v:* look down on with contempt or disgust; loathe; regard as inferior—ANT **admire**

The world *admires* heroes and *despises* cowards.

ebullient /i-ˈbùl-yənt/ *adj:* overflowing with enthusiasm; exuberant

Hundreds of *ebullient* fans thronged the airport to greet the new champions.

exaggerate /ig-ˈzaj-ə-ˌrāt/ *v:* enlarge a fact or statement beyond what is true; overstate—ANT **minimize**

You *exaggerated* when you called me an excellent student. I have a C average.

exhort /ig-ˈzȯrt/ *v:* arouse by words; advise strongly; urge

The newscaster *exhorted* drivers to leave their cars at home because of the slippery roads.

expertise /ˌek-spər-ˈtēz/ *n:* specialized skill or technical knowledge; know-how; expertness

Mrs. Waldo has an accountant prepare her tax return because she lacks the *expertise* to do it herself.

finicky /ˈfin-i-kē/ *adj:* excessively concerned with trifles or details; hard to please; fussy; particular

Abe showed me I had forgotten to dot one of my i's. He is very *finicky* about such matters.

gall /ˈgȯl/ *v:* make sore; irritate mentally; annoy; vex

Why are you in such a bad mood? What is *galling* you?

inane /in-ˈān/ *adj:* lacking significance or sense; pointless; silly; insipid— ANT **profound**

I asked him how the water was, and he said "wet." Now isn't that *inane?*

indemnify /in-'dem-nə-ˌfī/ *v:* compensate for loss, damage, or injury; reimburse; repay

Some of the tenants were not *indemnified* for their losses in the fire, as they carried no insurance.

Occident /'äk-sə-dənt/ *n:* West; countries of America and Europe—ANT **Orient**

The plane that landed in Shanghai brought tourists from the United States, Canada, Brazil, Italy, and other countries in the *Occident*.

peruse /pə-'rüz/ *v:* read; look at fairly attentively; study

Before signing a contract, you should *peruse* its contents and discuss any questions you may have with your attorney.

scuffle /'skəf-əl/ *n:* rough struggle with scrambling and confusion; fight

The dean broke up the *scuffle* and made all the participants promise that there would be no more fighting.

spurn /'spərn/ *v:* thrust aside with disdain or contempt; reject—ANT **accept**

We wanted to assist, but they *spurned* all offers of aid.

stipend /'stī-ˌpend/ *n:* fixed or regular pay for services; wage; salary

He earns a *stipend* of $800 a month.

surveillance /sər-'vā-ləns/ *n:* close watch over a person, group, or area; supervision

The patients in the intensive care ward are under continuous *surveillance*.

tepid /'tep-əd/ *adj:* moderately warm; lukewarm

The soup was served hot, but I didn't get to it for about five minutes, and by then it was *tepid*.

wager /'wā-jər/ *v:* risk (something) on the outcome of a contest or uncertain event; gamble; bet

Those who had *wagered* we would win are out of some money; we lost the game.

wane /'wān/ *v:* decrease in power or size; dwindle; decline; sink

The senator may not be reelected. His popularity is *waning*.

Apply What You Have Learned

EXERCISE 6.   Which choice, A or B, makes the sentence correct? Enter the *letter* of your answer on your paper.

1. They spurned my suggestion and did as __?__.
   (A) they pleased   (B) I advised

2. To send someone a birthday card __?__ her birthday is absolutely inane.
   (A) a month after   (B) three days before

3. The Independents have just __?__ two more seats; their influence is waning.
   (A) won   (B) lost

4. After four years of service in the American embassy in __?__, Williams is longing to return to the Occident.
   (A) Tokyo   (B) Madrid

5. Our guests are not finicky; they are __?__ to please.
   (A) hard   (B) easy

6. Asked if she were coming to Class Night, an ebullient senior answered: __?__.
   (A) "I guess so."   (B) "I wouldn't miss it for the world!"

7. The new cinema features an actress never before seen on the __?__.
   (A) screen   (B) stage

8. He is just under five eleven, and when he gives his height, he says: __?__. He does not exaggerate.
   (A) "six feet"   (B) "five ten"

9. We are keeping __?__ the suspects; they are under surveillance.
   (A) a lookout for   (B) an eye on

10. Surely you would not want to __?__ someone you despise.
    (A) ignore   (B) associate with

EXERCISE 7. Rewrite each sentence on your paper, replacing the italicized expression with a single word from the vocabulary list at the end of the exercise.

1. They get into one *rough struggle* after another.
2. Policyholders will be *compensated* for losses.
3. Do you know how many thousands he *risked on the outcome of uncertain events?*
4. My counselor *strongly advised* me to prepare for college.
5. The soda was *moderately warm*, so I added ice.
6. Where did you get your *technical knowledge* as a photographer?
7. The first paragraph *filled* me *with confusion*.
8. She *looked at* the report *fairly attentively*.
9. The position commands a *fixed pay* of $400 a week.
10. Her false charges *irritated* me *mentally*.

VOCABULARY LIST

indemnified	galled	expertise
baffled	scuffle	perused
tepid	stipend	wagered
	exhorted	

EXERCISE 8. *Synonyms and Antonyms.*

A. On your paper, enter a SYNONYM for the italicized word from the vocabulary list that follows.

1. These bills *annoy* me.
2. What is the name of the new *movie?*
3. The crowd was *exuberant*.
4. I got a *lukewarm* reception.
5. You are acquiring *know-how* in carpentry.

VOCABULARY LIST

expertise	despise	exaggerate
Occident	ebullient	inane
gall	spurn	tepid
	cinema	

B. On your paper, enter an ANTONYM for the italicized word from the preceding vocabulary list.

6. Do not *minimize* your achievements.
7. The freighter is bound for the *Orient*.
8. We *admire* them.
9. She said something very *profound*.
10. The winner will probably *accept* the award.

EXERCISE 9. *Identify the Situation.* Each sentence or passage below describes a situation that can be summed up in a word. Select that word from the following list and enter it on your paper.

exaggeration	finickiness	wagering
scuffle	exhortation	expertise
surveillance	ebullience	inanity
	indemnification	

1. Through closed-circuit TV, the security guard in the lobby can watch people as they go up or come down in the elevator.
2. Joyce was not satisfied with the way I had set the table because some spoons and forks were almost—but not exactly—parallel.
3. With a wrench and a screwdriver, Armand skillfully replaced the washer of the faucet that had been leaking.
4. She has been paid in full for the damage to her car.
5. Give to the Heart Fund today, if you have not already contributed. The life you save may be your own.
6. The article says the play opened to a full house, but I saw about a third of the seats unoccupied.
7. The suggestion he made was silly; it made no sense at all.
8. We think the proposed shopping mall is an excellent idea, and we support it very enthusiastically.
9. The pushing and shoving began when someone tried to get in at the head of the line. Two people were hurt.
10. "I bet you two millions you wouldn't stick in a cell even for five years."
"If you mean it seriously," replied the lawyer, "then I bet I'll stay not five but fifteen."—Anton Chekhov

EXERCISE 10. Answer each question in a sentence or two.

1. What kind of stipend would it be sensible to spurn?
2. Would you avoid a cinema that baffled your friends? Why, or why not?
3. How long should an employer maintain surveillance over a new employee with little expertise?
4. Why are some people galled by those who repeatedly make inane remarks?
5. How would you deal with someone asking to be indemnified who exaggerates the damage you did to his or her car?

3. "Commonsense" Contexts

Do you know what *reel* means in the following sentence?

> It weighs a ton, and strong porters *reel* under its weight.
> —W. Somerset Maugham

Note that the context contains neither a contrasting nor a similar word to help with the meaning of *reel*. Yet you can tell what it means by using a bit of **common sense.** You ask yourself:

> "How would I behave if I were to carry, or try to carry, something that feels like a ton?"

You realize that you would "sway dizzily," or "stagger." That is exactly what *reel* means.

Can you give a definition of *severed*? Do you know what *pinioned* means? If not, you should be able to discover their meanings from the following context by applying common sense.

> . . . I whirled about, grabbing the razor-sharp knife from my belt sheath, and slashed three or four times with a full sweep of my arms in the direction of the touch. By luck I *severed* two of the lassoing arms that were gripping me; in another instant the octopus would have had my two arms *pinioned* and I should have been helpless.
> —Victor Berge and Henry W. Lanier

What would you do to the arms of an octopus if you slashed them three or four times with a razor-sharp knife with a full sweep of your arms? You would *cut them off*, of course. *Severed* means "cut off."

And what would happen to your own arms if they were lassoed and gripped by the arms of an octopus? Obviously, they would be *bound fast*, so that you would not be able to use them. *Pinioned* means "bound fast."

The term *"commonsense" context*, as used in this book, means a context that yields the meaning of an unfamiliar word through clues other than by a synonym or antonym. Such contexts, as we have seen, involve a bit of reasoning on your part.

Pretest 3

On your paper, enter the meaning of the italicized word in each of the following "commonsense" contexts:

Do not write in this book. Enter all answers on separate paper.

---

1. A child wandering through a department store with its mother is *admonished* over and over again not to touch things.—Paul Gallico
2. My simple *repast* consisted of a sandwich and an apple.
3. Restrictions on the use of water will end as soon as our reservoirs are *replenished*.
4. A sufferer from *insomnia*, she lies awake most of the night.
5. The judge listened to the arguments of both attorneys before *rendering* her decision.
6. And take from seventy springs a *score*,
   It only leaves me fifty more.—A. E. Housman
7. In another year my father will have completed his first *decade* in business; he opened his shop nine years ago.
8. The blade slipped and cut my hand. Two *sutures* were needed to close the wound.
9. When the bald-headed fellow pretended he was the rightful King of France, Huck and Jim believed him. They were quite *gullible*.

10. While *confined* here in the Birmingham city jail, I came across your recent statement calling my present activities "unwise and untimely."—Martin Luther King, Jr.

11. A *probe* into the suspect's financial dealings disclosed evidence of large-scale fraud.

12. The dealer asked $90 for the radio, and I gave him his price; we did not *haggle*.

13. I know you asked for a hamburger, but I forgot to order it. I am sorry for the *lapse*.

14. We moved into first place, but our glory was *ephemeral*. The next day we lost a doubleheader and dropped to third.

15. It was not that he felt any emotion akin to love for Irene Adler. All emotions, and that one particularly, were *abhorrent* to his cold, precise but admirably balanced mind.—Arthur Conan Doyle

16. Jean greeted everyone, but when I said, "Hello," she walked past me as if I did not exist. The *snub* bothered me the rest of the day.

17. As I was leaving the meeting, I realized that I had *unwittingly* taken someone else's coat. Embarrassed, I ran back and apologized.

18. If the bomb had *detonated*, the consequences would have been frightful.

19. I *immersed* my hands in warm soapy water to loosen the dirt.

20. Perhaps in heaven, but certainly not until then, shall I ever taste anything so *ambrosial* as that fried chicken and coffee ice cream!
   —Dorothy Canfield Fisher

Study Your New Words

You have just attempted to learn the meanings of twenty words from "commonsense" clues in their contexts. Now, for a firmer grasp of these words, study the following:

abhorrent /ab-'hȯr-ənt/ *adj*: (followed by *to*) in conflict; utterly opposed; loathsome; repugnant—ANT **admirable**

Please do not ask me to tell an untruth; lying is *abhorrent* to me.

admonish /ad-'män-ish/ *v*: reprove gently but seriously; warn of a fault; caution—ANT **commend**

The teacher *commended* me on my improvement in writing, but *admonished* me for my lateness to class.

ambrosial /am-'brō-zhəl/ *adj:* extremely pleasing to taste or smell; delicious; like *ambrosia* (the food of the gods)

Taste this ripe pineapple; it has an *ambrosial* flavor.

confine /kən-'fīn/ *v:* shut up; imprison; keep in narrow cramped quarters —ANT **free**

On July 14, 1789, a Paris mob freed the prisoners *confined* in the Bastille.

decade /'dek-ˌād/ *n:* period of ten years

In the United States, the 1930's were the *decade* of the Great Depression.

detonate /'det-ə-ˌnāt/ *v:* explode with suddenness and violence; cause (something) to explode

Fallout shows that a nuclear device was probably *detonated* recently over the Pacific.

ephemeral /i-'fem-ə-rəl/ *adj:* lasting one day only; fleeting; transitory; short-lived—ANT **permanent**

Day lily blossoms are *ephemeral;* they last only for a day.

gullible /'gəl-ə-bəl/ *adj:* easily deceived or cheated; credulous—ANT **astute**

A few of the investors were *gullible* enough to buy the worthless stock, but most were too *astute* to be deceived.

haggle /'hag-əl/ *v:* dispute or argue over a price in a petty way; bargain; wrangle

Have they agreed on a price yet, or are they still *haggling?*

immerse /im-'ərs/ *v:* plunge or place into a liquid; dip; duck

I filled a basin with lukewarm water and *immersed* my foot in it.

insomnia /in-'säm-nē-ə/ *n:* inability to sleep; abnormal wakefulness; sleeplessness

The former hostages now get a normal amount of sleep; during their imprisonment they suffered from *insomnia.*

lapse /ˈlaps/ *n:* accidental mistake; slip; error; trivial fault

I wrote your name with one *t*, instead of two. Please forgive the *lapse*.

probe /ˈprōb/ *n:* critical inquiry into suspected illegal activity; investigation

A *probe* is being conducted to learn what happened to the missing funds.

render /ˈren-dər/ *v:* hand down officially; deliver (as a verdict); give

Tension was high in the courtroom as the jury filed in to *render* its verdict.

repast /ri-ˈpast/ *n:* food for one occasion of eating; meal

She eats little; her lunch would hardly make a *repast* for a sparrow.

replenish /ri-ˈplen-ish/ *v:* bring back to condition of being full; refill

Every 200 miles we stopped at a service station to *replenish* the gas tank.

score /ˈskȯ(ə)r/ *n:* group or set of twenty; twenty

We have nineteen signatures already, and if we get one more, we'll have an even *score*.

snub /ˈsnəb/ *n:* act or instance of *snubbing* (treating with contempt); rebuff; slight; insult

Why did Sharon invite everyone but me? Was it just an oversight, or a deliberate *snub*?

suture /ˈsü-chər/ *n:* strand or fiber used to sew parts of the living body; also, stitch made with such material

A few days after the cut finger was sewn together, the patient returned for the removal of the *sutures*.

unwittingly /ən-ˈwit-iŋ-lē/ *adv:* unintentionally; by accident; inadvertently—ANT **intentionally**

I *unwittingly* opened a letter addressed to you. Please forgive me.

Do not write in this book. Enter all answers on separate paper.

Apply What You Have Learned

EXERCISE 11. Which choice, A or B, makes the sentence correct? Enter the *letter* of your answer on your paper.

1. When you __?__, your body is totally immersed.
   (A) take a shower   (B) swim underwater

2. A probe of the corporation is under way; several of its top officers have been __?__.
   (A) questioned   (B) promoted

3. Dawson entered the House in __?__ and served for a score of years until his defeat in 1982.
   (A) 1962   (B) 1972

4. The guests __?__ about the ambrosial food.
   (A) raved   (B) complained

5. Shoppers will find the selection __?__ because the shelves have been replenished.
   (A) poor   (B) excellent

6. Do you regularly listen to the radio at 3 __?__? You must have insomnia.
   (A) A.M.   (B) P.M.

7. Remember how I offered my hand and __?__? I cannot forgive the snub.
   (A) we walked off the field together   (B) he didn't take it

8. Did you __?__ by yourself, or did someone join you in your repast?
   (A) study   (B) dine

9. For the first decade of her life, she lived on a farm. When she was __?__, her family moved to the city.
   (A) ten   (B) eleven

10. They haggled. Joan wanted three dollars for the used book and Audrey thought that was __?__.
    (A) too much   (B) a fair price

EXERCISE 12. Rewrite each sentence on your paper, replacing the italicized expression with a single word from the vocabulary list at the end of the exercise.

1. It is hard to fool them; they are not *easily deceived.*
2. What if the device had *exploded with suddenness and violence?*
3. A decision *handed down officially* by the Supreme Court carries a great deal of weight.
4. She was *reproved gently but firmly* and given another chance.
5. I walked off with your pen *by accident.*
6. Nobody likes to be *kept in narrow cramped quarters.*
7. Silk, nylon, or wire can be used as a *fiber to close a wound.*
8. When she said "Atkin," she meant "Atkins." It was a *trivial fault.*
9. Their behavior is *utterly opposed* to my principles.
10. The setback was *of a day's duration.*

VOCABULARY LIST

detonated	abhorrent	lapse
ephemeral	rendered	admonished
unwittingly	suture	confined
	gullible	

EXERCISE 13. *Synonyms and Antonyms.*

A. On your paper, enter a SYNONYM for the italicized word from the vocabulary list that follows:

1. We *bargained* for more than an hour.
2. She took it as an *insult.*
3. Has your glass been *refilled?*
4. What causes *sleeplessness?*
5. A mental *slip* prevented me from recalling your name.

VOCABULARY LIST

gullible	confined	replenished
insomnia	ephemeral	unwittingly
haggled	lapse	snub
	admonished	

B. On your paper, enter an ANTONYM for the italicized word from the preceding vocabulary list.

6. It was a *permanent* friendship.

7. Your opponent was quite *astute*.

8. Did she step on your foot *intentionally?*

9. The chief *commended* us.

10. On what grounds can the suspect be *freed?*

EXERCISE 14. *Thinking With Your New Vocabulary.*

A. Read all of the following statements:

As a child Jeff believed there were lions, tigers, and fire-breathing dragons in the woods near his home, as well as buried pirate treasure.

Andy ordered a seven-course dinner, but all Marie ate was a slice of cantaloupe.

Ben sold forty-two tickets, Stella twenty-nine, and Tony nineteen.

Louise called her home but she reached another party. Instead of 384-8349, she dialed 384-8439.

Bob did exceptionally well on opening day, but unfortunately business was very slow after that.

Rivers wanted to investigate to see if there had been any wrongdoing, but Thompson said it would be a waste of our time and money.

Mrs. Klein reminded Joe that he had not submitted a paper that was due yesterday, and she gave him until next Monday to hand it in.

Olga had to invent an excuse for her friend, and it was something she loathed doing.

Rita, the payroll secretary, complained of her cramped office; she said it was like a closet.

While Barry and Jim hesitated, wondering about the water temperature, Connie dived in and swam the length of the pool and back.

B. Enter the answers to the following questions on your paper:

1. Who enjoyed ephemeral success?

2. Who felt confined?

3. Who committed a lapse?

4. Who had an abhorrent experience?

5. Who was gullible?

6. Who opposed a probe?

7. Who was admonished?

8. Who had a meager repast?

9. Who was immersed?

10. Who was short of a score?

EXERCISE 15. Answer each question in a sentence or two.

1. How many decades are there in fourscore years?
2. Which could you more readily forgive, a snub or a lapse? Why?
3. Why is a gullible customer not likely to haggle?
4. Should someone who detonates firecrackers be admonished? Explain.
5. Describe one of the most ambrosial repasts you ever had.

4. Mixed Contexts

This is a review section. It contains contexts of all the types we have met up to now—those with a contrasting word, or a similar word, or a commonsense clue. By this time you should be able to deal with any of these types of contexts.

Pretest 4

On your paper, enter the meaning of the italicized word in each of the following contexts:

Do not write in this book. Enter all answers on separate paper.

---

1. . . . then we examined the house itself. We divided its entire surface into compartments, which we numbered, so that none might be missed; then we *scrutinized* each individual square inch throughout the premises, including the two houses immediately adjoining, with the microscope, as before.—Edgar Allan Poe
2. "The two houses adjoining!" I exclaimed. "You must have had a great deal of trouble."
   "We had; but the reward offered is *prodigious*."—Edgar Allan Poe
3. They meant to be of help, but they *hampered* us by getting in our way.
4. The vacation *rejuvenated* her. She returned looking years younger.
5. If *acquitted*, the accused will walk out of the courtroom a free person.

6. . . . I have known since childhood that faced with a certain kind of simple problem I have sometimes made it so *complex* that there is no way out.—Lillian Hellman

7. Most of the merchandise was sold early in the season at regular prices. The *residue* is being marked down 50% for a clearance sale.

8. Each of us carried a small cylinder of oxygen in his pack, but we used it only in emergencies and found that, while its immediate effect was *salutary*, it left us later even worse off than before.
—James Ramsey Ullman

9. In the twentieth century the automobile *superseded* the horse-drawn vehicle as a means of transportation.

10. I would never have had the *effrontery* to do what they did. What nerve they had!

11. When he *withdrew* his hands from his gloves, the cold wind seemed to leap forward and grasp his unprotected fingers in an iron grip.
—Edward A. Herron

12. Still another attempt will be made to reduce inflation and unemployment; they are *nettlesome* problems.

13. I was about to leave for the beach, *oblivious* of my appointment with the dentist, when Mother reminded me.

14. They do some *zany* things. For example, in one scene, having lost their employer's shopping money, they try to steal a chunk of meat from the cage of a hungry lion at the zoo. .

15. When the neighbor mainland would be *sweltering*, day and night alike, under a breathless heat, out here on the island there was always a cool wind blowing.—Sir Charles G. D. Roberts

16. It was an *excruciating* headache. I had to stay in bed.

17. The package was so *unwieldy* that it was hard to get a grip on it, and I dreaded taking it on the bus.

18. We have not complained up to now; but our *forbearance* is coming to an end.

19. I thought you would be nervous when you were unexpectedly asked to give the first talk, but you were *unruffled.*

20. It was even whispered that Whymper and the Taugwalders had deliberately cut the rope, *consigning* their companions to death to save their own skins.—James Ramsey Ullman

Study Your New Words

acquit /ə-'kwit/ *v:* relieve from an accusation; pronounce not guilty; discharge; exculpate—ANT **convict**

Two of the defendants were *convicted* of first-degree murder; the third was *acquitted.*

complex /käm-'pleks/ *adj:* having varied interrelated parts, and therefore hard to understand; complicated; intricate—ANT **simple**

I would never try to repair a mechanism so *complex* as a wristwatch, but I can easily replace a watchband.

consign /kən-'sīn/ *v:* give, transfer, or deliver, as if by signing over; hand over; commit

If she had married someone who could not earn a living, she would have *consigned* herself to a life of misery.

effrontery /i-'frənt-ə-rē/ *n:* shameless boldness; insolence; gall; temerity

When Roger was shown evidence that he had copied an answer from my paper, he had the *effrontery* to claim that I had copied from him.

excruciating /ik-'skrü-shē-ˌāt-iŋ/ *adj:* causing great pain or anguish; agonizing; unbearably painful

I had feared that the drilling of the tooth would be *excruciating*, but I barely felt any pain.

forbearance /fȯr-'ber-əns/ *n:* act of forbearing (refraining); abstaining; leniency; patience—ANT **anger**

If you stepped on my foot by accident, I would show *forbearance.* But if you tripped me on purpose, I would not be able to repress my *anger.*

hamper /'ham-pər/ *v:* interfere with; hinder; impede—ANT **aid**

We tried to leave the stadium quickly, but the heavy crowd *hampered* our progress.

nettlesome /'net-ᵊl-səm/ *adj:* literally, full of *nettles* (plants with stinging hairs); irritating; causing annoyance or vexation

How can we safely dispose of nuclear wastes? So far, no satisfactory answer has been found to this *nettlesome* question.

oblivious /ə-'bli-vē-əs/ *adj:* (usually followed by *of*) forgetful; unmindful; not aware

She had promised to wait, but she walked off without me, *oblivious* of her promise.

prodigious /prə-'dij-əs/ *adj:* extraordinary in amount or size; enormous; gigantic—ANT **tiny**

In one year there was a *prodigious* increase in the cost of oil; prices nearly tripled.

rejuvenate /ri-'jü-və-ˌnāt/ *v:* make young or youthful again; give new vigor to; reinvigorate; refresh

A good night's sleep will *rejuvenate* you, and you will wake up feeling refreshed.

residue /'rez-ə-ˌd(y)ü/ *n:* whatever is left after a part is taken, disposed of, or gone; remainder; rest

The floodwater receded, leaving a *residue* of mud in the streets.

salutary /'sal-yə-ˌter-ē/ *adj:* favorable to health; healthful; curative; beneficial—ANT **deleterious**

A winter in the South had a *salutary* effect on Agnes: her cough disappeared. The icy Northern climate would have been *deleterious* to her health.

scrutinize /'skrüt-ᵊn-ˌīz/ *v:* examine very closely; inspect

After *scrutinizing* my driver's license to see if there were any prior violations, the officer returned it to me.

supersede /ˌsü-pər-'sēd/ *v:* force out of use; displace; supplant; replace

In many businesses, paper wrapping has been *superseded* by plastic.

sweltering /'swel-tə-riŋ/ *adj:* oppressively hot; torrid—ANT **frigid**

It was a *sweltering* day; everyone was perspiring.

unruffled /ən-'rəf-əld/ *adj:* not upset or agitated; calm; cool; unflustered —ANT **discomposed**

Most of us were *discomposed* by the new developments, but Elinor remained *unruffled*.

unwieldy /ən-'wēl-dē/ *adj:* hard to *wield* (handle) because of size or weight; unmanageable; bulky

Will you please help me dispose of the empty refrigerator carton? It is too *unwieldy* for one person to carry out.

withdraw /wi<u>th</u>-'drȯ/ *v*

(1) take back; remove—ANT **deposit**

I *deposited* a check for $87.50 and *withdrew* $50 in cash.

(2) draw back; go away; retreat; leave—ANT **advance**

As the officers *advanced* toward the scene, the mob *withdrew*.

zany /'zā-nē/ *adj:* having the characteristics of a clown; mildly insane; crazy; clownish

Warren would squirt you with a water pistol for a laugh; he has a *zany* sense of humor.

Do not write in this book. Enter all answers on separate paper.

Apply What You Have Learned

EXERCISE 16. Which choice, A or B, makes the sentence correct? Enter the *letter* of your answer on your paper.

1. Your zany brother came to the meeting __?__.
   (A) with a list of complaints   (B) in a gorilla costume

2. The treatments were salutary; the patient's condition __?__.
   (A) improved   (B) worsened

3. Someone in the sweltering auditorium suggested that we turn off the __?__.
   (A) air conditioning   (B) heat

4. After saying your pie was soggy, Marge had the effrontery to __?__.
   (A) apologize for her remark   (B) ask for a second helping

5. They thought that when they would find __?__, they would become rejuvenated.
   (A) Captain Kidd's treasure   (B) the Fountain of Youth

6. A superseded regulation __?__.

 (A) is still in effect   (B) should be disregarded

7. In the imaginary country of Lilliput, where people were no more than six __?__ tall, an ordinary human like Gulliver must have seemed prodigious.

 (A) inches   (B) feet

8. After being acquitted, the suspect __?__.

 (A) requested a new trial   (B) thanked the jury

9. When your sister is criticized, she shows forbearance; she __?__.

 (A) becomes enraged   (B) listens patiently

10. Oblivious of the sudden drop in temperature, I left the house __?__.

 (A) without taking a sweater   (B) thinking it would snow

EXERCISE 17.   On your paper, rewrite each sentence, replacing the italicized expression with a single word from the vocabulary list at the end of the exercise.

1. The instructions were *hard to understand*.
2. At the entrance to the parking lot, she *handed over* her car to the custody of an attendant.
3. Soon afterward they *went away*.
4. If you make the bundle too large, it will be *hard to handle*.
5. *Not upset* by his failure, he hopes to try again.
6. By asking too many questions you *interfered with* my work.
7. If only part of the food was eaten, what happened to the *part that was left?*
8. She would not have screamed if the injury to her ankle had not been *unbearably painful*.
9. The outside of the safe was *examined very closely* for fingerprints.
10. It is a topic *that causes vexation*, so I try to avoid it.

VOCABULARY LIST

withdrew	residue	scrutinized
excruciating	consigned	complex
unruffled	nettlesome	hampered
	unwieldy	

EXERCISE 18. *Synonyms and Antonyms.*

A. On your paper, enter a SYNONYM for the italicized word from the vocabulary list that follows.

1. They remained *cool* throughout the crisis.
2. She chose wallpaper with an *intricate* pattern.
3. The situation is rapidly becoming *unmanageable*.
4. Would you have had the *temerity* to open someone else's mail?
5. He ordered the most expensive dinner, *unmindful* of the cost.

VOCABULARY LIST

prodigious	complex	effrontery
hampered	unruffled	acquitted
unwieldy	oblivious	salutary
	sweltering	

B. On your paper, enter an ANTONYM for the italicized word from the preceding vocabulary list.

6. The company ended the year with a *tiny* profit.
7. Why should the suspect have been *convicted?*
8. The suggested remedy may have *deleterious* effects.
9. We cannot remain in this *frigid* room.
10. The security staff *aided* our efforts to gain admission.

EXERCISE 19. *Thinking With Your New Vocabulary.*

A. Read all of the following statements:

When Martin asked permission to look through the files for the missing evidence, Muriel said, "Not now. Come back next week."

Rachel is more relaxed now that she has given up smoking, and her health has improved.

Mr. Bailey looked for a way to stop the almost daily bitter fights we were having over the use of the tennis courts.

Doug was not dismissed, but someone else is getting his job as floor manager.

Paul, like Enid and Arthur, had been on our committee for a year, and we wanted him to stay, but he left.

Jason's father had died, but Medea, an enchantress, brought him back to life and made him young again.

To our amusement, Tony, humming the "Blue Danube Waltz," danced around the room with a mopstick for a partner.

When Jonathan had finished cutting the boards, Florence swept up the sawdust and tossed it into the fireplace.

Gail has not paid back the dollar she borrowed from Eva last month, but so far Eva has said nothing.

"He was ten foot tall when he stood in his boots," said William Rose Benét in a poem about the outlaw Jesse James.

B. Enter the answers to the following questions on your paper:

1. Who is being superseded?
2. Who withdrew?
3. Who hampered an investigation?
4. Who rejuvenated someone?
5. Who made a salutary decision?
6. Who behaved in a zany way?
7. Who was portrayed as prodigious in size?
8. Who was faced with a nettlesome problem?
9. Who showed forbearance?
10. Who disposed of a residue?

EXERCISE 20.   Answer each question in a sentence or two.

1. How much forbearance should we have with a zany driver? Why?
2. May we conclude that a person who seems unruffled has no nettlesome problems? Explain.
3. Is it salutary to sunbathe for hours under a sweltering sun? Why, or why not?
4. Should an official who hampers an investigation be superseded? Explain.
5. Would you be joking or serious if you said that a friend who is oblivious of faces, names, and appointments has a prodigious memory? Why?

CHAPTER iii Building Vocabulary Through Central Ideas

One helpful way to build your vocabulary is to study groups of related words. According to this method, you may first take a group of words dealing with "joy"; then another group with an idea like "sadness," etc. You will soon discover that studying several related words at one time can be much more profitable than studying lists of unrelated words.

This chapter presents twenty-five groups, each consisting of words relating to a unifying central idea. Under each central idea there are several important words dealing with that idea, together with definitions and illustrative sentences. Each sentence has been specially constructed to help you fix in mind the definition and use of a new word.

Despite this assistance, you will not achieve the results that you should achieve unless you *apply yourself*. Expanding your vocabulary is a rewarding but *challenging* task. It calls for sustained effort and imagination. Here are a few suggestions that will enable you to get the most out of this chapter.

1. Pay careful attention to each illustrative sentence. Then construct, at least in your mind, a similar sentence using your own context.

2. Do the abundant drill exercises thoughtfully, not mechanically. Review the words you miss.

3. Deliberately *use* your new vocabulary as soon as possible in appropriate situations—in chats with friends, class discussions, letters, and compositions. Only by *exercising* new words will you succeed in making them part of your active vocabulary.

Study Your New Words

1. Joy, Pleasure

bliss /'blis/ *n:* perfect happiness

The young movie star could conceive of no greater *bliss* than winning an "Oscar."

blithe /'blīth/ *adj:* merry; cheerful; happy

I was so enraptured with the scenery that I drove right through the intersection in *blithe* disregard of the "Full Stop" sign.

buoyant /'bòi-ənt/ *adj*

(1) cheerful

We need your *buoyant* companionship to lift us from boredom.

(2) able to float

The raft is sinking; it is not *buoyant*.

complacent /kəm-'plās-ᵊnt/ *adj:* self-satisfied

We should not be *complacent* about our security; we must be alert to potential threats.

convivial /kən-'viv-ē-əl/ *adj*

fond of eating and drinking with friends; jovial

Our *convivial* host hates to dine alone.

delectable /di-'lek-tə-bəl/ *adj:* very pleasing; delightful

The food was *delectable;* we enjoyed every morsel.

ecstasy /'ek-stə-sē/ *n:* state of overwhelming joy; rapture

If we win tomorrow, there will be *ecstasy;* if we lose, gloom.

elated /i-'lāt-əd/ *adj:* in high spirits; joyful

Except for my sister, who misses the old neighborhood, the family is *elated* with the new house.

frolicsome /'fräl-ik-səm/ *adj:* full of merriment; playful

The clown's *frolicsome* antics amused the children.

gala /ˈgā-lə/ *adj:* characterized by festivity

The annual Mardi Gras in New Orleans is a *gala* carnival of parades and merriment.

jocund /ˈjäk-ənd/ *adj:* merry; cheerful

Our neighbor is a *jocund* fellow who tells amusing anecdotes.

jubilation /ˌjü-bə-ˈlā-shən/ *n:* rejoicing

On election night there usually is *jubilation* at the campaign headquarters of the victorious party.

2. Sadness

ascetic /ə-ˈset-ik/ *adj:* shunning pleasures; self-denying

The *ascetic* Puritans rigidly suppressed many forms of recreation.

ascetic /ə-ˈset-ik/ *n:* person who shuns pleasures

Carl never goes to the movies, plays, or parties. He must be an *ascetic*.

chagrin /shə-ˈgrin/ *n:* embarrassment; mortification; disappointment

Imagine my *chagrin* when I learned that I had not been invited to the party!

compunction /kəm-ˈpəŋ(k)-shən/ *n:* regret; remorse; misgiving; qualm

Mr. Jones had no *compunction* about failing the track star, as she had not done her work all term.

contrite /kən-ˈtrīt/ *adj:* showing deep regret and sorrow for wrongdoing; deeply penitent; repentant

Believing the young offender to be *contrite*, the dean decided to give him another chance.

dejected /di-ˈjek-təd/ *adj:* sad; in low spirits; depressed

We are elated when our team wins, but *dejected* when it loses.

disconsolate /dis-ˈkän-sə-lət/ *adj:* cheerless; inconsolable

The mother could not stop her *disconsolate* son from sobbing over the loss of his dog.

disgruntled /dis-'grənt-əld/ *adj:* in bad humor; displeased

From her *disgruntled* expression I could tell she was not satisfied with my explanation.

doleful /'dōl-fəl/ *adj:* full of sorrow; mournful; dolorous

The refugee told a *doleful* tale of hunger and persecution.

glum /'gləm/ *adj:* moody; gloomy; dour

As they emerged from the conference, both the Mayor and the Governor were *glum* and refused to talk to reporters.

lamentable /'lam-ən-tə-bəl/ *adj:* pitiable; rueful

He described the *lamentable* hardships of the three miners trapped in the underground chamber.

maudlin /'mȯd-lən/ *adj:* weakly sentimental and tearful

After presenting a couple of *maudlin* numbers, the quartet was asked to sing something more cheerful.

nostalgia /nə-'stal-jə/ *n*

(1) homesickness

Toward the end of a vacation away from home, we usually experience a feeling of *nostalgia*.

(2) yearning for the past

In moments of *nostalgia*, I long for the good old days.

pathetic /pə-'thet-ik/ *adj:* arousing pity

Despite his *pathetic* condition, the crippled lad had a ready smile.

pathos /'pā-thäs/ *n:* quality in events or in art (literature, music, etc.) that arouses our pity

The young seamstress who precedes Sydney Carton to the guillotine adds to the *pathos* of A TALE OF TWO CITIES.

pensive /'pen-siv/ *adj:* thoughtful in a sad way; melancholy

Unlike her cheerful, outgoing sister, Elizabeth was *pensive* and shy.

plight /'plīt/ *n:* unfortunate state; predicament

Numerous offers of assistance were received after the *plight* of the distressed family was publicized.

poignant /ˈpȯi-nyənt/ *adj:* painfully touching; piercing

One of the most *poignant* scenes in MACBETH occurs when Macduff learns that his wife and children have been slaughtered.

sullen /ˈsəl-ən/ *adj:* ill-humoredly silent; gloomy; morose

The *sullen* suspect refused to give his name and address.

throes /ˈthrōz/ *n pl:* anguish; pangs

Fortunate are those who have never experienced the *throes* of separation from a loved one.

tribulation /ˌtrib-yə-ˈlā-shən/ *n:* suffering; distress

The time between the final examinations and the announcement of the marks is a period of real *tribulation* for most students.

3. Stoutness

burly /ˈbər-lē/ *adj:* stout; husky and rough

Extra-large football uniforms were ordered to outfit our *burly* linemen.

buxom /ˈbək-səm/ *adj:* plump and attractive

By the side of her lean city cousin, the farm girl looked radiant and *buxom.*

cherubic /chə-ˈrü-bik/ *adj:* chubby and innocent-looking; like a *cherub* (angel in the form of a child)

Your well-nourished nephew, despite his *cherubic* face, can be quite mischievous.

obese /ō-ˈbēs/ *adj:* very fat; corpulent; portly

Prince Hal describes the *obese* Falstaff as a "huge hill of flesh."

pudgy /ˈpəj-ē/ *adj:* short and fat

My tall, athletic sister was rather *pudgy* as a child of ten.

4. Thinness

attenuate /ə-'ten-yə-ˌwāt/ *v:* make thin; weaken

Photographs of President Lincoln reveal how rapidly the cares of leadership aged and *attenuated* him.

emaciated /i-'mā-shē-ˌāt-əd/ *adj:* made unnaturally thin

Emaciated by his illness, the patient found that his clothes would no longer fit.

haggard /'hag-ərd/ *adj:* careworn; gaunt

Haggard from their long ordeal, the rescued miners were rushed to the hospital for treatment and rest.

lank /'laŋk/ *adj:* long and thin; slender

Every basketball team longs for a *lank*, agile center who can control the boards.

svelte /'svelt/ *adj:* slender; lithe

Ballet dancers observe a strict diet to maintain their *svelte* figures.

5. Flattery

adulation /ˌad-yə-'lā-shən/ *n:* excessive praise; flattery

True leaders can distinguish sincere praise from blind *adulation*.

blandishment /'blan-dish-mənt/ *n:* word or deed of mild flattery

Suitors often use terms of endearment, flowers, and similar *blandishments*.

cajole /kə-'jōl/ *v:* persuade by pleasant words; wheedle

Sister *cajoled* Dad into raising her allowance.

curry (*v.*) **favor** (*n.*) /'kər-ē fā-və(r)/: seek to gain favor by flattery

The candidate tried to *curry favor* with the voters by praising their intelligence and patriotism.

fulsome /ˈfūl-səm/ *adj:* offensive because of insincerity; repulsive; disgusting

How can you endure the *fulsome* praises of your subordinate who lauds your every decision, right or wrong?

ingratiate /in-ˈgrā-shē-ˌāt/ *v:* work (oneself) into favor

By trying to respond to every question, the new pupil tried to *ingratiate* herself with the teacher.

lackey /ˈlak-ē/ *n:* slavish follower

The queen could never get a frank opinion from the *lackeys* surrounding her, for they would always agree with her.

obsequious /əb-ˈsē-kwē-əs/ *adj:* slavishly attentive; fawning

The *obsequious* subordinates vied with one another in politeness and obedience, each hoping to win the manager's favor.

sycophant /ˈsik-ə-fənt/ *n:* parasitic flatterer

Sycophants live at the expense of vain persons who enjoy flattery.

truckle /ˈtrək-əl/ *v:* submit servilely to a superior

Some people, unfortunately, gain promotion by *truckling* to their supervisors.

Do not write in this book. Enter all answers on separate paper.

Apply What You Have Learned

EXERCISE 1. On your paper, enter the *letter* of the word NOT SIMILAR in meaning to the other words in each group.

1. (A) ecstatic (B) jubilant (C) rapturous (D) pensive
2. (A) svelte (B) slender (C) slippery (D) lithe
3. (A) comedian (B) lackey (C) flatterer (D) sycophant
4. (A) tribulation (B) insincerity (C) suffering (D) pangs
5. (A) cajolery (B) gloominess (C) dejection (D) melancholy
6. (A) elation (B) frolicsomeness (C) gaiety (D) adulation
7. (A) wheedle (B) attenuate (C) ingratiate (D) fawn
8. (A) pathos (B) pity (C) complacency (D) compassion
9. (A) portly (B) burly (C) buxom (D) contrite
10. (A) jovial (B) jocund (C) blithe (D) disconsolate

EXERCISE 2. On your paper, copy each word or expression from column I, and next to it enter the *letter* of its correct meaning from column II.

COLUMN I	COLUMN II
1. delightful	(A) predicament
2. arousing pity	(B) attenuated
3. plight	(C) nostalgia
4. blandishment	(D) haggard
5. careworn	(E) delectable
6. self-denying	(F) bliss
7. perfect happiness	(G) lackey
8. weakened	(H) mild flattery
9. slavish follower	(I) pathetic
10. homesickness	(J) ascetic

EXERCISE 3. If the italicized word is *correctly* used in the sentence, enter *C* on your paper. If *incorrectly* used, enter *X*.

1. The Browns are not going on vacation this year; a sharp reduction in income has compelled them to adopt a more *ascetic* way of life.
2. *Attenuated* by the addition of water, the soup was *thicker* than usual.
3. Happy as we are in our new home, we experience occasional pangs of *nostalgia* for our old apartment.
4. Refusing to *truckle* to the new owner, the manager behaved just as independently as in the past.
5. As she watched the *dolorous* drama on television, she suddenly burst into laughter.

EXERCISE 4. Which word, selected from the vocabulary list below, will correctly complete the sentence? Enter the appropriate word on your paper.

VOCABULARY LIST

poignant	cajole	tribulation
buxom	burly	emaciated
throes	pathos	gala
fulsome	jubilation	elated
pudgy	remorse	glum

1. The __?__ movers lifted the piano with surprising ease.
2. After the game there was wild __?__ as supporters rushed onto the field to congratulate their heroes.
3. The President looked __?__ as he announced the disappointing news.
4. To a young child, a birthday is certainly a (an) __?__ occasion.
5. Newspapers reported the __?__ details of the futile rescue attempt.
6. The leader was repelled by the __?__ compliments of some of her subordinates.
7. When Mr. Norwood was stopped for a traffic violation, he tried to __?__ the officer into not writing a ticket.
8. The __?__ appearance of the liberated prisoners shocked the world.
9. At the trial one of the suspects wept repeatedly, but the other showed no __?__.
10. Sarah's brother is short, but definitely not stout; he therefore cannot be called __?__.

EXERCISE 5. On your paper, enter the *letter* of the word that means the SAME as or the OPPOSITE of the italicized word.

1. *displeased*
   - (A) doleful
   - (B) disgruntled
   - (C) remorseful
   - (D) embarrassed
   - (E) maudlin
2. *festive*
   - (A) melancholy
   - (B) restless
   - (C) poignant
   - (D) complacent
   - (E) mortifying
3. *qualm*
   - (A) composure
   - (B) disadvantage
   - (C) complaint
   - (D) bliss
   - (E) compunction
4. *chagrin*
   - (A) ignorance
   - (B) misfortune
   - (C) gain
   - (D) delight
   - (E) blunder
5. *gaunt*
   - (A) clumsy
   - (B) fulsome
   - (C) haggard
   - (D) pensive
   - (E) skilled
6. *lamentable*
   - (A) utter
   - (B) joyous
   - (C) unexpected
   - (D) premature
   - (E) predictable

7. *sullen*
   (A) communicative   (C) soiled   (E) unprejudiced
   (B) lean   (D) cherubic

8. *servile*
   (A) acrobatic   (C) fawning   (E) disappointing
   (B) elastic   (D) glum

9. *buoyant*
   (A) comfortable   (C) navigable   (E) floatable
   (B) obsequious   (D) unseaworthy

10. *sociability*
    (A) ecstasy   (C) jubilation   (E) ingratitude
    (B) etiquette   (D) conviviality

EXERCISE 6. Answer each question in a sentence or two.

1. Who is more likely to come in ahead in a race, a lank runner or a burly one? Why?

2. Why would you rather be with convivial companions than with disgruntled ones?

3. Name two delectable foods that most of us may have to give up for a svelte waistline.

4. If you accidentally hurt someone, would you be complacent or contrite? Explain.

5. Would you work for a firm where most of the other employees are obsequious and truckle to the boss? Why, or why not?

EXERCISE 7. *Analogies.* On your paper, enter the *letter* of the pair of words related to each other in the same way as the capitalized pair.

Sample

ECSTASY : JOY

  a. thrift : wealth   *d.* terror : fear
  b. certainty : doubt   *e.* frigid : cold
  c. fondness : adoration

Answer: *d*

Solution

The first step is to find the relationship in the capitalized pair. Obviously ECSTASY is a state of overwhelming JOY. If we designate ECSTASY by the letter X, and JOY by the letter Y, we can express the ECSTASY : JOY relationship by saying, "X is a state of overwhelming Y."

a. Thrift : Wealth

> *Thrift* is a means by which one may acquire *wealth*. *Thrift* is NOT a state of overwhelming *wealth*.

b. Certainty : Doubt

> *Certainty* is the opposite of *doubt*. It is definitely NOT a state of overwhelming *doubt*.

c. Fondness : Adoration

> *Fondness* is a much milder expression of liking than *adoration*. Note that the trouble with this pair is the order. If it were reversed (ADORATION : FONDNESS), this pair would be a correct answer because *adoration* is a state of overwhelming *fondness*.

d. Terror : Fear

> *Terror* is a state of overwhelming *fear*. This choice looks very good, but let us also check the final pair.

e. Frigid : Cold

> *Frigid* is overwhelmingly *cold*. The relationship is correct. However, *frigid* and *cold* are adjectives, whereas the capitalized pair, ECSTASY : JOY, are nouns. If choice *e* were changed to FRIGIDITY : COLD (*nouns*), it would be acceptable.

> Note that *terror* and *fear* in choice *d* are both nouns. This, plus the fact that *terror* is a state of overwhelming *fear*, makes *d* the correct choice.

1. NOSTALGIA : PAST

    a. regret : deed   *d.* absence : presence
    b. yearning : eternity   *e.* memory : forgetfulness
    c. anticipation : future

2. SYCOPHANT : SINCERITY

 a. thief : cleverness   *d.* friend : loyalty
 b. deceiver : truth   *e.* hero : courage
 c. coward : fear

3. ASCETIC : PLEASURE

 a. politician : votes   *d.* root : water
 b. plant : light   *e.* hermit : society
 c. scientist : truth

4. FOOD : OBESITY

 a. slip : fall   *d.* rainfall : flood
 b. spark : explosion   *e.* landslide : earthquake
 c. fatigue : work

5. DISCONSOLATE : CHEER

 a. intrepid : fear   *d.* frolicsome : merriment
 b. compassionate : sympathy   *e.* plaintive : sorrow
 c. repentant : regret

Going Over the Answers

Since this is our first exercise in analogies, check your answers with the following, paying careful attention to the reasoning involved.

QUESTION	RELATIONSHIP OF X AND Y	ANSWER AND EXPLANATION
1.	*Nostalgia* is a yearning for the *past*.	*c.* *Anticipation* is a yearning for the *future*.
2.	A *sycophant* makes a pretense of *sincerity*.	*b.* A *deceiver* makes a pretense of *truth*.
3.	An *ascetic* shuns *pleasure*.	*e.* A *hermit* shuns *society*.
4.	Excessive *food* intake may cause *obesity*.	*d.* Excessive *rainfall* may cause a *flood*.
5.	A *disconsolate* person is without *cheer*.	*a.* An *intrepid* person is without *fear*.

Study Your New Words

6. Animal

apiary /'ā-pē-ˌer-ē/ *n:* place where bees are kept
A beekeeper maintains an *apiary*.

aviary /'ā-vē-ˌer-ē/ *n:* place where birds are kept
Some birds of prey are confined in an *aviary* on the zoo grounds.

badger /'baj-ə(r)/ *v:* tease; annoy; nag (originally to harass a trapped badger)
Badgered by the children's persistent pleas, the mother finally relented and allowed them to go to the movies.

halcyon /'hal-sē-ən/ *adj:* calm; peaceful (from *halcyon*, a bird thought to calm the waves)
Most adults nostalgically recall the *halcyon* days of their youth.

lionize /'lī-ə-ˌnīz/ *v:* treat as highly important
With the first publication of his poems, Robert Burns gained immediate fame and was *lionized* by Edinburgh society.

molt /'mōlt/ *v:* shed feathers, skin, hair, etc.
Birds, mammals, and snakes *molt* periodically.

ornithology /ˌȯr-nə-'thäl-ə-jē/ *n:* study of birds
Ellen developed an interest in *ornithology* after reading John Burroughs' writings on birds.

parasite /'par-ə-ˌsīt/ *n:* animal, plant, or person living on others
Instead of seeking employment, he lived as a *parasite* on his brother.

parrot /'par-ət/ *v:* repeat mechanically (like a parrot)
Does he really understand what he is saying, or is he merely *parroting* his teacher?

scavenger /'skav-ən-jə(r)/ *n:* animal or person removing refuse, decay, etc.
Sea gulls are useful harbor *scavengers*, since they feed on garbage.

7. Health, Medicine

antidote /'ant-i-ˌdōt/ *n:* remedy for a poison or evil

A bottle containing poison must have the *antidote* specified on the label.

astringent /ə-'strin-jənt/ *n:* substance that shrinks tissues and checks flow of blood

According to its label, this after-shave lotion acts as an *astringent* by helping to check the bleeding of nicks and scrapes.

benign /bi-'nīn/ *adj*

(1) not dangerous—ANT **malignant**

The patient was relieved to learn that his tumor was *benign*, not *malignant*.

(2) gentle; kindly

The doorman is a kind, elderly man with a *benign* smile.

convalesce /ˌkän-və-'les/ *v:* recover health after illness; recuperate

After the appendectomy, you will have to *convalesce* for about a week before returning to school.

fester /'fes-tə(r)/ *v:* form pus; rankle; rot; putrefy

When a wound *festers*, it becomes inflamed, swollen, and painful.

hypochondriac /ˌhī-pə-'kän-drē-ˌak/ *n:* one who is morbidly anxious about personal health, or suffering from imagined illness.

The *hypochondriac* often interprets a normal condition as a symptom of serious illness.

immunity /im-'yü-nət-ē/ *n*

(1) resistance (to a disease)

Most people acquire life-long *immunity* to German measles once they have had that disease.

(2) freedom (from an obligation)

Federal and state properties within the city limits enjoy *immunity* from taxation.

lesion /'lē-zhən/ *n:* injury; hurt

The slightest *lesion* on a tree's bark, if left untended, may kill the tree.

malignant /mə-'lig-nənt/ *adj*

   (1) threatening to cause death—ANT **benign**

An operation was scheduled to remove the *malignant* tissues.

   (2) very evil

The brothers came under the *malignant* influence of a neighborhood criminal who taught them to steal.

morbid /'mȯr-bəd/ *adj*

   (1) gruesome

In describing his illness, he discreetly omitted the *morbid* details.

   (2) having to do with disease

In her present *morbid* condition, the patient is troubled by hallucinations and fantasies.

pestilential /ˌpes-tə-'len-shəl/ *adj*

   (1) morally harmful

Parents, teachers, and spiritual leaders have attacked certain TV programs as *pestilential*.

   (2) pertaining to a pestilence

The flu is a *pestilential* disease.

regimen /'rej-ə-mən/ *n:* set of rules to improve health

After the operation, I had to follow a *regimen* of diet and exercise prescribed by my physician.

salubrious /sə-'lü-brē-əs/ *adj:* healthful

Southern Florida's *salubrious* climate attracts many convalescents.

sebaceous /si-'bā-shəs/ *adj:* greasy; secreting fatty matter

The *sebaceous* glands in the skin secrete an oily substance essential for skin health.

therapeutic /ˌther-ə-'pyüt-ik/ *adj:* curative

The "get-well" cards have had a *therapeutic* effect on the hospitalized patient.

toxic /'täk-sik/ *adj:* poisonous

Operating a gasoline engine in a closed garage may cause death, because the exhaust fumes are dangerously *toxic*.

unguent /ˈəŋ-gwənt/ *n:* salve; ointment

Flora's skin irritation was relieved after she applied the *unguent* prescribed by her physician.

virulent /ˈvir-(y)ə-lənt/ *adj*

(1) extremely poisonous; deadly; venomous

Some insecticides and weed killers contain arsenic, a *virulent* substance.

(2) very bitter

The rebels show a *virulent* antagonism to the present ruler.

virus /ˈvī-rəs/ *n*

(1) disease-causing organism too small to be seen through a microscope

Polio is caused by a *virus*, an organism visible only through the electron microscope.

(2) corruptive force

What further measures are needed to combat the *virus* of prejudice?

8. Praise

acclaim /ə-ˈklām/ *v:* welcome with approval; applaud loudly

I did not enjoy that novel although it was *acclaimed* by several leading reviewers.

encomium /en-ˈkō-mē-əm/ *n:* speech or writing of high praise; tribute

Lincoln's "Gettysburg Address" is, in part, an *encomium* of those who fought at Gettysburg.

eulogize /ˈyü-lə-ˌjīz/ *v:* praise; extol

The police commissioner *eulogized* the officer for his alertness and bravery.

laudable /ˈlȯd-ə-bəl/ *adj:* praiseworthy; commendable

The bus driver's *laudable* safety record evoked high praise from her superiors.

laudatory /'lȯd-ə-ˌtȯr-ē/ *adj:* expressing praise, eulogistic

Most of the critics wrote *laudatory* reviews of the new film; only one found fault with it.

plaudit /'plȯd-ət/ *n:* (used mainly in the plural) applause; enthusiastic praise

Responding to the *plaudits* of her admirers, the singer reappeared for an encore.

9. Defamation

calumnious /kə-'ləm-nē-əs/ *adj:* falsely and maliciously accusing; defamatory; slanderous

Witnesses who heard the *calumnious* attack offered to testify in behalf of the slandered person.

derogatory /di-'räg-ə-ˌtȯr-ē/ *adj:* expressing low esteem; belittling; disparaging

On examining the culprit's permanent record card, the dean found few laudatory comments but several *derogatory* ones.

imputation /ˌim-pyə-'tā-shən/ *n:* insinuation; accusation

You have tried to besmirch my character with the cowardly *imputation* that I have robbed the poor.

libel /'lī-bəl/ *n:* false and defamatory printed (or written) statement

We shall certainly sue the newspaper that printed this *libel* against our company.

malign /mə-'līn/ *v:* speak evil of; vilify; traduce

I cannot bear to hear you *malign* so good a man.

slander /'slan-d ə(r)/ *n:* false and defamatory spoken statement; calumny

The rumor that I was discharged is a vicious *slander;* the fact is that I resigned.

stigma /'stig-mə/ *n:* mark of disgrace

With the *stigma* of a prison record, the ex-convict had difficulty in finding employment.

stigmatize /ˈstig-mə-ˌtīz/ *v:* brand with a mark of disgrace

Surely no one would enjoy being *stigmatized* by a nickname like "Dopey."

10. Jest

banter /ˈbant-ə(r)/ *n:* playful teasing; joking; raillery

The retiring employee was subjected to gentle *banter* about his coming life of ease.

caricature /ˈkar-i-kə-ˌchù(ə)r/ *n:* drawing, imitation, or description that ridiculously exaggerates peculiarities or defects

The Class Night skit that drew the loudest plaudits was a *caricature* of the first day in high school.

droll /ˈdrōl/ *adj:* odd and laughter-provoking

The essay had the *droll* title "On Eating Crackers in Bed."

facetious /fə-ˈsē-shəs/ *adj*

(1) in the habit of joking

Our *facetious* club president has a way of turning almost every comment into a joke.

(2) said in jest without serious intent

Of course she was only joking when she introduced you as a "math genius"; it was just a *facetious* remark.

flippant /ˈflip-ənt/ *adj:* treating serious matters lightly

Don't be so *flippant* about the need for studying; it is a serious matter that may affect your graduation.

harlequin /ˈhär-li-k(w)ən/ *n:* buffoon; clown

The *harlequin's* clowning endeared him to all.

hilarity /hil-ˈar-ət-ē/ *n:* noisy gaiety; mirth; jollity; glee

The laughter and shouting resulted in the entry of the principal, curious to learn what all the *hilarity* was about.

irony /ˈī-rə-nē/ *n*

(1) species of humor whose intended meaning is the opposite of the words used

In *irony*, the basketball players nicknamed their 6'6" center "Shorty."
   (2) state of affairs contrary to what would normally be expected
The breakdown occurred just after the car was inspected and found
to be in perfect condition. What *irony!*

jocose /jō-'kōs/ *adj:* given to jesting; playfully humorous; jocular
Some columnists write in a *jocose* vein; others are inclined to be
serious.

levity /'lev-ət-ē/ *n:* lack of proper seriousness; trifling gaiety; frivolity
During the assembly program George kept giggling, a *levity* for which
his teacher scolded him later.

ludicrous /'lüd-ə-krəs/ *adj:* exciting laughter; ridiculous; farcical; absurd
Pie-throwing, falling down stairs, and similar *ludicrous* antics were
common in early film comedies.

parody /'par-əd-ē/ *n:* humorous imitation of a serious writing
The Washington press corps entertained the Chief Executive with
a *parody* of a Presidential message to Congress.

sarcasm /'sär-ˌkaz-əm/ *n:* sneering language intended to hurt a person's
   feelings
Instead of helping, he offered such *sarcasm* as "You have made your
bed; now lie in it."

sardonic /sär-'dän-ik/ *adj:* bitterly sarcastic; mocking; sneering
Villains are often portrayed with a *sardonic* grin that suggests contempt for others.

satire /'sa-ˌtī(ə)r/ *n:* language or writing that exposes follies or abuses
   by holding them up to ridicule
Jonathan Swift's GULLIVER'S TRAVELS is a brilliant *satire* on human follies.

travesty /'trav-ə-stē/ *n:* imitation that makes a serious thing seem ridiculous; mockery
That a notorious criminal should escape trial because of a technicality
seems like a *travesty* of justice.

Apply What You Have Learned

EXERCISE 8. Each word or expression in column I has an ANTONYM (opposite) in column II. On your paper, enter the *letter* of the correct ANTONYM.

COLUMN I	COLUMN II
1. mark of honor	(A) laudatory
2. susceptible	(B) poisonous
3. nontoxic	(C) halcyon
4. treat (someone) as unimportant	(D) doleful
5. hilarious	(E) levity
6. derogatory	(F) stigma
7. turbulent	(G) encomium
8. seriousness	(H) lionize
9. denunciation	(I) condemn
10. extol	(J) immune

EXERCISE 9. On your paper, enter the *letter* of the word NOT SIMILAR in meaning to the other words in each group.

1. (A) joking (B) gaping (C) banter (D) teasing (E) raillery
2. (A) improve (B) recuperate (C) impute (D) recover (E) convalesce
3. (A) imitation (B) caricature (C) parody (D) lesion (E) travesty
4. (A) satire (B) applause (C) plaudit (D) encomium (E) commendation
5. (A) rot (B) putrefy (C) fester (D) rankle (E) molt
6. (A) defamation (B) libel (C) virus (D) calumny (E) slander
7. (A) vulture (B) parrot (C) mimic (D) ape (E) copy
8. (A) sarcastic (B) mocking (C) sardonic (D) eulogistic (E) sneering
9. (A) healthful (B) salubrious (C) benign (D) therapeutic (E) environmental
10. (A) nag (B) mare (C) badger (D) harass (E) annoy

EXERCISE 10. On your paper, enter the *letter* of the word or expression that has most nearly the SAME MEANING as the italicized word.

1. *Astringent* rebuke
   - (A) mild
   - (B) friendly
   - (C) undeserved
   - (D) stern

2. Effective *antidote*
   - (A) harlequin
   - (B) punishment
   - (C) remedy
   - (D) precaution

3. *Derogatory* comment
   - (A) unfair
   - (B) belittling
   - (C) congratulatory
   - (D) false

4. *Benign* ruler
   - (A) healthful
   - (B) aging
   - (C) kindly
   - (D) tyrannical

5. *Ironical* development
   - (A) contrary to expectation
   - (B) very sudden
   - (C) discouraging
   - (D) unfortunate

6. *Festering* slums
   - (A) decaying
   - (B) crime-ridden
   - (C) poverty-stricken
   - (D) spreading

7. Utterly *farcical*
   - (A) hopeless
   - (B) incompetent
   - (C) irresponsible
   - (D) absurd

8. Prescribed *regimen*
   - (A) rules
   - (B) medicine
   - (C) dose
   - (D) enforcement

9. *Venomous* fangs
   - (A) vigorous
   - (B) virulent
   - (C) dangerous
   - (D) pointed

10. *Halcyon* atmosphere
    - (A) cloudy
    - (B) noisy
    - (C) calm
    - (D) clear

EXERCISE 11. On your paper, enter the *letter* of the word (or set of words) that best completes the sentence.

1. In crime reporting, newspapers withhold the names of offenders under sixteen so as not to __?__ them.
   - (A) popularize
   - (B) libel
   - (C) stigmatize
   - (D) slander
   - (E) traduce

2. DON QUIXOTE, a __?__ novel by Cervantes, ridicules exaggerated notions of chivalry.
   - (A) satirical
   - (B) sentimental
   - (C) historical
   - (D) realistic
   - (E) eulogistic

3. The __?__ currently being exhibited in the __?__ have attracted numerous students of ornithology.
   - (A) apes . . aviary
   - (B) parrots . . apiary
   - (C) bees . . aviary
   - (D) monkeys . . apiary
   - (E) vultures . . aviary

4. For her laudable feat, the Olympic medal winner was __?__ by the citizens of her hometown.
   - (A) badgered
   - (B) parodied
   - (C) maligned
   - (D) lionized
   - (E) caricatured

5. Winston Churchill __?__ the heroes of the Battle of Britain in his memorable __?__: "Never was so much owed by so many to so few."
   - (A) congratulated . . travesty
   - (B) defended . . encomium
   - (C) vilified . . plaudit
   - (D) acclaimed . . tribute
   - (E) extolled . . oration

EXERCISE 12. As clues to each mystery word below, you are given its first letter and the number of its missing letters. On your paper, enter the complete word.

1. At the dedication ceremony, the mayor will e____7____ the scientist for whom the school is being named.

2. Fearing that a failing grade would s ____9____ her, Margaret did her best to pass the course.

3. It is i____7____ that the severely paralyzed lad should have the name Hale, which means "healthy."

4. The biochemist claimed that the substance has t___10___ properties useful in the treatment of diseases of the lungs.
5. F___8___ remarks on solemn occasions are entirely inappropriate.
6. The person who accidentally swallowed the poison was given an a___7___ and rushed to the hospital.
7. Several newspaper editors commended the Governor for his l___7___ efforts to prevent the strike.
8. Beneath the outer layer of the skin are the s___8___ glands, which secrete oil to lubricate the skin and the hair.
9. Many a life has been saved by the timely surgical removal of a m___8___ growth.
10. Though responsible for the fatal collision, the envoy could not be arrested because of diplomatic i___7___.

EXERCISE 13.   Answer each question in a sentence or two.

1. Why is it cruel to badger someone who is convalescing?
2. Suppose you are ill, and someone calls you a hypochondriac. Would you feel maligned? Why, or why not?
3. Is it a travesty for a suspect who testifies against his or her accomplices to receive immunity from prosecution? Explain.
4. Why is it derogatory to be called a "parasite"?
5. Why would it be irony if an ordinary high school tennis player defeated someone acclaimed as the world champion?

EXERCISE 14.   On your paper, enter the *letter* of the word that best completes the analogy.

Sample

Aviary is to *birds* as *apiary* is to __?__.
  a. flowers *b.* apes *c.* worms *d.* reptiles *e.* bees

Solution

The first step is to find the relationship of *aviary* and *birds*. As you have learned, an *aviary* is a "place where birds are kept." Then say to yourself, an *apiary* is a "place in which what is kept?" The answer, of course, is *e*, bees.

1. *Invalid* is to *hypochondriac* as *real* is to ___?___.
   a. sickly *b.* genuine *c.* healthful *d.* imagined *e.* impossible

2. *Birds* are to *ornithologist* as *poisons* are to ___?___.
   a. bacteriologist *b.* pharmacist *c.* toxicologist *d.* physician
   e. coroner

3. *Waste* is to *scavenger* as *dirt* is to ___?___.
   a. oil *b.* parasite *c.* cleanser *d.* ant *e.* weed

4. *Photograph* is to *caricature* as *fact* is to ___?___.
   a. drawing *b.* exaggeration *c.* sketch *d.* truth *e.* description

5. *Laughter* is to *ludicrous* as *sorrow* is to ___?___.
   a. dolorous *b.* droll *c.* facetious *d.* jocose *e.* flippant

Study Your New Words

11. Willingness—Unwillingness

alacrity /ə-'lak-rət-ē/ *n:* cheerful willingness; readiness; liveliness
An ideal class is one which pupils attend with *alacrity* and leave with reluctance.

aversion /ə-'vər-zhən/ *n:* strong dislike; repugnance; antipathy
Philip's *aversion* to work led to his dismissal.

loath /'lōth/ *adj:* unwilling; averse; disinclined; reluctant
We were *loath* to leave our friends, but Dad's transfer to California left us no choice.

volition /vō-'lish-ən/ *n:* will
Were you discharged or did you leave of your own *volition?*

12. Height

acclivity /ə-'kliv-ət-ē/ *n:* upward slope—ANT **declivity**
The sharp *acclivity* compelled us to drive in low gear.

acme /'ak-mē/ *n:* highest point; pinnacle; summit

With the completion of the MONA LISA, Leonardo da Vinci is generally believed to have reached his *acme* as a painter.

apogee /'ap-ə-jē/ *n*

(1) farthest point from the earth in the orbit of a man-made satellite or heavenly body

At its *apogee* the satellite was 560 miles (903 kilometers) from the earth, and at its perigee 150 miles (242 kilometers).

(2) highest point—ANT **perigee**

Solar energy as a means of heating homes is being used more widely, but it is still far from its *apogee*.

climactic /klī-'mak-tik/ *adj:* arranged in order of increasing force and interest—ANT **anticlimactic**

Notice the *climactic* order of ideas in this sentence: "Swelled by heavy rains, brooks became creeks, creeks rivers, and rivers torrents."

consummate /kən-'səm-ət/ *adj:* perfect; carried to the highest degree

The pilot guided the liner into its berth with *consummate* skill.

eminence /'em-ə-nəns/ *n:* high rank

Raised suddenly to an *eminence* for which he was ill qualified, the executive could not get along with his new subordinates.

ethereal /i-'thir-ē-əl/ *adj:* of the heavens; celestial; airy; delicate; intangible

Charles was told by his employer, "Get rid of your *ethereal* notions and come down to earth."

exalt /ig-'zȯlt/ *v*

(1) lift up with joy, pride, etc.; elate—ANT **humiliate**

My parents were *exalted* to learn that I had been admitted to Arista.

(2) raise in rank, dignity, etc.; extol; glorify

Some films have *exalted* criminals to the level of heroes.

precipice /'pres-ə-pəs/ *n:* very steep, overhanging place; cliff

The climbers had to make a lengthy detour around an insurmountable *precipice*.

precipitous /pri-'sip-ət-əs/ *adj*

(1) steep as a precipice

She descended from the summit in low gear, using her brakes all the way, since the road was so *precipitous*.

(2) hasty; rash

Don't rush into a *precipitous* action that you may later regret. Take your time.

preeminent /prē-'em-ə-nənt/ *adj*: standing out above others; superior

As a violinmaker, Stradivarius remains *preeminent*.

sublimate /'səb-lə-ˌmāt/ *v*

(1) redirect the energy of a person's bad impulses into socially and morally higher channels

With the aid of dedicated social workers, energies that now find release in gang fights can be *sublimated* into wholesome club activities and sports.

(2) purify; refine

The alchemists failed in their efforts to *sublimate* baser metals, such as lead and copper, into gold.

sublime /sə-'blīm/ *adj*: elevated; noble; exalted; uplifting

Visitors to the Grand Canyon are uplifted and refreshed by its *sublime* scenery.

vertex /'vər-ˌteks/ *n*: farthest point opposite the base, as in a triangle or pyramid; apex

The *vertex* of the largest Egyptian pyramid was originally 482 feet (147 meters) from the base.

zenith /'zē-nəth/ *n*

(1) highest point; culmination—ANT **nadir**

His election as President marked the *zenith* of his long career in politics.

(2) point in the heavens directly overhead

At noon, the sun reaches the *zenith*.

13. Lowness, Depth

abject /'ab-,jekt/ *adj:* deserving contempt; sunk to a low condition; wretched

For your *abject* submission to your tyrannical associate we have the utmost contempt.

abyss /ə-'bis/ *n:* bottomless, immeasurably deep space

The sudden death of his closest friend threw Tennyson into an *abyss* of despair.

anticlimax /,ant-i-'klī-maks/ *n:* abrupt decline in dignity or importance at the end; comedown; bathos—ANT **climax**

Jane Austen uses *anticlimax* with comic effect when she describes a mother who in the same breath inquires about her daughter's "welfare and poultry."

chasm /'kaz-əm/ *n:* deep breach; wide gap or rift

Prospects for a settlement became remote, as the *chasm* between the rival parties deepened.

declivity /di-'kliv-ət-ē/ *n:* downward slope—ANT **acclivity**

The hill was ideal for beginning skiers because of its gentle *declivity*.

dregs /'dregz/ *n pl:* most worthless part; sediment at the bottom of a liquid

Gamblers, thieves, and hoodlums are among the *dregs* of society.

earthy /'ər-thē/ *adj:* coarse; low

Though we are satisfied with your helpers' work, we do not care for their *earthy* humor.

humble /'həm-bəl/ *adj*

(1) of low position or condition

Despite his *humble* origin, Lincoln rose to the highest office in the land.

(2) not proud; unpretentious; modest; courteously respectful

Though Stella has done far more than anyone else, she has never boasted of her achievement; she is *humble*.

humiliate /hyü-'mil-ē-ˌāt/ *v:* lower the pride, position, or dignity of; abase; degrade; mortify—ANT **exalt**

Rose feels I *humiliated* her in class today when I said her answer was wrong.

humility /hyü-'mil-ət-ē/ *n:* freedom from pride; humbleness; lowliness; modesty

Boasters and braggarts need a lesson in *humility.*

menial /'mē-nē-əl/ *adj:* low; mean; subservient; servile

Many college students do *menial* work, such as waiting on tables, to help pay their tuition.

nadir /'nā-də(r)/ *n:* lowest point—ANT **zenith**

Hopes of the American Revolutionary forces were at their *nadir* in the bitter winter of 1777–78 at Valley Forge.

plumb /'pləm/ *v:* get to the bottom of; ascertain the depth of; fathom

Sherlock Holmes amazes readers by his ability to *plumb* the deepest mysteries.

profound /prə-'faund/ *adj:* very deep; deeply felt; intellectually deep

Einstein's theories are understood by relatively few because they are so *profound.*

ravine /rə-'vēn/ *n:* deep, narrow gorge worn by running water

Survivors of the plane that crashed in the mountain *ravine* were rescued by helicopter.

14. Relatives

filial /'fil-ē-əl/ *adj:* of or like a son or daughter

The youngest daughter looked after her ailing father with *filial* devotion.

fraternal /frə-'tərn-əl/ *adj:* of or like a brother

There was much *fraternal* affection between the brothers; they were devoted to one another.

genealogy /ˌjē-nē-ˈäl-ə-jē/ *n:* a person's or family's descent; lineage; pedigree

The *genealogy* of every American but the Indian can be traced back to an immigrant.

gentility /jen-ˈtil-ət-ē/ *n*

(1) good manners

George Bernard Shaw's PYGMALION shows how a cockney flower girl quickly acquires the *gentility* necessary to pass as a duchess.

(2) aristocratic birth; membership in the upper class

It is not unusual for sons and daughters of aristocrats to go to work, despite their *gentility*.

kith and kin /ˈkith; ˈkin/ *n pl:* friends and relatives; kindred

Because he married in a distant state, the soldier had few of his *kith and kin* at the wedding.

maternal /mə-ˈtərn-ᵊl/ *adj:* of or like a mother

The kindergarten teacher has a kindly, *maternal* concern for each pupil.

nepotism /ˈnep-ə-ˌtiz-əm/ *n:* favoritism to relatives by those in power

Whenever a President appoints a relative to a government position, the cry of *nepotism* is raised by the opposition party.

paternal /pə-ˈtərn-ᵊl/ *adj:* of or like a father

The molding of a child's character is an important maternal and *paternal* obligation.

progenitor /prō-ˈjen-ət-ə(r)/ *n:* forefather

Adam is the Biblical *progenitor* of the human race.

progeny /ˈpräj-ə-nē/ *n:* offspring; children; descendants

Josiah Franklin's *progeny* numbered seventeen, the fifteenth being a lad named Benjamin.

sibling /ˈsib-liŋ/ *n:* one of two or more children of a family

Eileen has three *siblings*—two younger brothers and an older sister.

15. Smell

aroma /ə-ˈrō-mə/ *n:* pleasant odor; bouquet

What a smoker may describe as a rich tobacco *aroma*, a nonsmoker may consider a disgusting stench.

fragrant /ˈfrā-grənt/ *adj:* having a pleasant odor; pleasantly odorous or odoriferous

A florist's shop is a *fragrant* place.

fusty /ˈfəs-tē/ *adj*

(1) stale-smelling; musty; moldy

To rid the unused room of its *fusty* smell, we opened the windows and let the fresh air in.

(2) old-fashioned

The *fusty* elderly tenant refused to have a washing machine, a dryer, or a dishwasher in the apartment.

incense /ˈin-ˌsens/ *n:* substance yielding a pleasant odor when burned

Ancient Greek and Roman worshipers often burned *incense* to please their gods.

malodorous /mal-ˈōd-ə-rəs/ *adj:* ill-smelling; stinking; fetid; unpleasantly odorous

Brewing coffee makes a kitchen aromatic; boiling cabbage makes it *malodorous*.

noisome /ˈnȯi-səm/ *adj*

(1) offensive to smell; disgusting

Buses discharge *noisome* exhaust fumes that offend our nostrils.

(2) harmful; noxious

Why don't you leave this *noisome* factory neighborhood and move to a more healthful, more wholesome area?

olfactory /äl-ˈfak-t(ə-)rē/ *adj:* pertaining to the sense of smell

Because of their superior *olfactory* sense, bloodhounds can pick up the trails of fleeing criminals.

pungent /ˈpən-jənt/ *adj:* sharp in smell or taste; acrid; biting; stimulating

As she sliced the onions, the *pungent* fumes made her eyes tear.

putrid /ˈpyü-trəd/ *adj*

    (1) stinking from decay

An occasional rinse with a soapy solution will keep garbage cans free of *putrid* odors.

    (2) extremely bad; corrupt

Any system that requires applicants for promotion to pay bribes is *putrid*.

rancid /ˈran-səd/ *adj:* unpleasant to smell or taste from being spoiled or stale

If butter or fish has a *rancid* odor, it is unfit to eat.

rank /ˈraŋk/ *adj*

    (1) having a strong, bad odor or taste; offensively gross or coarse

When threatened, a skunk protects itself effectively by emitting a *rank* odor.

    (2) extreme

Many felt that the murderer's acquittal on the grounds of insanity was a *rank* injustice.

reek /ˈrēk/ *v:* emit a strong, disagreeable smell; be permeated with

Even after the fire was extinguished and the tenants were allowed to return, the building *reeked* of smoke.

scent /ˈsent/ *n:* smell; perfume

The room was fragrant with the *scent* of freshly cut lilacs.

scent /ˈsent/ *v:* get a suspicion of

When I saw my two rivals putting their heads together in a whispered conference, I *scented* a plot.

unsavory /ˈən-ˈsāv(-ə)-rē/ *adj*

    (1) unpleasant to taste or smell

The *unsavory* odor was traced to a decaying onion in the vegetable bin.

    (2) morally offensive

Opponents of the nominee alleged that he was an *unsavory* character with connections to the underworld.

Apply What You Have Learned

EXERCISE 15. On your paper, copy each word or expression from column I, and next to it enter the *letter* of its correct meaning from column II.

COLUMN I	COLUMN II
1. spicy	(A) abyss
2. most worthless part	(B) high rank
3. chasm	(C) humility
4. consummate	(D) precipitous
5. disinclined	(E) dregs
6. humiliated	(F) loath
7. descent	(G) pungent
8. eminence	(H) lineage
9. hasty	(I) humbled
10. freedom from pride	(J) perfect

EXERCISE 16. On your paper, enter the *letter* of the word NOT SIMILAR in meaning to the other words in each group.

1. (A) contemptible (B) abject (C) reluctant (D) wretched (E) low
2. (A) putrid (B) unsavory (C) menial (D) fusty (E) malodorous
3. (A) children (B) offspring (C) scent (D) progeny (E) descendants
4. (A) vertex (B) apex (C) climax (D) acme (E) base
5. (A) rank (B) position (C) gross (D) offensive (E) coarse
6. (A) abyss (B) precipice (C) elevation (D) peak (E) cliff
7. (A) modesty (B) humility (C) unpretentiousness (D) pride (E) humbleness
8. (A) unwillingness (B) repugnance (C) antipathy (D) aversion (E) alacrity
9. (A) rift (B) acclivity (C) breach (D) ravine (E) gorge
10. (A) servile (B) paternal (C) obsequious (D) submissive (E) subservient

EXERCISE 17. On your paper, enter the *letter* of the word in each group that means either the SAME as or the OPPOSITE of the italicized word.

1. *profound*
   (A) earthy
   (B) shallow
   (C) corrupt
   (D) damp
   (E) noxious

2. *pedigree*
   (A) genealogy
   (B) pinnacle
   (C) nepotism
   (D) perigee
   (E) apogee

3. *zenith*
   (A) drop
   (B) rise
   (C) nadir
   (D) gain
   (E) setback

4. *sibling*
   (A) uncle
   (B) nephew
   (C) aunt
   (D) sister
   (E) cousin

5. *noisome*
   (A) quiet
   (B) mild
   (C) loud
   (D) disgusting
   (E) calm

6. *glorification*
   (A) gentility
   (B) volition
   (C) humiliation
   (D) dislike
   (E) incense

7. *acrid*
   (A) deep
   (B) pungent
   (C) steep
   (D) bottomless
   (E) rash

8. *preeminent*
   (A) degrading
   (B) astringent
   (C) superior
   (D) mortifying
   (E) putrid

9. *unbrotherly*
   (A) cowardly
   (B) filial
   (C) flippant
   (D) fraternal
   (E) ethereal

10. *sublimated*
   (A) postponed
   (B) plumbed
   (C) unrelated
   (D) extended
   (E) purified

EXERCISE 18. Which word, selected from the vocabulary list below, will correctly complete the sentence? Enter the appropriate word on your paper.

VOCABULARY LIST

maternal	progeny	exalted
rancid	bathos	kith and kin
attraction	aversion	chasm
gentility	delectable	humiliated
filial	climax	declivity

1. Janet's __?__ to the water made her dread our swimming class.
2. It is only natural that we should be __?__ by our successes.

3. Mother's Day gives children an opportunity to express their __?__ devotion.
4. The gripping suspense at the __?__ of the play held the audience breathless.
5. As we came down the steep __?__, the speed of our car increased sharply.
6. The meal was wholesome and delicious except for the butter, which was __?__.
7. The youngsters received kinder treatment from total strangers than from their own __?__.
8. Coming as it did after three excellent skits, the rather dull final number produced an effect of __?__.
9. Your companion's earthy manner of speaking suggests that he has no __?__.
10. I felt __?__ when I was notified that I had not passed the driving test.

EXERCISE 19. Which choice, A or B, makes the sentence correct? Enter the *letter* of your answer on your paper.

1. A genealogist may help you learn more about your __?__.
   (A) progenitors   (B) descendants

2. To a writer, winning the Nobel Prize means achieving the __?__ of literary fame.
   (A) perigee   (B) pinnacle

3. The employer cannot be accused of nepotism, since none of his employees is __?__ him.
   (A) critical of   (B) related to

4. Mr. Myers was __?__ to write a letter of recommendation for Audrey because of her laudable record in his class.
   (A) eager   (B) loath

5. The ideas in the following quotation are arranged in __?__ order: "Tony has been an excellent outfielder, our most dependable hitter, and the best all-around player on our team."
   (A) climactic   (B) anticlimactic

EXERCISE 20. Answer each question in a sentence or two.

1. Why might you have an aversion to telling a friend that his or her breath reeks of garlic?
2. Would you be loath to take a menial job? Why, or why not?
3. Name one thing a parent can do to bridge a chasm between siblings.
4. Why is it unsavory for a public official in a democracy to practice nepotism?
5. Would you feel humiliated if someone said you were a student of consummate intelligence? Explain.

EXERCISE 21. On your paper, enter the *letter* of the word-pair that best expresses a relationship similar to that existing between the capitalized word-pair.

1. INFINITE : END

   a. wealthy : money
   b. blithe : happiness
   c. abysmal : bottom
   d. contrite : repentance
   e. delectable : delight

2. AUDITORY : HEARING

   a. keen : observing
   b. gustatory : touching
   c. tactile : tasting
   d. olfactory : smelling
   e. irritable : feeling

3. VERTEX : TRIANGLE

   a. peak : mountain
   b. summit : foot
   c. slope : base
   d. hill : ravine
   e. index : preface

4. PROGENY : PROGENITOR

   a. root : branch
   b. river : source
   c. genius : protector
   d. bricks : house
   e. orchestra : conductor

5. FETID : FRAGRANT

   a. imperfect : consummate
   b. humble : pretentious
   c. shallow : profound
   d. fresh : stale
   e. reeking : aromatic

Study Your New Words

16. Age

adolescent /ˌad-ᵊl-ˈes-ᵊnt/ *adj:* growing from childhood to adulthood; roughly, of the teenage period

In their early *adolescent* years, boys and girls usually attend junior high school.

adolescent /ˌad-ᵊl-ˈes-ᵊnt/ *n:* teenager

As *adolescents* develop into adults, they tend to become more self-confident.

antediluvian /ˌant-i-dᵊ-ˈlü-vē-ᵊn/ *adj:* antiquated; belonging to the time before the Biblical Flood (when all except Noah and his family perished)

Compared with today's supersonic jets, the plane the Wright brothers flew in 1903 seems *antediluvian.*

archaic /är-ˈkā-ik/ *adj:* no longer used, except in a special context; old-fashioned

An *archaic* meaning of the word "quick" is "living," as in the Biblical phrase "the quick and the dead."

callow /ˈkal-ō/ *adj:* young and inexperienced; unfledged

A prudent executive cannot be expected to entrust the management of a company to a *callow* youth just out of college.

contemporary /kən-ˈtem-pə-ˌrer-ē/ *adj:* of the same period or duration

The English Renaissance was not *contemporary* with the Italian Renaissance; it came two centuries later.

contemporary /kən-ˈtem-pə-ˌrer-ē/ *n:* person who lives at the same time as another

Benjamin Franklin was a *contemporary* of Thomas Jefferson.

crone /ˈkrōn/ *n:* withered old woman

The use of the word *crone* is unfair to women because there is no corresponding word for a "withered old man."

decrepit /di-'krep-ət/ *adj:* weakened by old age

Several *decrepit* inmates had to be carried to safety when the home for the aged was evacuated during the fire.

defunct /di-'fəŋ(k)t/ *adj:* dead; deceased; extinct

The Acme Lumber Company is still in business, but the Equity Appliance Corporation has long been *defunct*.

forebear /'fȯr-ˌbe(ə)r/ *n:* forefather, ancestor

Her *forebears* on her father's side had settled in New Jersey before the Civil War.

hoary /'hȯr-ē/ *adj*

(1) white or gray with age

Santa Claus is usually portrayed as an elderly, stout man with a *hoary* beard.

(2) ancient

The plot of the novel is based on one of the *hoary* legends of Ancient Greece.

infantile /'in-fən-ˌtīl/ *adj:* of or like an infant or infancy; childish

A child may revert to the *infantile* act of thumb-sucking when insecure.

inveterate /in-'vet-ə-rət/ *adj*

(1) firmly established by age; deep-rooted

From their ancestors, Americans have inherited an *inveterate* dislike of tyranny.

(2) habitual

My cousin would like to give up tobacco, but it will not be easy; she's an *inveterate* smoker.

juvenile /'jü-və-ˌnīl/ *adj*

(1) of or for youth; youthful

Books for grade-school children are usually located in the *juvenile* section of the library.

(2) immature

Jody suggested we play hide-and-seek, but I told her not to be *juvenile*.

longevity /län-ʼjev-ət-ē/ *n*

(1) long life

Methuselah is renowned for his *longevity;* according to the Bible, he lived for 969 years.

(2) length of life

The average *longevity* for a woman is at least five years more than for a man.

mature /mə-ʼt(y)ů(ə)r/ *adj*

(1) full-grown; ripe

Though an excellent worker, Rita was not appointed manager as she was only twenty-three; the employer wanted a more *mature* person in that position.

(2) carefully thought out

These are *mature* plans; they were not devised hastily.

nonage /ʼnän-ij/ *n:* legal minority; period before maturity

On his twenty-first birthday, the heir assumed control of his estate from the trustees who had administered it during his *nonage.*

nonagenarian /ˌnō-nə-jə-ʼner-ē-ən/ *n:* person in his or her 90's

(Note also **octogenarian**, person in the 80's, and **septuagenarian**, person in the 70's.)

George Bernard Shaw, among his many other distinctions, was a *nonagenarian,* for he lived to be 94.

obsolescent /ˌäb-sə-ʼles-ᵊnt/ *adj:* going out of use; becoming obsolete

Our firm's machinery is *obsolescent;* it will have to be replaced within the next two years if we are to meet competition.

obsolete /ˌäb-sə-ʼlēt/ *adj:* no longer in use; out-of-date

The modern refrigerator has replaced the icebox, now *obsolete.*

patriarch /ʼpā-trē-ˌärk/ *n*

(1) venerable old man

Practically all of the *patriarch's* children, grandchildren, and great-grandchildren attended the celebration of his eightieth birthday.

(2) father and ruler of a family or tribe; founder

According to the Bible, the human family is descended from the *patriarch* Adam and his wife Eve.

posthumous /'päs-chə-məs/ *adj*

(1) published after the author's death

Only two of Emily Dickinson's poems were published before her death; the rest are *posthumous*.

(2) occurring after death

Posthumous fame is of no use to an artist who struggles for a lifetime and dies unknown.

primeval /prī-'mē-vəl/ *adj:* pertaining to the world's first ages; primitive

From the exposed rock strata in the Grand Canyon, scientists have learned much about *primeval* life on this planet.

primordial /prī-'mȯrd-ē-əl/ *adj*

(1) existing at the very beginning

Humanity's *primordial* conflict with the environment has continued to the present day.

(2) elementary; primary; first in order

One of the *primordial* concepts of science is that matter and energy can neither be created nor destroyed.

pristine /'pris-ₜtēn/ *adj:* in original, long-ago state; uncorrupted

A diamond in its *pristine* state as it comes from the mine looks altogether different from the diamond in a ring.

puberty /'pyü-bərt-ē/ *n:* physical beginning of manhood or womanhood (at about age 14 for boys and 12 for girls)

Among the changes in boys at *puberty* are a deepening of the voice and the growth of hair on the face.

puerile /'pyu̇(-ə)r-əl/ *adj:* foolish for a grown person to say or do; childish

Some thought it was fun to throw objects at passing cars, but I considered it *puerile*.

senile /'sēn-ₜīl/ *adj:* showing the weakness of age

Grandfather often forgets things. He is becoming *senile*.

superannuated /ˌsü-pər-'an-yə-wāt-əd/ *adj:* retired on a pension; too old for work

Despite their age, some *superannuated* citizens can be more productive than many still in the work force.

venerable /'ven-ər-ə-bəl/ *adj:* worthy of respect because of advanced age, religious association, or historical importance

At family reunions our *venerable* grandmother, now past 80, is accorded the greatest respect.

veteran /'vet-ə-rən/ *n*

(1) person experienced in some occupation, art, or profession

In her bid for reelection, the Mayor, a *veteran* of twenty years in public service, cited her opponent's lack of experience.

(2) ex-member of the armed forces

Many *veterans* of the Vietnam War found it hard to readjust to civilian life.

yore /'yȯ(ə)r/ *n:* (always preceded by *of*) long ago

In days of *yore* there was trial by combat; today, we have trial by jury.

17. Sobriety—Intoxication

abstemious /ab-'stē-mē-əs/ *adj:* sparing in eating and drinking; temperate; abstinent

Employers usually do not hire known alcoholics, preferring personnel who are *abstemious* in their habits.

carousal /kə-'raù-zəl/ *n:* jovial feast; drinking party

While the enemy was celebrating Christmas Eve in a merry *carousal*, Washington and his troops, quite sober, crossed the Delaware and took them by surprise.

dipsomania /ˌdip-sə-'mā-nē-ə/ *n:* abnormal, uncontrollable craving for alcohol; alcoholism

An organization that has helped many persons to overcome *dipsomania* is Alcoholics Anonymous.

inebriated /in-'ē-brē-ˌāt-əd/ *adj:* drunk; intoxicated

Captain Billy Bones, *inebriated* from too much rum, terrorized the other patrons of the Admiral Benbow Inn.

sober /'sō-bə(r)/ *adj*

(1) not drunk; temperate

The motorist's obligation to be *sober* must be emphasized in driver-training programs.

(2) serious; free from excitement or exaggeration

My immediate thought was to leave, but after *sober* consideration, I decided not to.

sot /'sät/ *n:* person made foolish by excessive drinking; drunkard

Don't ask a *sot* for direction; consult someone whose mind is clear.

teetotaler /'tē-'tōt-ᵊl-ə(r)/ *n:* person who totally abstains from intoxicating beverages

Former dipsomaniacs who are now *teetotalers* deserve admiration for their courage and will power.

18. Sea

bow /'bau̇/ *n:* forward part of a ship; prow—ANT **stern**

A search from *bow* to *stern* before sailing disclosed that no stowaways were on board.

brine /'brīn/ *n*

(1) salty water

Brine can be converted to drinking water, but at high cost.

(2) ocean; sea; the deep

Anything on deck that was not firmly secured would have been blown into the *brine*.

doldrums /'dōl-drəmz/ *n pl*

(1) calm, windless part of the ocean near the equator

Becalmed in the *doldrums*, the sailing vessel was "As idle as a painted ship/Upon a painted ocean."

(2) listlessness

The rise in sales and employment shows that we are emerging from the economic *doldrums* of the past two years.

flotsam /ˈflät-səm/ *n:* wreckage of a ship or its cargo found floating on the sea; driftage

Flotsam from the sunken freighter littered the sea for miles around.

jetsam /ˈjet-səm/ *n:* goods cast overboard to lighten a ship in distress

Jetsam washed ashore indicated that frantic efforts had been made to lighten the ship's cargo.

jettison /ˈjet-ə-sən/ *v:* throw (goods) overboard to lighten a ship or plane; discard

The pilot of the distressed plane *jettisoned* his surplus fuel before attempting an emergency landing.

leeward /ˈlē-wərd/ *adj:* in the direction away from the wind—ANT **windward**

To avoid the wind, we chose deck chairs on the *leeward* side of the ship.

marine /mə-ˈrēn/ *adj:* of the sea or shipping; nautical; maritime

If you are fascinated by undersea plants and animals, you may want to study *marine* biology.

starboard /ˈstär-bərd/ *adj:* pertaining to the right-hand side of a ship when you face the bow (forward)—ANT **port**

When a ship follows a southerly course, sunrise is on the port side and sunset on the *starboard* side.

19. Cleanliness—Uncleanliness

carrion /ˈkar-ē-ən/ *n:* decaying flesh of a carcass

Vultures fed for several days on the air-polluting *carrion* left by hunters.

contaminate /kən-ˈtam-ə-ˌnāt/ *v:* make impure by mixture; pollute

Many of our rivers are being *contaminated* by sewage and industrial wastes.

dross /'dräs/ *n:* waste; refuse

When you revise your composition, eliminate all meaningless expressions, repetitions, and similar *dross.*

expurgate /'ek-spər-ˌgāt/ *v:* remove objectionable material from a book; bowdlerize; purify

In his FAMILY SHAKESPEARE (published 1818), Bowdler *expurgated* Shakespeare's works, removing words and expressions that he considered improper for reading aloud in a family.

immaculate /im-'ak-yə-lət/ *adj:* spotless; absolutely clean; pure; faultless

With some water, a cloth, and a little energy, a dirty windshield can be made *immaculate.*

offal /'ä-fəl/ *n:* waste parts of a butchered animal; refuse; garbage

Sea gulls hover about wharves where fish is sold, waiting to scoop up any *offal* cast into the water.

purge /'pərj/ *v:* cleanse; purify; rid of undesired element or person

If elected, the candidate vowed she would *purge* the county administration of corruption and inefficiency.

slatternly /'slat-ərn-lē/ *adj:* untidy; dirty from habitual neglect

There were cobwebs on the walls, dust on the shelves, and dirty dishes in the sink; it was a *slatternly* kitchen.

sloven /'sləv-ən/ *n:* person habitually untidy, dirty, or careless in dress, habits, etc.

It is difficult for an immaculate person to share a room with a *sloven.*

sordid /'sȯrd-əd/ *adj:* filthy; vile

As soon as the athlete received the bribe offer, he informed his coach of the *sordid* affair.

squalid /'skwäl-əd/ *adj:* filthy from neglect; dirty; degraded

The neglectful owner of the *squalid* tenements was ordered to correct all violations of the Sanitary Code within thirty days.

sully /'səl-ē/ *v:* tarnish; besmirch; defile

The celebrity felt that his name had been *sullied* by the publicity given his son's arrest for speeding.

20. Nearness

adjacent /ə-'jās-ᵊnt/ *adj:* lying near or next to; bordering; adjoining
Alaska is *adjacent* to northwestern Canada.

approximate /ə-'präk-sə-mət/ *adj:* nearly correct
The *approximate* length of a year is 365 days; its exact length is 365 days, 5 hours, 48 minutes, and 46 seconds.

contiguous /kən-'tig-yə-wəs/ *adj:* touching; adjoining
England and France are not *contiguous;* they are separated by the English Channel.

environs /in-'vī-rənz/ *n pl:* districts surrounding a place; suburbs
Many of the city's former residents now live in its immediate *environs.*

juxtaposition /ˌjək-stə-pə-'zish-ən/ *n:* close or side-by-side position
Soap should not be placed in *juxtaposition* with foods because it may impart its scent to them.

propinquity /prō-'piŋ-kwət-ē/ *n*
  (1) kinship
Disregarding *propinquity,* the executive gave the post to a highly recommended stranger rather than to his own nephew.
  (2) nearness of place; proximity
There were large shrubs too close to the house, and their *propinquity* added to the dampness indoors.

Do not write in this book. Enter all answers on separate paper.

Apply What You Have Learned

EXERCISE 22. Each word or expression in column I has an ANTONYM (opposite) in column II. On your paper, enter the *letter* of the correct ANTONYM.

COLUMN I		COLUMN II
1. full-fledged	(A)	descendant
2. vigorous	(B)	abstinent
3. forebear	(C)	filthy
4. right	(D)	callow
5. intemperate	(E)	bow
6. windward	(F)	maturity
7. nonage	(G)	inveterate
8. immaculate	(H)	leeward
9. stern	(I)	decrepit
10. not habitual	(J)	port

EXERCISE 23. On your paper, enter the *letter* of the word NOT SIMILAR in meaning to the other words in each group.

1. (A) immaturity (B) adolescence (C) senility (D) nonage
   (E) childhood
2. (A) cleansed (B) tarnished (C) expurgated (D) sublimated
   (E) purged
3. (A) boredom (B) doldrums (C) inactivity (D) listlessness
   (E) longevity
4. (A) sordid (B) sober (C) abstinent (D) temperate
   (E) abstemious
5. (A) venerable (B) aged (C) patriarchal (D) hoary
   (E) convalescent
6. (A) antiquated (B) archaic (C) obsolescent (D) obsolete
   (E) antediluvian
7. (A) port (B) bow (C) tow (D) stern (E) starboard
8. (A) original (B) habitual (C) primitive (D) pristine
   (E) uncorrupted
9. (A) carouser (B) sot (C) alcoholic (D) teetotaler
   (E) dipsomaniac

10. (A) unsullied   (B) slovenly   (C) defiled   (D) squalid
     (E) besmirched

EXERCISE 24. On your paper, enter the *letter* of the word that has most nearly the SAME MEANING as the italicized word.

1. *Unexpurgated* edition
  (A) abbreviated
  (B) unpurified
  (C) purified
  (D) bowdlerized

2. Jefferson's *forebears*
  (A) contemporaries
  (B) rivals
  (C) ancestors
  (D) followers

3. *Defunct* princess
  (A) dead
  (B) infantile
  (C) intemperate
  (D) slatternly

4. *Inveterate* latecomer
  (A) strange
  (B) extinct
  (C) juvenile
  (D) habitual

5. *Sober* estimates
  (A) approximate
  (B) calm
  (C) exaggerated
  (D) inaccurate

6. Venerable *patriarch*
  (A) founder
  (B) martyr
  (C) monument
  (D) philosopher

7. *Jettisoned* cargo
  (A) surplus
  (B) wrecked
  (C) discarded
  (D) loaded

8. *Primordial* rights
  (A) inherited
  (B) secondary
  (C) elementary
  (D) royal

9. Surface *dross*
  (A) waste
  (B) flotsam
  (C) dregs
  (D) polish

10. *Contiguous* properties
  (A) sordid
  (B) contagious
  (C) noxious
  (D) touching

EXERCISE 25. Which word, selected from the vocabulary list below, will correctly complete the sentence? Enter the appropriate word on your paper. (Hint: For a clue to the missing word, study the italicized expression.)

VOCABULARY LIST

juxtaposition	puberty	primeval
obsolescent	abstemious	dross
squalid	puerile	obsolete
senility	immaculate	nonage
longevity	jetsam	carrion

1. Aunt Matilda thinks it *childish* for grown-ups to yell and boo at ball games. She cannot understand their __?__ behavior.
2. When individuals distinguished for their *length of life* are interviewed by the press, they are usually asked for the secret of their __?__.
3. The horse-drawn carriage has long been *out of date*. It became __?__ with the invention of the automobile.
4. In the hospital, every room was *spotless*. The corridors, too, were __?__.
5. During his *legal minority*, the young monarch had heeded his advisers, but, once past his __?__, he took absolute personal control.
6. The school physician can easily distinguish those eighth-graders who are at *the physical beginning of manhood or womanhood* from those who have not yet arrived at __?__.
7. The two troublemakers occupied desks in *a side-by-side position*. Such __?__ gave them ample opportunity to create disturbances.
8. Jackals feed on *the decaying flesh of a carcass*. Kites, hawks, and buzzards also subsist on __?__.
9. By studying fossils, scientists have established many facts *pertaining to the world's first ages* and have learned a great deal about __?__ plants and animals.
10. When pedestrians track in mud from *dirty* streets, the custodial staff has to mop the halls and stairways frequently to keep them from becoming __?__.

EXERCISE 26. On your paper, enter the *letter* of the word (or set of words) that best completes the sentence.

1. A struggling artist knows that __?__ recognition will not help battle poverty.
   (A) contemporary   (C) sober   (E) posthumous
   (B) ample   (D) fulsome

2. At __?__, Grandfather, with a powerful handshake, vigorous stride, and wiry figure, is in excellent condition for an octogenarian.
   (A) 73   (C) 91   (E) 78
   (B) 84   (D) 69

3. __?__ and __?__ are in relatively close proximity.

(A) Vermont . . . Rhode Island
(B) Maine . . . Maryland
(C) Florida . . . Texas
(D) Alaska . . . Hawaii
(E) Pennsylvania . . . South Dakota

4. Anyone whose room is as untidy as Ralph's must be a (an) __?__.

(A) crone   (C) sot   (E) nonagenarian
(B) adolescent   (D) sloven

5. The new commander, a staunch believer in sobriety, would not tolerate __?__ in any of his subordinates.

(A) disrespect   (C) inebriation   (E) frivolity
(B) propinquity (D) bantering

EXERCISE 27.   Answer each question in a sentence or two.

1. What can residents do to prevent an adjacent vacant lot from becoming squalid?
2. Is it puerile for a mature person to play follow-the-leader? Explain.
3. Why would you prefer an abstemious chauffeur to an inebriated one?
4. Are all septuagenarians senile? Why, or why not?
5. Can oil tankers jettison sludge without harm to marine plants and animals? Explain.

EXERCISE 28.   On your paper, enter the *letter* of the word that best completes the analogy.

1. *Drought* is to *rain* as *doldrums* is to __?__.
   a. sea *b.* calm *c.* sails *d.* sunshine *e.* wind
2. *Refrigerator* is to *chill* as *brine* is to __?__.
   a. moisten *b.* preserve *c.* spoil *d.* fill *e.* spill
3. *Employed* is to *salary* as *superannuated* is to __?__.
   a. bonus *b.* wages *c.* pension *d.* royalties *e.* commission
4. *Banana* is to *peel* as *carcass* is to __?__.
   a. offal *b.* meat *c.* game *d.* hunter *e.* carrion
5. *Front* is to *rear* as *bow* is to __?__.
   a. leeward *b.* prow *c.* port *d.* stern *e.* starboard

21. Reasoning

analogy /ə-'nal-ə-jē/ *n:* likeness in some respects between things otherwise different; similarity; comparison

An *analogy* is frequently made between life and a candle, since each lasts a relatively short time and is capable of being snuffed out.

arbitrary /'är-bə-ˌtrer-ē/ *adj:* proceeding from a whim or fancy; capricious; despotic

A promotion should depend on an employee's record rather than on some official's *arbitrary* decision.

arbitrate /'är-bə-ˌträt/ *v:* decide a dispute, acting as *arbiter* (judge); submit a dispute to an arbiter

When the opposing claimants asked me to *arbitrate*, it was understood they would abide by my decision.

axiomatic /ˌak-sē-ə-'mat-ik/ *adj:* self-evident; universally accepted as true

It is *axiomatic* that expenditures must not exceed income.

bias /'bī-əs/ *n:* opinion formed before there are grounds for it; prejudice; predilection; partiality

Prospective jurors with a *bias* for or against the defendant were not picked for the jury.

bigoted /'big-ət-əd/ *adj:* intolerant; narrow-minded

It is futile to argue with *bigoted* persons; they hold stubbornly to their prejudices.

cogitate /'käj-ə-ˌtāt/ *v:* think over; consider with care; ponder

Since the matter is important, I must have time to *cogitate* before announcing my decision.

criterion /krī-'tir-ē-ən/ *n:* standard; rule or test for judging—PL **criteria**

Two of the *criteria* that experts consider in judging an automobile are fuel consumption and frequency of repair.

crux /'krəks/ *n:* most important point; essential part

Skip over the minor points and get to the *crux* of the matter.

deduce /di-'d(y)üs/ *v:* derive by reasoning; infer

From the fact that the victim's wallet and jewelry were not taken, we *deduced* that robbery had not been a motive for the murder.

dilemma /də-'lem-ə/ *n:* situation requiring a choice between two equally bad alternatives; predicament

Trapped by the flames, the guests on the upper stories faced the *dilemma* of leaping or waiting for an uncertain rescue.

dogmatic /dȯg-'mat-ik/ *adj:* asserting opinions as if they were facts; opinionated; asserted without proof

If, without offering any proof at all, you keep insisting that the plan will not work, you are being *dogmatic*.

eclectic /e-'klek-tik/ *adj:* choosing (ideas, methods, etc.) from various sources

In some matters I follow the progressives and in others the conservatives; you may consider me *eclectic*.

fallacious /fə-'lā-shəs/ *adj:* based on a *fallacy* (erroneous idea); misleading; deceptive

For centuries people held the *fallacious* view that the sun revolves around the earth.

fallible /'fal-ə-bəl/ *adj:* liable to be mistaken

Umpires occasionally make mistakes; like other human beings, they too are *fallible*.

heterodox /'het-ə-rə-ˌdäks/ *adj:* rejecting regularly accepted beliefs or doctrines; heretical—ANT **orthodox**

Political dissenters in dictatorships are often persecuted for their *heterodox* beliefs.

hypothetical /ˌhī-pə-'thet-i-kəl/ *adj:* supposed; having the characteristics of a *hypothesis*, a supposition made as a basis for reasoning or research. (If supported by considerable evidence, a hypothesis becomes a *theory*, and eventually, if no exceptions are found, a *law*.)

The detective investigated each employee because of a *hypothetical* notion that the robber had received "inside" information.

illusion /il-'ü-zhən/ *n:* misleading appearance; false impression; misconception

Barbara had thought that no college student could be dishonest, but the theft of her textbooks shattered that *illusion*.

indubitable /in-'d(y)ü-bət-ə-bəl/ *adj:* certain; incontrovertible; indisputable

The defendant's confession, added to the witnesses' testimony, makes his guilt *indubitable*.

orthodox /'òr-thə-,däks/ *adj:* generally accepted, especially in religion; conventional; approved—ANT **heterodox**

At the dinner table it is *orthodox* to use a knife and fork, instead of your fingers.

paradoxical /,par-ə-'däk-si-kəl/ *adj:* having the characteristics of a *paradox* (a self-contradictory statement which may nevertheless be true)

It is *paradoxical* but true that teachers may be taught by their pupils.

plausible /'plò-zə-bəl/ *adj:* superficially true or reasonable; apparently trustworthy

To people of ancient times the notion that the earth is flat seemed *plausible*.

preposterous /pri-'päs-t(ə-)rəs/ *adj:* senseless; absurd; irrational

The choice of Stella for the leading role is *preposterous;* she can't act.

rational /'rash-ə-n ᵊl/ *adj*

(1) able to think clearly; intelligent; sensible

Humans are *rational;* animals have little power of reason.

(2) based on reason

Mobs, as a rule, do not make *rational* decisions.

rationalize /'rash-ə-n ᵊl-,īz/ *v:* devise excuses for one's actions, desires, failures, etc.

The fox in the fable *rationalized* his failure to get at the grapes by saying that they were sour.

sophistry /'säf-ə-strē/ *n:* clever but deceptive reasoning

Imagine the *sophistry* of that child! He denied having a water pistol because, as he later explained, he had two.

specious /'spē-shəs/ *adj:* apparently reasonable, but not really so

The contractor's claim that his men have an average experience of five years is *specious;* one has had twenty years of experience, but the other three practically none.

speculate /'spek-yə-ˌlāt/ *v*

(1) reflect; meditate; conjecture

Space exploration may solve a problem on which we have long *speculated*—whether or not human life exists elsewhere in the universe.

(2) buy or sell with the hope of profiting by price fluctuations

Aunt Susan never invests in risky stocks; she does not *speculate.*

tenable /'ten-ə-bəl/ *adj:* capable of being maintained or defended

An argument supported by facts is more *tenable* than one based on hearsay.

22. Shape

amorphous /ə-'mòr-fəs/ *adj:* shapeless

At first my ideas for a term paper were *amorphous*, but now they are beginning to assume a definite shape.

concave /kän-'kāv/ *adj:* curved inward, creating a hollow space—ANT **convex**

In its first and last quarters the moon is crescent-shaped; its inner edge is *concave* and its outer *convex.*

contour /'kän-ˌtu̇(ə)r/ *n:* outline of a figure

The *contour* of our Atlantic coast is much more irregular than that of our Pacific coast.

distort /dis-'tȯrt/ *v*

(1) twist out of shape

My uncle suffered a minor stroke that temporarily *distorted* his face.

(2) change from the true meaning

A company that speaks of the "average experience" of its technicians may be *distorting* the truth, as some of them may have had no experience.

malleable /ˈmal-yə-bəl/ *adj*

(1) capable of being shaped by hammering, as a metal

Copper is easily shaped into thin sheets because it is very *malleable*.

(2) adaptable

Had they asked me, I would not have reduced the price, but they bargained with my partner, who is more *malleable*.

rotund /rō-ˈtənd/ *adj*

(1) rounded out; plump

A *rotund* figure is usually a sign of overweight.

(2) full-toned

The announcer introduced each of the players in a clear, *rotund* voice.

sinuous /ˈsin-yə-wəs/ *adj*: bending in and out; winding; serpentine

Signs that forewarn motorists of a *sinuous* stretch of road usually indicate a safe speed for negotiating the curves.

symmetrical /sə-ˈme-tri-kəl/ *adj*: balanced in arrangement; capable of division by a central line into similar halves—ANT **asymmetrical**

This misshapen bumper was perfectly *symmetrical* before the crash.

23. Importance—Unimportance

grave /ˈgrāv/ *adj*: deserving serious attention; weighty; momentous

The President summoned his cabinet into emergency session on receipt of the *grave* news.

nugatory /ˈn(y)ü-gə-ˌtȯr-ē/ *adj*: trifling; worthless; useless

My last-minute cramming was *nugatory;* at the examination, I didn't remember a thing.

paltry /ˈpȯl-trē/ *adj*: practically worthless; trashy; piddling; petty

I complain not because of the *paltry* few pennies I was overcharged but because of the principle involved.

paramount /'par-ə-ˌmaunt/ *adj:* chief; above others; supreme

A mother's *paramount* concern is her children's welfare.

relevant /'rel-ə-vənt/ *adj:* bearing upon the matter in hand; pertinent

The prosecutor objected that the witness' testimony had nothing to do with the case, but the judge ruled that it was *relevant*.

24. Modesty

coy /'koi/ *adj:* pretending to be shy

Annabelle's shyness was just a pretense; she was being *coy*.

demure /di-'myu̇(ə)r/ *adj*

(1) falsely modest or serious; coy

The students giggled behind the teacher's back, but as soon as he turned around they looked *demure*.

(2) grave; prim

Who would have guessed that so *demure* a person as Mr. Lee was addicted to betting on horse races?

diffident /'dif-əd-ənt/ *adj:* lacking self-confidence; unduly timid; shy

Why is it that students who should be the most confident about passing are usually the most *diffident?*

modest /'mäd-əst/ *adj:* not thinking too highly of one's merits; unpretentious; humble

Joe is the real hero, but he is too *modest* to talk about it.

staid /'stād/ *adj:* of settled, quiet disposition; sedate

Shocking pink is much too loud; beige is more *staid*.

25. Vanity

brazen /'brāz-ᵊn/ *adj*

(1) shameless; impudent

Two persons in the audience were smoking in *brazen* defiance of the "No Smoking" sign.

(2) made of brass or bronze

We have a pair of *brazen* candlesticks.

egoism /'ē-gə-ˌwiz-əm/ *n:* conceit; selfishness

By assuming full credit for our committee's hard work, the chairman has disclosed his *egoism*.

ostentatious /ˌäs-tən-'tā-shəs/ *adj:* done to impress others; showy; pretentious

Parked next to our staid family car was an *ostentatious* red convertible.

overweening /ˌō-və(r)-'wē-niŋ/ *adj:* thinking too highly of oneself; arrogant; presumptuous

After his initial victories, the *overweening* pugilist boasted that he was invincible.

pert /'pərt/ *adj:* too free in speech or action; bold; saucy; impertinent

Most of us addressed the speaker as "Dr. Bell," but one sophomore began a question with a *pert* "Doc."

vain /'vān/ *adj*

(1) conceited; excessively proud

Oscar boasts about his marks to everyone, even strangers. I have never seen such a *vain* person.

(2) empty; worthless

We have had enough of your *vain* promises; you never keep your word.

(3) futile

Anna made a valiant but *vain* effort to get her sister to stop smoking.

vainglorious /vān-'glōr-ē-əs/ *adj:* excessively proud or boastful; elated by vanity

Vainglorious Ozymandias had these words inscribed on the pedestal of his statue, now shattered: "Look on my works, ye Mighty, and despair!"

Apply What You Have Learned

EXERCISE 29. On your paper, copy each word or expression from column I, and next to it enter the *letter* of its correct meaning from column II.

COLUMN I

1. asserted without proof
2. curved outward
3. importance
4. conventional
5. excuse for failure
6. change from the truth
7. shameless
8. predicament
9. indefensible
10. unable to think clearly

COLUMN II

(A) gravity
(B) rationalization
(C) brazen
(D) untenable
(E) dilemma
(F) orthodox
(G) distortion
(H) dogmatic
(I) irrational
(J) convex

EXERCISE 30. On your paper, enter the *letter* of the word NOT SIMILAR in meaning to the other words in each group.

1. (A) deceptive (B) infallible (C) erroneous (D) fallacious
2. (A) bold (B) immodest (C) pertinent (D) impudent
3. (A) intolerance (B) prejudice (C) impartiality (D) bias
4. (A) concave (B) buxom (C) rotund (D) corpulent
5. (A) unrelated (B) impertinent (C) rude (D) irrelevant
6. (A) petty (B) piddling (C) paltry (D) prim
7. (A) specious (B) unpretentious (C) illusory (D) sophistical
8. (A) preposterous (B) vain (C) proud (D) conceited
9. (A) shy (B) diffident (C) arrogant (D) coy
10. (A) indisputable (B) axiomatic (C) incontrovertible (D) hypothetical

EXERCISE 31. Which word, selected from the vocabulary list below, will correctly complete the sentence? Enter the appropiate word on your paper.

VOCABULARY LIST

axiomatic	analogy	saucy
dilemma	staid	hypothesis
theory	paradox	dogmatic
nugatory	illusion	speculating
sophistry	relevant	ostentatious

1. Scientific research usually begins with a (an) __?__ .
2. Grandmother and Grandfather look dignified and __?__ in their wedding picture.
3. Jack never wears any of his medals because he doesn't want to appear __?__ .
4. On a sinking ship, all considerations except the paramount one of saving the lives of the passengers are __?__ .
5. When exasperated with my little brother, I call him a "snake," but my parents do not like the __?__ .
6. It is __?__ that the shortest distance between any two points on a plane surface is a straight line.
7. As we were discussing tomorrow's picnic, Dinah interrupted with a (an) __?__ question about the weather forecast.
8. The company faces the __?__ of going into bankruptcy or seeing its debts mount further.
9. __?__ always involves risk, as prices fluctuate.
10. What I had been reasonably certain was a ship approaching on the horizon turned out to be a mere __?__ .

EXERCISE 32. On your paper, enter the *letter* of the word in each group that means either the SAME as or the OPPOSITE of the italicized word.

1. *coyly*
   (A) selfishly   (C) courteously   (E) indubitably
   (B) bashfully   (D) arbitrarily

2. *heretic*
    (A) believer   (C) heir   (E) rival
    (B) veteran   (D) patriarch

3. *winding*
    (A) heterodox   (C) serpentine   (E) narrow
    (B) precipitous   (D) misleading

4. *vanity*
    (A) tolerance   (C) prejudice   (E) bigotry
    (B) bias   (D) worthlessness

5. *shapeless*
    (A) sinuous   (C) momentous (E) morbid
    (B) deductive   (D) amorphous

6. *impudent*
    (A) serious   (C) fallible   (E) respectful
    (B) capricious   (D) egoistic

7. *criteria*
    (A) symmetry   (C) decisions   (E) outcomes
    (B) standards   (D) criticisms

8. *paramount*
    (A) steep   (C) piddling   (E) rocky
    (B) overweening (D) paradoxical

9. *analogy*
    (A) crux   (C) hypothesis (E) axiom
    (B) dilemma   (D) similarity

10. *adaptable*
    (A) callow   (C) malleable   (E) plausible
    (B) unattached   (D) demure

EXERCISE 33. If the italicized word is *correctly* used in the sentence, enter *C* on your paper. If *incorrectly* used, enter *X*.

1. Myra carefully cut the apple into two exactly *asymmetrical* halves.
2. The assertions of a person who is known to be prejudiced are quite likely to be *opinionated*.
3. A digest magazine may be called *eclectic* because its articles are chosen from various publications.
4. A true sport like Lorna will always *rationalize* her defeat and praise the winner's superior performance.
5. How could you be so *brazen* as to push your way into the bus ahead of the people waiting on line?

EXERCISE 34. Answer each question in a sentence or two.

1. Why is it difficult for vain individuals to admit that they are fallible?
2. Who is more likely to be popular with the fans—a modest champion, or an overweening one? Why?
3. Name an important criterion you would follow in arbitrating a dispute.
4. Would you regard it as nugatory if your opponent in a debate distorted one of your statements? Why, or why not?
5. Why is it preposterous for a person with a bias against consumers to be nominated to head a consumer protection agency?

EXERCISE 35. On your paper, enter the *letter* of the word-pair that best expresses a relationship similar to that existing between the capitalized word-pair.

1. CONTOUR : STATUE
   a. shadow : body
   b. coastline : island
   c. peak : mountain
   d. area : surface
   e. original : imitation

2. CRUX : ARGUMENT
   a. title : book
   b. bridge : river
   c. kernel : nut
   d. door : house
   e. costume : actor

3. CONCAVE : CONVEX
   a. bowl : platter
   b. bulge : dent
   c. cup : saucer
   d. cavity : swelling
   e. building : dome

4. HYPOTHESIS : TRUTH
   a. supposition : fact
   b. proof : conclusion
   c. deceit : honesty
   d. folly : wisdom
   e. guess : blunder

5. RATIONALIZING : SELF-DECEPTION
   a. speculating : thrift
   b. egoism : shyness
   c. cogitating : brain
   d. brazenness : courtesy
   e. boasting : vanity

Chapter iv **Words Derived From Greek**

A great revival of interest in ancient Greek and Latin civilizations took place in England during the years 1500–1650, a period known as the Renaissance. At that time numerous ancient Greek and Latin words and their derivatives were incorporated into our language. This pattern of language growth has continued to the present day. When modern scientists need to name a new idea, process, or object, they tend to avoid existing English words because these already may have several other meanings. Instead they prefer to construct a new English word out of one or more ancient Greek or Latin words. Though ancient Greek has not given us so many English words as Latin, it has been especially preferred as a source of new words in the scientific and technical fields.

Here are twenty-five ancient Greek prefixes and roots that have enriched our language. Each one, as you can see, has produced a separate group of useful English words.

1. PHOBIA: "fear," "dislike," "aversion"

acrophobia /ˌak-rə-ˈfō-bē-ə/ *n:* fear of being at a great height

agoraphobia /ˌag-ə-rə-ˈfō-bē-ə/ *n:* fear of open spaces

Anglophobia /ˌaŋ-glə-ˈfō-bē-ə/ *n:* dislike of England or the English

claustrophobia /ˌklȯ-strə-ˈfō-bē-ə/ *n:* fear of enclosed or narrow spaces

Germanophobia /jer-ˌman-ə-ˈfō-bē-ə/ *n:* dislike of Germany or the Germans

hydrophobia /ˌhī-drə-ˈfō-bē-ə/ *n:* rabies (literally, "fear of water")

monophobia /ˌmä-nō-ˈfō-bē-ə/ *n:* fear of being alone

phobia /ˈfō-bē-ə/ *n:* fear; dislike; aversion

photophobia /ˌfōt-ə-ˈfō-bē-ə/ *n:* morbid (abnormal) aversion to light

xenophobia /ˌzen-ə-ˈfō-bē-ə/ *n:* aversion to foreigners

The form *phobe* at the end of a word means "one who fears or dis-likes." For example:

Russophobe /ˈrə-sə-ˌfōb/ *n:* one who dislikes Russia or the Russians

Also: **Francophobe, Anglophobe, Germanophobe,** etc.

EXERCISE 1. On your paper, enter the most appropriate word from group 1, *phobia*, for completing the sentence.

1. You would not expect a professional mountain climber to have __?__.
2. As we grow up, we overcome our childhood __?__ of the dark.
3. Passage of the Chinese Exclusion Act of 1882 proves that some de-gree of __?__ existed in our nation at that time.
4. Youngsters who suffer from __?__ do not make a habit of hiding in closets.
5. After many decades of __?__, the French joined the West Germans in close economic ties following World War II.

2. PHIL (PHILO): "loving," "fond of"

philanthropist /fə-ˈlan-thrə-pəst/ *n:* lover of humanity; person active in promoting human welfare

philanthropy /fə-ˈlan-thrə-pē/ *n:* love of humanity, especially as shown in donations to charitable and socially useful causes

philately /fə-ˈlat-ᵊl-ē/ *n:* collection and study of stamps

philharmonic /ˌfil-ər-ˈmän-ik/ *adj:* pertaining to a musical organization, such as a symphony orchestra (originally, "loving music")

philhellenism /fil-ˈhel-ə-ˌniz-əm/ *n:* support of Greece or the Greeks

philogyny /fə-ˈläj-ə-nē/ *n:* love of women

philology /fə-'läl-ə-jē/ *n:* study (love) of language and literature

philosopher /fə-'läs-ə-fə(r)/ *n:* lover of, or searcher for, wisdom or knowledge; person who regulates his or her life by the light of reason

The form *phile* at the end of a word means "one who loves or supports." For example:

Anglophile /'aŋ-glə-ˌfīl/ *n:* supporter of England or the English

bibliophile /'bib-lē-ə-ˌfīl/ *n:* lover of books

Francophile /'fraŋ-kə-ˌfīl/ *n:* supporter of France or the French

EXERCISE 2. On your paper, enter the most appropriate word from group 2, *phil* (*philo*), for completing the sentence.

1. Socrates, the great Athenian __?__, devoted his life to seeking truth and exposing error.
2. The __?__ was proud of his fine collection of beautifully bound volumes.
3. Do you collect stamps? I, too, was once interested in __?__.
4. A (An) __?__ was known as a Tory at the time of the American Revolution.
5. In her will the __?__ bequeathed more than a million dollars to charity.

3. MIS: "hate"
(MIS means the opposite of PHIL.)

misandry /'mi-ˌsan-drē/ *n:* hatred of males

misanthrope /'mis-ᵊn-ˌthrōp/ *n:* hater of humanity

misanthropy /mis-'an-thrə-pē/ *n:* hatred of humanity

misogamy /mə-'säg-ə-mē/ *n:* hatred of marriage

misogyny /mə-'säj-ə-nē/ *n:* hatred of women

misology /mə-'säl-ə-jē/ *n:* hatred of argument or discussion

misoneism /ˌmis-ə-'nē-ˌiz-əm/ *n:* hatred of anything new

EXERCISE 3. On your paper, enter the most appropriate word from group 3, *mis*, for completing the sentence.

1. Many employers used to hire men only, not because of __?__, but from an unfounded supposition that men could do the work better.
2. When Gulliver returned from his travels, he could not endure the sight of fellow humans; he had become a __?__.
3. Surprisingly, the first of the fraternity members to marry was the one who had been the loudest advocate of __?__.
4. Isabel likes to discuss, argue, and debate; she cannot be accused of __?__.
5. Some oppose innovation out of sheer __?__; they do not want any change.

4. DYS: "bad," "ill," "difficult"

dysentery /ˈdis-ᵊn-ˌter-ē/ *n:* inflammation of the large intestine

dysfunction /dis-ˈfəŋk-shən/ *n:* abnormal functioning, as of an organ of the body

dyslexia /də-ˈslek-sē-ə/ *n:* impairment of the ability to read

dyspepsia /dis-ˈpep-shə/ *n:* difficult digestion; indigestion—ANT **eupepsia** /yù-ˈpep-shə/ good digestion

dysphagia /dis-ˈfā-jə/ *n:* difficulty in swallowing

dysphasia /dis-ˈfā-zhə/ *n:* speech difficulty resulting from brain injury

dystrophy /ˈdis-trə-fē/ *n:* faulty nutrition

EXERCISE 4. On your paper, enter the most appropriate word from group 4, *dys*, for completing the sentence.

1. To aid digestion, eat slowly; rapid eating may cause __?__.
2. Those who ate the contaminated food became ill with __?__.
3. Injury to the brain may result in __?__, a complicated speech disorder.
4. Muscular __?__ is a disease in which the muscles waste away.
5. When your throat is badly inflamed, you may experience some __?__ at meal time.

5. EU: "good," "well," "advantageous" (EU means the opposite of DYS.)

eugenics /yu̇-'jen-iks/ *n:* science dealing with improving the hereditary qualities of the human race

eulogize /'yü-lə-ˌjīz/ *v:* write or speak in praise of someone

eupepsia /yu̇-'pep-shə/ *n:* good digestion—ANT **dyspepsia** /dis-'pep-shə/ difficult digestion; indigestion

euphemism /'yü-fə-ˌmiz-əm/ *n:* substitution of a "good" expression for an unpleasant one. Example: *passed away* for *died.*

euphonious /yu̇-'fō-nē-əs/ *adj:* pleasing in sound—ANT **cacophonous** /ka-'käf-ə-nəs/ harsh-sounding

euphoria /yu̇-'fȯr-ē-ə/ *n:* sense of well-being

euthanasia /ˌyü-thə-'nā-zhə/ *n:* illegal practice of painlessly putting to death a person suffering from an incurable, painfully distressing disease (literally "advantageous death")

euthenics /yu̇-'then-iks/ *n:* science dealing with improving living conditions

EXERCISE 5. On your paper, enter the most appropriate word from group 5, *eu*, for completing the sentence.

1. The audience liked the organist's __?__ melodies.
2. Before conferring the award, the presiding officer will probably __?__ the recipient.
3. The employee formerly called a "janitor" is now known by a __?__ such as "superintendent" or "custodian."
4. In the eyes of the law, anyone who commits __?__, regardless of the circumstances, is a murderer.
5. The __?__ I felt when my teacher complimented my work this morning stayed with me for the rest of the day.

6. MACRO: "large," "long"
7. MICRO: "small"

MACRO

macrocosm /ˈmak-rə-ˌkaz-əm/ *n:* great world; universe—ANT **microcosm** little world

macron /ˈmāk-ˌrän/ *n:* horizontal mark indicating that the vowel over which it is placed is long

macroscopic /ˌmak-rə-ˈskäp-ik/ *adj:* large enough to be visible to the naked eye—ANT **microscopic** invisible to the naked eye

MICRO

microbe /ˈmī-ˌkrōb/ *n:* very minute organism; a microorganism

microbicide /mī-ˈkrō-bə-ˌsīd/ *n:* agent that destroys microbes

microcosm /ˈmī-krə-ˌkäz-əm/ *n:* little world—ANT **macrocosm** great world; universe

microdont /ˈmī-krə-ˌdänt/ *adj:* having small teeth

microfilm /ˈmī-krə-ˌfilm/ *n:* film of very small size

micrometer /mī-ˈkräm-ət-ə(r)/ *n:* instrument for measuring very short distances

microscopic /ˌmī-krə-ˈskäp-ik/ *adj:* invisible to the naked eye—ANT **macroscopic** large enough to be visible to the naked eye

microsecond /ˈmī-krə-ˌsek-ənd/ *n:* unit of time equal to one millionth of a second

microwave /ˈmī-krə-wāv/ *n:* very short electromagnetic wave

EXERCISE 6. On your paper, enter the most appropriate word from groups 6 and 7, *macro* and *micro*, for completing the sentence.

1. Documents can be recorded in a minimum of space if photographed on __?__.

2. Space exploration has made us more aware of the vastness of the __?__.

3. A __?__ enables us to measure very minute distances that cannot be measured accurately with a ruler.
4. An ant is visible to the naked eye, but an ameba is __?__.
5. By means of a __?__, we are informed that the *e* in *ēra* is a long vowel.

8. A (AN): "not," "without"

amoral /ā-'mȯr-əl/ *adj:* without sense of moral responsibility

amorphous /ə-'mȯr-fəs/ *adj:* without (having no) definite form or shape

anemia /ə-'nē-mē-ə/ *n:* lack of a normal number of red blood cells

anesthesia /ˌan-əs-'thē-zhə/ *n:* loss of feeling or sensation resulting from ether, chloroform, novocaine, etc.

anhydrous /an-'hī-drəs/ *adj:* destitute of (without) water

anomaly /ə-'näm-ə-lē/ *n:* deviation from the common rule

anonymous /ə-'nän-ə-məs/ *adj:* nameless; of unknown or unnamed origin

anoxia /a-'näk-sē-ə/ *n:* deprivation of (state of being without) oxygen

aseptic /ā-'sep-tik/ *adj:* free from disease-causing microorganisms

atheism /'ā-thē-ˌiz-əm/ *n:* godlessness; denial of the existence of a Supreme Being

atrophy /'a-trə-fē/ *n:* lack of growth from disuse or want of nourishment —ANT **hypertrophy** /hī-'pər-trə-fē/ enlargement of a body part, as from excessive use

atypical /ā-'tip-i-kəl/ *adj:* unlike the typical

EXERCISE 7. On your paper, enter the most appropriate word from group 8, *a (an)*, for completing the sentence.

1. The __?__ donor of the large contribution stipulated that under no circumstances was his name to be disclosed.
2. In the tropics a snowstorm would be a (an) __?__.

3. The administration of __?__ prevents the patient from feeling pain during and immediately after an operation.
4. Wendy is __?__ in one respect: she doesn't care for ice cream.
5. In __?__ surgery, rigid precautions are taken to exclude disease-causing microorganisms.

9. MONO (MON): "one," "single," "alone"
10. POLY: "many"

monarchy /'män-ər-kē/ *n:* rule by a single person

polyarchy /'pä-lē-ˌär-kē/ *n:* rule by many

monochromatic /ˌmän-ə-krō-'mat-ik/ *adj:* of one color

polychromatic /ˌpäl-i-krō-'mat-ik/ *adj:* showing a variety of colors

monogamy /mə-'näg-ə-mē/ *n:* marriage with one mate at a time

polygamy /pə-'lig-ə-mē/ *n:* marriage to several mates at the same time

monomorphic /ˌmän-ō-'mȯr-fik/ *adj:* having a single form

polymorphic /ˌpäl-i-'mȯr-fik/ *adj:* having various forms

monosyllabic /ˌmän-ə-sə-'lab-ik/ *adj:* having one syllable

polysyllabic /ˌpäl-i-sə-'lab-ik/ *adj:* having more than three syllables

monotheism /'män-ə-thē-ˌiz-əm/ *n:* belief that there is one God

polytheism /'päl-i-thē-ˌiz-əm/ *n:* belief that there is a plurality of gods

MONO

monocle /'män-i-kəl/ *n:* eyeglass for one eye

monogram /'män-ə-ˌgram/ *n:* two or more letters interwoven to represent a name

monograph /'män-ə-ˌgraf/ *n:* written account of a single thing or class of things

monolith /'män-ᵊl-ˌith/ *n:* single stone of large size

monolog(ue) /ˈmän-ᵊl-ˌog/ *n:* long speech by one person in a group

monomania /ˌmän-ə-ˈmā-nē-ə/ *n:* derangement of mind on one subject only

monotonous /mə-ˈnät-ᵊn-əs/ *adj:* continuing in an unchanging tone; wearying

POLY

polyglot /ˈpäl-i-ˌglät/ *adj:* speaking several languages

polyglot /ˈpäl-i-ˌglät/ *n:* person who speaks several languages

polygon /ˈpäl-i-ˌgän/ *n:* closed plane figure having, literally, "many angles" (and, therefore, many sides)

polyphonic /ˌpäl-i-ˈfän-ik/ *adj:* having many sounds or voices—ANT **homophonic** /ˌhäm-ə-ˈfän-ik/ having the same sound

polytechnic /ˌpäl-i-ˈtek-nik/ *adj:* dealing with many arts or sciences

EXERCISE 8.   On your paper, enter the most appropriate word from groups 9 and 10, *mono* and *poly*, for completing the sentence.

1. So intense was Ahab's desire for revenge on Moby Dick, the white whale, that it amounted to a __?__.
2. Books for beginning readers should contain relatively few __?__ words.
3. The Romans practiced __?__, for they worshiped many gods.
4. A relative gave me some handkerchiefs embroidered with my own __?__.
5. A discussion in which Janet takes part is usually a __?__; she doesn't give anyone else a chance to speak.
6. Our __?__ neighbor speaks French, German, Russian, and English.
7. The young chemist's __?__ on garden insecticides is being widely read.
8. A __?__ institute offers instruction in many applied sciences and technical arts.
9. George longed for a change because he found the work __?__.
10. The 555-foot Washington Monument dominates the skyline of our nation's capital like a huge __?__.

Review Exercises

EXERCISE 9. On your paper, copy each Greek prefix or root from column I, and next to it enter the *letter* of its correct meaning from column II.

COLUMN I	COLUMN II
1. PHOBIA	*a.* bad; ill; difficult
2. MACRO	*b.* small
3. PHIL (PHILO)	*c.* not; without
4. MONO (MON)	*d.* one; single; alone
5. A (AN)	*e.* fear; dislike; aversion
6. DYS	*f.* one who loves or supports
7. POLY	*g.* many
8. PHOBE	*h.* loving; fond of
9. MIS	*i.* large; long
10. MICRO	*j.* good; well; advantageous
11. EU	*k.* hate
12. PHILE	*l.* one who fears or dislikes

EXERCISE 10. On your paper, enter the word that means the OPPOSITE of each word defined below. For your guidance, your first answer should be *atheism*.

1. *theism* (belief in God)
2. *Russophile* (supporter of Russia)
3. *typical* (conforming to a type)
4. *eupepsia* (good digestion)
5. *Anglophobe* (one who dislikes England)
6. *philanthropist* (lover of humanity)
7. *monotheistic* (believing there is but one God)
8. *cacophonous* (harsh in sound)
9. *polychromatic* (showing a variety of colors)
10. *septic* (infected)

11. *Francophobe* (one who dislikes France)
12. *polygamous* (married to several mates at the same time)
13. *microscopic* (invisible to the naked eye)
14. *hypertrophy* (enlargement, as from excessive use)
15. *polyarchy* (rule by many)
16. *Germanophile* (supporter of Germany)
17. *misogyny* (hatred of women)
18. *monosyllabic* (having but one syllable)
19. *macrocosm* (the great world; universe)
20. *polymorphic* (having various forms)

EXERCISE 11. Which word, selected from the vocabulary list below, will correctly complete the sentence? Enter the appropriate word on your paper.

VOCABULARY LIST

euphemistic	euphoria	dysentery
monogram	dysphagia	acrophobia
euthanasia	anesthesia	dystrophy
misanthropy	anomalous	philatelist
anonymous	monograph	xenophobia

1. The practice of __?__ is illegal in every civilized society.
2. A two-headed horse would be a (an) __?__ sight.
3. The new regime dislikes foreigners; it exhibits a profound __?__.
4. Though the letter was __?__, I was able to discover who had written it.
5. The term "mortician" is a (an) __?__ term for "undertaker."
6. As a result of drinking contaminated water, he contracted __?__, an inflammation of the large intestine.
7. A (An) __?__ specializes in collecting stamps.
8. I had no dread of heights, but my companion's __?__ became more severe as we approached the summit.
9. So effective was the local __?__ that I scarcely felt any pain during the minor surgery.
10. The biology professor, a skilled writer, has completed a (an) __?__ on earthworms.

EXERCISE 12. On your paper, enter the *letter* of the word in each group that means either the SAME as or the OPPOSITE of the italicized word.

1. *claustrophobia*   *a.* acrophobia   *b.* rabies   *c.* philanthropy
   d. agoraphobia   *e.* xenophobia
2. *monotonous*   *a.* philharmonic   *b.* interesting   *c.* polyglot
   d. polysyllabic   *e.* amorphous
3. *anhydrous*   *a.* waterless   *b.* hydrophobic   *c.* dyspeptic
   d. gaseous   *e.* anemic
4. *polytheism*   *a.* atheism   *b.* monotheism   *c.* disbelief
   d. godlessness   *e.* theism
5. *euphonious*   *a.* polyphonic   *b.* misanthropic   *c.* cacophonous
   d. homophonic   *e.* euphemistic

EXERCISE 13. Answer each question in a sentence or two.

1. Why is it monotonous to listen to a monologue?
2. How would the presence of hundreds of cacophonous birds affect the euphoria of people living in the neighborhood?
3. Would it be an anomaly for a well-known Francophobe to choose to live permanently in France? Why, or why not?
4. Why would it surprise you to learn that a distinguished bibliophile has been suffering from dyslexia?
5. Is it atypical for an immigrant to encounter no xenophobia? Explain.

EXERCISE 14. On your paper, enter the *letter* of the word that best completes the analogy.

1. *Anemia* is to *red blood cells* as *anoxia* is to __?__.
   a. corpuscles   *b.* disease   *c.* oxygen   *d.* tissue   *e.* surgery
2. *Euthenics* is to *environment* as *eugenics* is to __?__.
   a. surroundings   *b.* heredity   *c.* nutrition   *d.* health   *e.* education
3. *Dysphagia* is to *swallowing* as *dysphasia* is to __?__.
   a. digestion   *b.* hearing   *c.* sight   *d.* speech   *e.* tasting
4. *Misanthropy* is to *humanity* as *misogamy* is to __?__.
   a. women   *b.* novelty   *c.* marriage   *d.* argument   *e.* foreigners
5. *Polychromatic* is to *colors* as *polytechnic* is to __?__.
   a. arts   *b.* sounds   *c.* forms   *d.* syllables   *e.* angles

11. LOGY: "science," "study," "account"

anthropology /ˌan-thrə-'päl-ə-jē/ *n:* science dealing with the origin, races, customs, and beliefs of humankind

bacteriology /bak-ˌtir-ē-'äl-ə-jē/ *n:* science dealing with the study of bacteria

biology /bī-'äl-ə-jē/ *n:* science dealing with the study of living organisms

cardiology /ˌkärd-ē-'äl-ə-jē/ *n:* science dealing with the action and diseases of the heart

criminology /ˌkrim-ə-'näl-ə-jē/ *n:* scientific study of crimes and criminals

dermatology /ˌdər-mə-'täl-ə-jē/ *n:* science dealing with the skin and its diseases

ecology /i-'käl-ə-jē/ *n:* science dealing with the relation of living things to their environment and to each other

ethnology /eth-'näl-ə-jē/ *n:* science dealing with human races, their origin, distribution, culture, etc.

genealogy /ˌjē-nē-'äl-ə-jē/ *n:* account of the descent of a person or family from an ancestor

geology /jē-'äl-ə-jē/ *n:* science dealing with the earth's history as recorded in rocks

meteorology /ˌmēt-ē-ə-'räl-ə-jē/ *n:* science dealing with the atmosphere and weather

morphology /mȯr-'fäl-ə-jē/ *n:* scientific study of the forms and structures of plants and animals

mythology /mith-'äl-ə-jē/ *n:* account or study of myths

necrology /nə-'kräl-ə-jē/ *n:* register of persons who have died

neurology /n(y)u̇-'räl-ə-jē/ *n:* scientific study of the nervous system and its diseases

paleontology /ˌpā-lē-än-'täl-ə-jē/ *n:* science dealing with life in the remote past as recorded in fossils

pathology /pə-'thäl-ə-jē/ *n:* science dealing with the nature and causes of disease

petrology /pə-'träl-ə-jē/ *n:* scientific study of rocks

physiology /ˌfiz-ē-'äl-ə-jē/ *n:* science dealing with the functions of living things or their organs

psychology /sī-'käl-ə-jē/ *n:* science of the mind

sociology /ˌsō-sē-'äl-ə-jē/ *n:* study of the evolution, development, and functioning of human society

technology /tek-'näl-ə-jē/ *n:* industrial science

theology /thē-'äl-ə-jē/ *n:* study of religion and religious ideas

EXERCISE 15. On your paper, enter the most appropriate word from group 11, *logy*, for completing the sentence.

1. Both ethnology and __?__ deal with the origin and races of humankind.
2. The tale of Pyramus and Thisbe is one of the most appealing in Greek __?__.
3. Advances in __?__ have enabled industries to manufacture products at lower costs.
4. Sherlock Holmes is a fictional character who excels in __?__, bringing numerous felons to justice.
5. Patients suffering from skin disorders are often referred to a specialist in __?__.

12. BIO: "life"

abiogenesis /ˌā-ˌbī-ō-'jen-ə-səs/ *n:* spontaneous generation (development of life from lifeless matter)—ANT biogenesis

amphibious /am-'fib-ē-əs/ *adj:* able to live both on land and in water

antibiotic /ˌant-i-bī-'ät-ik/ *n:* antibacterial substance produced by a living organism

autobiography /ˌȯt-ə-bī-'äg-rə-fē/ *n:* story of a person's life written by that person

biochemistry /ˌbī-ō-'kem-ə-strē/ *n:* chemistry dealing with chemical compounds and processes in living plants and animals

biogenesis /ˌbī-ō-'jen-ə-səs/ *n:* development of life from preexisting life —ANT **abiogenesis**

biography /bī-'äg-rə-fē/ *n:* story of a person's life written by another person

biology /bī-'äl-ə-jē/ *n:* science dealing with the study of living organisms

biometry /bī-'äm-ə-trē/ *n:* calculation of the probable duration of human life—or **biometrics** /ˌbī-ō-'me-triks/

biopsy /'bī-ˌäp-sē/ *n:* diagnostic examination of a piece of tissue from the living body

biota /bī-'ōt-ə/ *n:* the living plants (flora) and living animals (fauna) of a region

microbe /'mī-ˌkrōb/ *n:* very minute living organism

symbiosis /ˌsim-bi-'ō-səs/ *n:* the living together in mutually helpful association of two dissimilar organisms

EXERCISE 16. On your paper, enter the most appropriate word from group 12, *bio*, for completing the sentence.

1. Fish can live only in water, but frogs are __?__.
2. One __?__ widely used to arrest the growth of harmful bacteria is penicillin.
3. In his __?__ AN AMERICAN DOCTOR'S ODYSSEY, Victor Heiser tells how he survived the Johnstown flood.
4. An example of __?__ is provided by the fungus that lives in a mutually beneficial partnership with the roots of an oak tree.
5. A (An) __?__ is a microscopic living organism.

13. TOMY (TOM): "cutting," "operation of incision"

anatomy /ə-'nat-ə-mē/ *n*

(1) dissection of plants or animals for the purpose of studying their structure, (2) structure of a plant or animal

appendectomy /ˌap-ən-'dek-tə-mē/ *n:* surgical removal of the appendix

atom /'at-əm/ *n:* smallest particle of an element (literally, "not cut," "indivisible")

atomizer /'at-ə-ˌmī-zə(r)/ *n:* instrument for reducing to a fine spray

dichotomy /dī-'kät-ə-mē/ *n:* cutting or division into two; division

gastrectomy /ga-'strek-tə-mē/ *n:* surgical removal of part or all of the stomach

lobotomy /lō-'bät-ə-mē/ *n:* brain surgery for treatment of certain mental disorders

phlebotomy /fli-'bät-ə-mē/ *n:* opening of a vein to diminish the blood supply

tonsillectomy /ˌtän-sə-'lek-tə-mē/ *n:* surgical removal of the tonsils

tracheotomy /ˌtrā-kē-'ät-ə-mē/ *n:* surgical operation of cutting into the *trachea* (windpipe)

EXERCISE 17. On your paper, enter the most appropriate word from group 13, *tomy (tom)*, for completing the sentence.

1. The sharp __?__ between your promises and your deeds suggests that you are not reliable.
2. Even though I have had a number of colds and sore throats, my physician feels I do not need a (an) __?__.
3. In former times __?__ (*bleeding*) was used indiscriminately as a treatment for practically all illnesses.
4. You will learn about the structure of the skeleton, the muscles, the heart, and other parts of the body when you study human __?__.
5. Only in extremely serious mental illness is a (an) __?__ performed.

14. POD: "foot"

antipodes /an-ˈtip-ə-ˌdēz/ *n pl:* parts of the globe (or their inhabitants) diametrically opposite (literally, "with the feet opposite")

arthropod /ˈär-thrə-ˌpäd/ *n:* any invertebrate (animal having no backbone) with jointed legs. Example: insects.

chiropodist /kə-ˈräp-əd-əst/ *n:* one who treats ailments of the human foot

dipody /ˈdip-əd-ē/ *n:* verse (line of poetry) consisting of two feet; a dimeter

podiatrist /pə-ˈdī-ə-trəst/ *n:* chiropodist

podium /ˈpōd-ē-əm/ *n*
  (1) dais; raised platform
  (2) low wall serving as a foundation

pseudopod /ˈsüd-ə-ˌpäd/ *n:* (literally, "false foot") temporary extension of the protoplasm, as in the ameba, to enable the organism to move and take in food—or **pseudopodium** /ˌsüd-ə-ˈpōd-ē-əm/

tripod /ˈtrī-ˌpäd/ *n:* utensil, stool, or caldron having three legs

unipod /ˈyü-nə-ˌpäd/ *n:* one-legged support

EXERCISE 18.   On your paper, enter the most appropriate word from group 14, *pod*, for completing the sentence.

1. One who treats ailments of the feet is known as a chiropodist or a (an) __?__.
2. The English often call Australia and New Zealand the __?__, since these countries are almost diametrically opposite England on the globe.
3. As the guest conductor stepped onto the __?__, the audience burst into applause.
4. A crab is a (an) __?__; so, too, are lobsters, bees, flies, spiders, and other invertebrates with segmented legs.
5. Having only three legs, a (an) __?__ is less stable than a four-legged support.

15. HOMO: "one and the same," "like"
16. HETERO: "different"

homochromatic /ˌhō-mō-krə-ˈmat-ik/ *adj:* having the same color

heterochromatic /ˌhet-ə-rō-krə-ˈmat-ik/ *adj:* having different colors

homogeneous /ˌhō-mə-ˈjē-nē-əs/ *adj:* of the same kind; similar

heterogeneous /ˌhet-ə-rə-ˈjē-nē-əs/ *adj:* differing in kind; dissimilar

homology /hō-ˈmäl-ə-jē/ *n:* fundamental similarity of structure

heterology /ˌhet-ə-ˈräl-ə-jē/ *n:* lack of correspondence between parts

homomorphic /ˌhō-mə-ˈmȯr-fik/ *adj:* exhibiting similarity of form

heteromorphic /ˌhet-ə-rō-ˈmȯr-fik/ *adj:* exhibiting diversity of form

homonym /ˈhäm-ə-ˌnim/ *n:* word that sounds like another but differs in meaning and spelling. Examples: *principal* and *principle*.

heteronym /ˈhet-ə-rə-ˌnim/ *n:* word spelled like another, but differing in sound and meaning. Examples: *bass* (the tone, pronounced "base") and *bass* (the fish, rhyming with "pass").

HOMO

homocentric /hō-mō-ˈsen-trik/ *adj:* having the same center

homophonic /ˌhäm-ə-ˈfän-ik/ *adj:* having the same sound—ANT **polyphonic** /ˌpäl-i-ˈfän-ik/ having many sounds or voices

HETERO

heteroclite /ˈhet-ə-rə-ˌklīt/ *adj:* deviating from the common rule

heteroclite /ˈhet-ə-rə-ˌklīt/ *n:* person or thing deviating from the common rule

heterodox /ˈhet-ə-rə-ˌdäks/ *adj:* contrary to some acknowledged standard—ANT **orthodox** / ȯr-thə-ˌdäks/ conforming to an acknowledged standard

EXERCISE 19. On your paper, enter the most appropriate word from groups 15 and 16, *homo* and *hetero*, for completing the sentence.

1. The butterfly is __?__; it goes through four stages in its life cycle, and in each of these it has a different form.
2. An archery target usually consists of several __?__ circles.
3. People of many races and religions can be found in the __?__ population of large American cities.
4. The words *write* and *right* are __?__.
5. The foreleg of a horse and the wing of a bird exhibit __?__, for they have a fundamental similarity of structure.
6. To escape persecution for his __?__ views, Roger Williams fled from Massachusetts Bay Colony and founded the colony of Rhode Island.
7. *Lower* (which means "inferior") and *lower* (which means "look sullen" and rhymes with "our") are a pair of __?__s.
8. Stained-glass windows are __?__, since they are composed of glass sections of many colors.
9. The newly admitted students, though fairly __?__ in age, were quite heterogeneous in ability.
10. One would not expect heteroclite opinions from a (an) __?__ person.

17. HYPER: "over," "above," "beyond the ordinary"

18. HYPO: "under," "beneath," "less than the ordinary"

hyperacidity /ˌhī-pər-ə-ˈsid-ət-ē/ *n:* excessive acidity

hypoacidity /ˌhī-pō-ə-ˈsid-ət-ē/ *n:* weak acidity

hyperglycemia /ˌhī-pər-glī-ˈsēm-ē-ə/ *n:* excess of sugar in the blood

hypoglycemia /ˌhī-pə-glī-ˈsēm-ē-ə/ *n:* low level of sugar in the blood

hypertension /ˌhī-pər-ˈten-shən/ *n:* abnormally high blood pressure

hypotension /ˌhī-pō-ˈten-shən/ *n:* low blood pressure

hyperthyroid /ˌhī-pər-ˈthī-ˌroid/ *adj:* marked by excessive activity of the thyroid gland

hypothyroid /ˌhī-pō-ˈthī-ˌroid/ *adj:* marked by deficient activity of the thyroid gland

HYPER

hyperactive /ˌhī-pə-ˈrak-tiv/ *adj:* overactive

hyperbole /hī-ˈpər-bə-lē/ *n:* extravagant exaggeration of statement

hypercritical /ˌhī-pər-ˈkrit-i-kəl/ *adj:* overcritical

hyperemia /ˌhī-pə-ˈrē-mē-ə/ *n:* superabundance of blood

hyperopia /ˌhī-pə-ˈrō-pē-ə/ *n:* farsightedness—ANT **myopia** /mī-ˈō-pē-ə/ nearsightedness

hypersensitive /ˌhī-pər-ˈsen-sət-iv/ *adj:* excessively sensitive; super-sensitive

hypertrophy /ˌhī-ˈpər-trə-fē/ *n:* enlargement of a body part or organ, as from excessive use—ANT **atrophy** /ˈa-trə-fē/ lack of growth from want of nourishment or from disease

HYPO

hypodermic /ˌhī-pə-ˈdər-mik/ *adj:* injected under the skin

hypothesis / hī-ˈpäth-ə-səs/ *n:* theory or supposition assumed as a basis for reasoning (something "placed under")

hypothetical /ˌhī-pə-ˈthet-i-kəl/ *adj:* assumed without proof for the purpose of reasoning; conjectural

EXERCISE 20. On your paper, enter the most appropriate word from groups 17 and 18, *hyper* and *hypo*, for completing the sentence.

1. Try not to hurt Ann's feelings when you criticize her work, as she is ___?___.

2. In ___?___, the blood pressure is lower than normal.

3. The student who judged the composition was ___?___; he exaggerated minor faults and gave no credit at all for the author's style and humor.

4. Nobody finished the lemonade because of its __?__. Evidently, too much lemon juice had been used.
5. The following statement is an example of __?__: "I've told you a *million* times to wear your boots when it rains."
6. A (An) __?__ syringe and needle are used to administer injections under the skin.
7. Billy is a (an) __?__ youngster; he won't sit still for a minute.
8. If your __?__ is disproved by facts, you should abandon it.
9. In __?__, the blood pressure is abnormally high.
10. Excessive activity of the thyroid gland is a (an) __?__ condition.

19. ENDO: "within"
20. EXO: "out of," "outside"

endocrine /'en-də-krən/ *adj:* secreting internally

exocrine /'ek-sə-krən/ *adj:* secreting externally

endogamy /en-'däg-ə-mē/ *n:* marriage within the tribe, caste, or social group

exogamy /ek-'säg-ə-mē/ *n:* marriage outside the tribe, caste, or social group

endogenous /en-'däj-ə-nəs/ *adj:* produced from within; due to internal causes

exogenous /ek-'säj-ə-nəs/ *adj:* produced from without; due to external causes

endoskeleton /ˌen-dō-'skel-ət-ᵊn/ *n:* internal skeleton or supporting framework in an animal

exoskeleton /ˌek-sō-'skel-ət-ᵊn/ *n:* hard protective structure developed outside the body, as the shell of a lobster

endosmosis /ˌen-ˌdäs-'mō-səs/ *n:* osmosis inward

exosmosis /ˌek-ˌsäs-'mō-səs/ *n:* osmosis outward

endocarditis /ˌen-dō-kär-ˈdīt-əs/ *n:* inflammation of the lining of the heart

endoderm /ˈen-də-ˌdərm/ *n:* membranelike tissue lining the digestive tract

endoparasite /ˌen-dō-ˈpar-ə-ˌsīt/ *n:* parasite living in the internal organs of an animal—ANT **ectoparasite** /ˌek-tō-ˈpar-ə-ˌsīt/ parasite living on the exterior of an animal

endophyte /ˈen-də-ˌfīt/ *n:* plant growing within another plant

exoteric /ˌek-sə-ˈter-ik/ *adj:* external; exterior; readily understandable—ANT **esoteric** /ˌes-ə-ˈter-ik/ inner; private; difficult to understand

exotic /eg-ˈzät-ik/ *adj*

(1) introduced from a foreign country

(2) excitingly strange

EXERCISE 21. On your paper, enter the most appropriate word from groups 19 and 20, *endo* and *exo*, for completing the sentence.

1. Algae that live within other plants are known as __?__s.
2. Foreign visitors can often be identified by their __?__ dress.
3. __?__ glands discharge their secretions externally through ducts or tubes.
4. __?__ glands, having no ducts or tubes, secrete internally.
5. Some primitive tribes observe __?__, forbidding marriage outside the tribe.
6. The body louse is a most annoying __?__, as it moves freely over the body of its host.
7. The lobster has a thick protective shell known as an __?__.
8. Unlike lobsters, humans have an inside skeleton called an __?__.
9. Refusing to admit that the rebellion was __?__, the dictator blamed "foreign agitators."
10. Once established in the intestines of its host, an __?__ can lead a life of comparative ease.

21. ARCHY: "rule"

anarchy /ˈan-ər-kē/ *n:* total absence of rule or government; confusion; disorder

autarchy /ˈȯ-ˌtär-kē/ *n:* rule by an absolute sovereign

hierarchy /ˈhī-ə-ˌrär-kē/ *n:* body of rulers or officials grouped in ranks, each being subordinate to the rank above it

matriarchy /ˈmā-trē-ˌär-kē/ *n:* form of social organization in which the mother rules the family or tribe, descent being traced through the mother

monarchy /ˈmän-ər-kē/ *n:* state ruled over by a single person, as a king or queen

oligarchy /ˈäl-ə-ˌgär-kē/ *n:* form of government in which a few people have the power

patriarchy /ˈpā-trē-ˌär-kē/ *n:* form of social organization in which the father rules the family or tribe, descent being traced through the father

---

EXERCISE 22. On your paper, enter the most appropriate word from group 21, *archy*, for completing the sentence.

1. In the naval __?__, a rear admiral ranks below a vice admiral.
2. Many a supposedly "democratic" organization is controlled by a (an) __?__ of three or four influential members.
3. In a constitutional __?__, the power of the king or queen is usually limited by a constitution and a legislature.
4. A family in which the mother alone makes all the final decisions could be called a (an) __?__.
5. Those who declare that the best form of government is no government at all are advocating __?__.

22. GEO: "earth," "ground"

geocentric /ˌjē-ō-'sen-trik/ *adj:* measured from the earth's center; having the earth as a center

geodetic /ˌjē-ə-'det-ik/ *adj:* pertaining to *geodesy* (mathematics dealing with the earth's shape and dimensions)

geography /jē-'äg-rə-fē/ *n:* study of the earth's surface, climate, continents, people, products, etc.

geology /jē-'ȧl-ə-jē/ *n:* science dealing with the earth's history as recorded in rocks

geometry /jē-'äm-ə-trē/ *n:* mathematics dealing with lines, angles, surfaces, and solids (literally, "measurement of land")

geomorphic /ˌjē-ə-'mȯr-fik/ *adj:* pertaining to the shape of the earth or the form of its surface

geophysics /ˌjē-ə-'fiz-iks/ *n:* science treating of the forces that modify the earth

geopolitics /ˌjē-ō-'päl-ə-ˌtiks/ *n:* study of government and its policies as affected by physical geography

geoponics /ˌjē-ə-'pän-iks/ *n:* art or science of agriculture (literally, "working of the earth")

georgic /'jȯr-jik/ *adj:* agricultural

georgic /'jȯr-jik/ *n:* poem on husbandry (farming)

geotropism /jē-'ä-trə-ˌpiz-əm/ *n:* response to earth's gravity, as the growing of roots downward in the ground

The form *gee* is used at the end of a word. For example:

apogee /'ap-ə-jē/ *n:* farthest point from the earth in the orbit of a satellite

perigee /'per-ə-jē/ *n:* nearest point to the earth in the orbit of a satellite

EXERCISE 23. On your paper, enter the most appropriate word from group 22, *geo*, for completing the sentence.

1. At its apogee the moon is nearly 252,000 miles from the earth; at its __?__ it is less than 226,000 miles away.
2. Heliotropism attracts leaves to sunlight; __?__ draws roots downward in the earth.
3. To make precise earth measurements, __?__ engineers use sensitive instruments.
4. Some earthquakes have little effect on the form of the earth's surface, but others result in noticeable __?__ changes.
5. The atmosphere, the sun, and other forces that modify the earth are dealt with in the science of __?__.

23. PATH (PATHO, PATHY): (1) "feeling," "suffering"; (2) "disease"

FEELING, SUFFERING

antipathy /an-ˈtip-ə-thē/ *n:* aversion ("feeling against"); dislike—ANT **sympathy**

apathy /ˈap-ə-thē/ *n:* lack of feeling, emotion, interest, or excitement; indifference

empathy /ˈem-pə-thē/ *n:* the complete understanding of another's feelings, motives, etc.

pathetic /pə-ˈthet-ik/ *adj:* arousing pity

pathos /ˈpā-thäs/ *n:* quality in speech, writing, music, events, etc., that arouses a feeling of pity or sadness

sympathy /ˈsim-pə-thē/ *n:* a sharing of ("feeling with") another's trouble; compassion—ANT **antipathy**

telepathy /tə-ˈlep-ə-thē/ *n:* transference of the thoughts and feelings of one person to another by no apparent means of communication

homeopathy /ˌhō-mē-'äp-ə-thē/ *n:* system of medical practice that treats disease by administering minute doses of a remedy which, if given to healthy persons, would produce symptoms of the disease treated

osteopath /'äs-tē-ə-ˌpath/ *n:* practitioner of *osteopathy* (treatment of diseases by manipulation of bones, muscles, nerves, etc.)

pathogenic /ˌpath-ə-'jen-ik/ *adj:* causing disease

pathological /ˌpath-ə-'läj-i-kəl/ *adj:* due to disease

psychopathic /ˌsī-kə-'path-ik/ *adj*
    (1) pertaining to mental disease
    (2) insane

EXERCISE 24. On your paper, enter the most appropriate word from group 23, *path* (*patho, pathy*), for completing the sentence.

1. Among the diseases caused by __?__ bacteria are pneumonia and scarlet fever.
2. Sometimes, as if by __?__, one may know the thoughts of an absent friend or relative.
3. The __?__ expression on the youngster's face made everyone feel sorry for him.
4. Such intense __?__ resulted from their quarrel that the sisters haven't spoken to each other for years.
5. The reunion of the rescued miners with their families was full of __?__.

24. MORPH: "form"

amorphous /ə-'mȯr-fəs/ *adj:* without definite form; shapeless

anthropomorphic /ˌan-thrə-pə-'mȯr-fik/ *adj:* attributing human form or characteristics to beings not human, especially gods

dimorphous /dī-'mȯr-fəs/ *adj:* occurring under two distinct forms

endomorphic /ˌen-də-'mȯr-fik/ *adj:* occurring within; internal

heteromorphic /'het-ə-rō-'mȯr-fik/ *adj:* exhibiting diversity of form

metamorphosis /ˌmet-ə-'mȯr-fə-səs/ *n:* change of form

monomorphic /ˌmän-ō-'mȯr-fik/ *adj:* having a single form

morphology /mȯr-'fäl-ə-jē/ *n:* branch of biology dealing with the form and structure of animals and plants

EXERCISE 25. On your paper, enter the most appropriate word from group 24, *morph*, for completing the sentence.

1. As the fog slowly lifted, __?__ objects began to assume definite shapes.
2. When you study cell __?__, you will learn about the nucleus, the cell membrane, and other features of cell structure.
3. The drastic __?__ from slum area to attractive residential neighborhood was accomplished in less than three years.
4. Individual members of a (an) __?__ species are identical or similar in form.
5. The ancient Greeks had a (an) __?__ conception of deity; they gave their gods and goddesses the characteristics of men and women.

25. PERI: "around," "about," "near," "enclosing"

pericardium /ˌper-ə-'kärd-ē-əm/ *n:* membranous sac enclosing the heart

perigee /'per-ə-jē/ *n:* nearest point to the earth in the orbit of a satellite—ANT **apogee** /'ap-ə-jē/ farthest point from the earth in the orbit of a satellite

perihelion /ˌper-ə-'hēl-yən/ *n:* nearest point to the sun in the orbit of a planet or comet—ANT **aphelion** /a-'fēl-yən/ farthest point from the sun in the orbit of a planet or comet

perimeter /pə-'rim-ət-ə(r)/ *n:* the whole outer boundary or measurement of a surface or figure

periphery /pə-'rif-ə-rē/ *n:* outside boundary

periphrastic /ˌper-ə-'fras-tik/ *adj:* expressed in a roundabout way

periscope /'per-ə-ˌskōp/ *n:* instrument permitting those in a submarine a view ("look around") of the surface

peristalsis /ˌper-ə-'stȯl-səs/ *n:* wavelike contraction of the walls of the intestines which propels contents onward

peristyle /'per-ə-ˌstīl/ *n*
   (1) row of columns around a building or court
   (2) the space so enclosed

peritonitis /ˌper-ət-ᵊnᴶīt-əs/ *n:* inflammation of the *peritoneum* (membrane lining the abdominal cavity and covering the organs)

EXERCISE 26. On your paper, enter the most appropriate word from group 25, *peri*, for completing the sentence.

1. The __?__ of a rectangle is twice its width plus twice its length.

2. At its aphelion, the earth is 152,516,120 kilometers (94,560,000 miles) from the sun; at its __?__, it is only 147,496,770 kilometers (91,448,000 miles) away.

3. The sections of an orange are narrowest at its center and widest at its __?__, or rind.

4. By a series of wavelike contractions, known as __?__, food is moved through the intestines.

5. Before changing its position, the cautious turtle raised its head like a __?__ to survey surrounding conditions.

Do not write in this book. Enter all answers on separate paper.

Review Exercises

EXERCISE 27. On your paper, enter the word that means the OPPOSITE of each word defined below.

1. *heterogeneous* (differing in kind)
2. *orthodox* (conforming to an acknowledged standard)
3. *atrophy* (lack of growth from want of nourishment)
4. *sympathy* (a feeling of accord)
5. *polyphonic* (having many sounds)
6. *esoteric* (difficult to understand)
7. *homology* (fundamental similarity in structure)
8. *ectoparasite* (parasite living on the exterior of an animal)
9. *hypotension* (low blood pressure)
10. *myopia* (nearsightedness)
11. *hyperacidity* (excessive acidity)
12. *exosmosis* (osmosis outward)
13. *endocrine* (secreting internally)
14. *hyperglycemia* (excess of sugar in the blood)
15. *perigee* (nearest point to the earth in the orbit of a satellite)
16. *biogenesis* (development of life from preexisting life)
17. *exogenous* (due to external causes)
18. *perihelion* (nearest point to the sun in the orbit of a planet)
19. *heteromorphic* (exhibiting diversity of form)
20. *exogamy* (marriage outside the tribe, caste, or social group)

EXERCISE 28. As clues to each mystery word below, you are given its first letter, the number of its missing letters, and its definition. On your paper, enter the complete word.

1. Only 9 percent of the registered voters actually voted in the last primary. How can we explain such a ___5___ (*lack of interest*)?
2. The p___8___ (*outer boundary*) of a 7-inch square measures 28 inches.
3. Some TV weather programs have enlarged our m___13___ (*dealing with the atmosphere*) knowledge.
4. Occasionally we prefer e___5___ (*introduced from a foreign country*) dishes to American cookery.
5. Further progress in t___9___ (*industrial science*) may ultimately bring about a shorter workweek.

6. It is very easy to hurt the feelings of a h____13____ (*excessively sensitive*) person.

7. Between the toppling of the dictatorship and the setting up of the republic, there was a five-day period of violent a____6____ (*total absence of government*).

8. Some of the lecturer's remarks were so e____7____ (*difficult to understand*) that only advanced scholars could fully comprehend them.

9. While it is noon here, it is midnight in the a____8____ (*diametrically opposite parts of the globe*).

10. By means of a b____5____ (*diagnostic examination of a piece of tissue from the living body*), a surgeon can usually tell whether a growth is benign or malignant.

EXERCISE 29. On your paper, copy each Greek prefix or root from column I, and next to it enter the *letter* of its correct meaning from column II.

COLUMN I	COLUMN II
1. POD	*a.* different
2. EXO	*b.* life
3. HETERO	*c.* under; beneath; less than ordinary
4. GEO	*d.* one and the same; like
5. LOGY	*e.* rule
6. HYPO	*f.* around; about; near; enclosing
7. BIO	*g.* cutting; operation of incision
8. MORPH	*h.* feeling; suffering; disease
9. PATH (PATHO, PATHY)	*i.* earth; ground
10. ARCHY	*j.* within
11. PERI	*k.* foot
12. TOMY (TOM)	*l.* form
13. HYPER	*m.* out of; outside
14. ENDO	*n.* over; above; beyond the ordinary
15. HOMO	*o.* science; study; account

EXERCISE 30. On your paper, enter the *letter* of the word or expression that has most nearly the SAME MEANING as the italicized word.

1. *hypercritical* reviewer
   a. uncritical   *b.* hypersensitive   *c.* esoteric   *d.* overcritical
2. complete *metamorphosis*
   a. change   *b.* course   *c.* process   *d.* misunderstanding
3. eminent *podiatrist*
   a. criminologist   *b.* world traveler   *c.* foot specialist   *d.* osteopath
4. trace one's *genealogy*
   a. career   *b.* descent   *c.* downfall   *d.* personality
5. *hypothetical* statement
   a. conjectural   *b.* introductory   *c.* unbiased   *d.* incontrovertible
6. *anatomical* defect
   a. minor   *b.* irremediable   *c.* structural   *d.* inherited
7. *homogeneous* in size
   a. different   *b.* perfect   *c.* heteromorphic   *d.* similar
8. *psychopathic* behavior
   a. pathetic   *b.* indifferent   *c.* mentally disturbed
   d. unsympathetic
9. powerful *oligarchy*
   a. conservatives   *b.* ruling few   *c.* hierarchy   *d.* rank and file
10. *amorphous* ideas
   a. organized   *b.* original   *c.* exaggerated   *d.* shapeless

EXERCISE 31. Answer each question in a sentence or two.

1. Is our nation's population homogeneous or heterogeneous? Explain.
2. Which subject should you specialize in if you want to be a weather forecaster, meteorology or psychology? Why?
3. Why would most Americans have an antipathy to the establishment of a monarchy?
4. Is it more difficult to dislodge an ectoparasite than an endoparasite? Explain.
5. Would it help or hurt a biography if the author used hyperbole? Why?

6. Suppose you are afraid of meeting with apathy in a talk you are to give on amphibious animals. Would it help if you were permitted to bring a living frog into the classroom? Why, or why not?

7. How does a hypersensitive individual react when criticized by a hypercritical person? Explain.

8. Which operation saves the lives of patients suffering a blockage of air above the windpipe—an appendectomy or a tracheotomy? Explain.

9. Name one metamorphosis that you hope technology will soon bring about in an American product.

10. Whom do we have in mind when we discuss the geopolitics of our antipodes—the Chinese or the Russians? Explain.

EXERCISE 32. On your paper, enter the *letter* of the word that best completes the analogy.

1. *Environment* is to *ecology* as *skin* is to __?__.
   a. osteopathy *b.* dermatology *c.* peritonitis *d.* neurology
   e. endoderm

2. *Lobotomy* is to *brain* as *phlebotomy* is to __?__.
   a. throat *b.* nerve *c.* foot *d.* vein *e.* muscle

3. *Government* is to *anarchy* as *sympathy* is to __?__.
   a. pathos *b.* compassion *c.* apathy *d.* empathy *e.* telepathy

4. *Pathology* is to *disease* as *morphology* is to __?__.
   a. structure *b.* function *c.* descent *d.* health *e.* race

5. *Animal* is to *tapeworm* as *plant* is to __?__.
   a. earthworm *b.* biota *c.* microbe *d.* ectoparasite
   e. endophyte

CHAPTER V **Words**
Derived From Latin

When the **Latin-speaking Romans** ruled Britain, approximately 75–410 A.D., there was no English language. The native Britons spoke Celtic, a language akin to Irish and Welsh. After the Romans withdrew, the Britons were overwhelmed by Germanic invaders, the Angles and Saxons. The English we speak today is a continuation of the language of the Angles and Saxons.

Before invading Britain, the Angles and Saxons had adopted some Latin words from contacts with the vast neighboring Roman Empire. In Britain, they undoubtedly acquired a few more Latin words from the Britons, who had lived so long under Roman domination. And after 597, when the Roman monk St. Augustine introduced Christianity and the Holy Scripture—in Latin—to Britain, the Anglo-Saxons absorbed more words from Latin. But Latin had no major impact on English until 1066, when the Normans conquered England.

The Normans spoke French, a *Romance* language, i.e., a language developed from the language of the *Romans*. French, which is 85 percent descended from Latin, was England's official language for two hundred years after the Norman Conquest. The language of the Normans gradually blended with the Anglo-Saxon spoken by the common people. In the process, a considerable number of Latin words were incorporated into English indirectly, by way of French.

Later, a substantial number of other words came into English directly from Latin itself. From the Renaissance, in the sixteenth century, to the present day, as English-speaking authors and scientists have needed new words to express new ideas, they have been able to form them from Latin (or Greek).

It is no wonder, then, that more than 50 percent of the vocabulary of English derives directly or indirectly from Latin.

To boost your word power, study the common Latin prefixes and roots presented in this chapter. Each of them, as the following pages will show, can help you learn a cluster of useful English words.

Latin Prefixes 1–15

PREFIX   MEANING   SAMPLE WORDS

1. **a, ab**   away, from   *a*vert (turn *away*), *ab*duct (lead *from*)

2. **ad**   to   *ad*mit (grant entrance *to*)

3. **ante**   before   *ante*room (a room *before* another)

4. **bi**   two   *bi*cycle (a vehicle having *two* wheels)

5. **circum**   around   *circum*navigate (sail *around*)

6. **con (col, com, cor)**   together, with   *con*spire (plot *together* or *with*), *col*loquy (a talking *together;* conference), *com*pose (put *together*), *cor*respond (agree *with;* communicate *with* by exchange of letters)

7. **contra**   against   *contra*dict (speak *against;* deny)

8. **de**   from, down   *de*duction (a conclusion drawn *from* reasoning), *de*mote (move *down* in rank)

9. **dis**   apart, away   *dis*rupt (break *apart*), *dis*miss (send *away*)

10. **e, ex**   out   *e*mit (send *out;* utter), *ex*pel (drive *out*)

11. **extra**   beyond   *extra*ordinary (*beyond* the ordinary)

12. **in (il, im, ir)**   not   *in*significant (*not* significant), *il*legal (*not* legal), *im*moral (*not* moral), *ir*regular (*not* regular)

13. **in (il, im, ir)**   in, into, on   *in*ject (throw or force *in*), *il*luminate (direct light *on;* light up), *im*port (bring *into* one country from another), *ir*rigate (pour water *on*)

14. **inter**   between   *inter*rupt (break *between;* stop)

15. **intra**   within   *intra*mural (*within* the walls; inside)

EXERCISE 1. Which prefix, added to the stated root, will produce the word we are seeking? Here is the complete first answer. Use it as your model.

IN (*not*) + TANGIBLE (*able to be touched*) = INTANGIBLE (*not able to be touched*).

1. __?__ (*not*) + TANGIBLE (*able to be touched*) = __?__ (*not able to be touched*).

2. __?__ (*against*) + VENE (*come; go*) = __?__ (*go against or contrary to*).

3. __?__ (*out*) + HALE (*breathe*) = __?__ (*breathe out*).

4. __?__ (*down*) + MOTE (*move*) = __?__ (*reduce to lower rank*).

5. __?__ (*to*) + HERE (*stick*) = __?__ (*stick to*).

6. __?__ (*together*) + GREGATE (*gather*) = __?__ (*gather together; assemble*).

7. __?__ (*from*) + NORMAL = __?__ (*deviating from the normal*).

8. __?__ (*around*) + SCRIBE (*write; draw*) = __?__ (*write or draw a line around; encircle; limit*).

9. __?__ (*between*) + CEDE (*go*) = __?__ (*go between arguing parties; mediate*).

10. __?__ (*two*) + SECT (*cut*) = __?__ (*cut into two parts*).

11. __?__ (*beyond*) + MURAL (*pertaining to a wall*) = __?__ (*occurring beyond the walls*).

12. __?__ (*before*) + DILUVIAN (*pertaining to a flood*) = __?__ (*belonging to the period before the Biblical Flood; therefore, very old*).

13. __?__ (*within*) + VENOUS (*pertaining to a vein*) = __?__ (*within a vein*).

14. __?__ (*apart*) + PEL (*drive*) = __?__ (*drive apart; scatter*).

15. __?__ (*in*) + FUSE (*pour*) = __?__ (*pour in; fill; instill*).

16. __?__ (*down*) + SCEND (*climb*) = __?__ (*climb down*).

17. __?__ (*beyond*) + SENSORY (*pertaining to the senses*) = __?__ (*beyond the scope of the senses*).

18. __?__ (*apart*) + SECT (*cut*) = __?__ (*cut apart*).

19. __?__ (*from*) + SOLVE (*loose*) = __?__ (*loose from; release from*).

20. __?__ (*apart*) + PUTE (*think*) = __?__ (*think apart—differently from others; argue*).

EXERCISE 2. On your paper, copy each Latin prefix from column I, and next to it enter the *letter* of its correct meaning from column II.

COLUMN I

1. contra
2. ante
3. de
4. extra
5. a, ab
6. in (il, im, ir)
7. bi
8. intra
9. dis
10. e, ex
11. ad
12. inter
13. circum
14. con (col, com, cor)

COLUMN II

a. within
b. between
c. in; into; on
d. from; down
e. out
f. against
g. around
h. beyond
i. apart; away
j. to
k. together
l. before
m. two
n. away; from

Latin Prefixes 16–30

PREFIX   MEANING   SAMPLE WORDS

16. **ob**   against   *ob*loquy (a talking *against;* censure)

17. **per**   through, thoroughly   *per*ennial (lasting *through* the years; enduring), *per*vert (*thoroughly* turn from the right way; corrupt)

18. **post**   after   *post*war (*after* the war)

19. **pre**   before   *pre*monition (a warning *before;* forewarning)

20. **preter**   beyond   *preter*human (*beyond* what is human)

21. **pro**   forward   *pro*gressive (moving *forward*)

22. **re** again, back *re*vive (make alive *again*), *re*tort (hurl *back;* reply sharply)

23. **retro** backward *retro*gression (act of moving *backward*)

24. **se** apart *se*cede (move *apart;* withdraw)

25. **semi** half *semi*circle (*half* of a circle)

26. **sub** under *sub*merge (put *under* or plunge into water)

27. **super** above *super*natural (*above* what is natural; miraculous)

28. **trans** across, through *trans*continental (extending *across* a continent), *trans*mit (send *through*)

29. **ultra** beyond, exceedingly *ultra*conservative (*exceedingly* conservative)

30. **vice** in place of *vice*-president (officer acting *in place of* the president)

EXERCISE 3. On your paper, copy each Latin prefix from column I, and next to it enter the *letter* of its correct meaning from column II.

COLUMN I	COLUMN II
1. semi	*a.* against
2. ob	*b.* beyond; exceedingly
3. sub	*c.* again; back
4. trans	*d.* before
5. vice	*e.* after
6. ultra	*f.* half
7. super	*g.* apart
8. re	*h.* under
9. pro	*i.* in place of
10. post	*j.* above
11. se	*k.* forward
12. pre	*l.* across; through

EXERCISE 4. Which prefix, added to the stated root, will produce the word we are seeking?

1. __?__ (*in place of*) + CHANCELLOR = __?__ (*person acting in place of a chancellor*).

2. __?__ (*half*) + ANNUAL = __?__ (*occurring every half year*).

3. __?__ (*under*) + VERT (*turn*) = __?__ (*turn under; undermine*).

4. __?__ (*apart*) + CLUDE (*shut*) = __?__ (*shut or keep apart; isolate*).

5. __?__ (*above*) + SEDE (*sit*) = __?__ (*sit above; take the place of; replace*).

6. __?__ (*forward*) + MOTE (*move*) = __?__ (*move foward; raise in rank*).

7. __?__ (*against*) + DURATE (*hardened*) = __?__ (*hardened against; unyielding; stubborn*).

8. __?__ (*through*) + IENT (*going*) = __?__ (*going through—not staying; short-lived*).

9. __?__ (*against*) + STRUCT (*pile up*) = __?__ (*pile up—an obstacle—against; hinder*).

10. __?__ (*back*) + CALCITRANT (*kicking*) = __?__ (*kicking back; rebellious*).

11. __?__ (*after*) + PONE (*put*) = __?__ (*put after; defer; delay*).

12. __?__ (*exceedingly*) + NATIONALISTIC = __?__ (*exceedingly nationalistic*).

13. __?__ (*before*) + REQUISITE (*required*) = __?__ (*required before; necessary as a preliminary*).

14. __?__ (*backward*) + ACTIVE = __?__ (*acting backward; effective in a prior time*).

15. __?__ (*through*) + MEATE (*pass*) = __?__ (*pass through*).

16. __?__ (*again*) + SUME (*take*) = __?__ (*take up or begin again*).

17. __?__ (*thoroughly*) + TURB (*disturb*) = __?__ (*disturb thoroughly; agitate*).

18. __?__ (*beyond*) + NATURAL = __?__ (*beyond what is natural*).

19. __?__ (*apart*) + GREGATE (*gather*) = __?__ (*set apart; gather into separate groups*).

20. __?__ (*under*) + MARINE (*pertaining to the sea*) = __?__ (*used or existing under the sea's surface*).

Review Exercises

EXERCISE 5. On your paper, copy each numbered word below, and next to it enter its basic meaning. Let your knowledge of Latin prefixes and the hints given below guide you to the answers. Your first answer should appear as follows on your paper:

1. report—carry back

Hint for Words 1–5: -port means "carry."

1. report
2. import
3. transport
4. deport
5. export

Hint for Words 6–10: -ject means "throw."

6. interject
7. eject
8. object
9. project
10. inject

Hint for Words 11–15: -scribe means "write."

11. superscribe
12. transcribe
13. prescribe
14. inscribe
15. subscribe

Hint for Words 16–20: -pel means "drive."

16. dispel
17. propel
18. expel
19. impel
20. repel

Hint for Words 21–25: -voke means "call."

21. evoke
22. convoke
23. provoke
24. revoke
25. invoke

Hint for Words 26–30: -mit means "send."

26. permit
27. admit
28. transmit
29. emit
30. remit

Hint for Words 31–35: -tract means "drag," "draw."

31. protract
32. subtract
33. distract
34. retract
35. detract

Hint for Words 36–40: -duce means "lead," "draw."

36. seduce
37. induce
38. produce
39. deduce
40. reduce

Hint for Words 41–45: -cede or -ceed means "go."
41. intercede   43. secede   45. recede
42. proceed   44. exceed

Hint for Words 46–50: -fer means "carry," "bring," "bear."
46. transfer   48. refer   50. defer
47. prefer   49. infer

LATIN ROOTS
1. RUPT: "break," "burst"

abrupt /ə-'brəpt/ *adj*
  (1) broken off
  (2) sudden

corrupt /kə-'rəpt/ *adj:* changed ("broken to pieces") from good to bad; vicious

corrupt /kə-'rəpt/ *v:* change ("break to pieces") from good to bad; debase; pervert; falsify

disrupt /dis-'rəpt/ *v:* break apart

erupt /i-'rəpt/ *v:* burst or break out

incorruptible /ˌin-kə-'rəp-tə-bəl/ *adj:* inflexibly honest; incapable of being corrupted or bribed

interrupt /ˌint-ə-'rəpt/ *v:* break into or between; hinder; stop

rupture /'rəp-chə(r)/ *n*
  (1) break; breaking
  (2) hostility

EXERCISE 6. On your paper, enter the most appropriate word from group 1, *rupt*, for completing the sentence.

1. The simmering antipathy between the rival groups may __?__ into open combat.
2. The star's __?__ withdrawal from the cast took the producer by surprise.
3. Both sides had faith in the judge's honesty, for he was known to be __?__.
4. Many homes were flooded as a result of a (an) __?__ in a water main.
5. Please don't __?__ me when I am speaking on the telephone.

2. CIDE: "killing," "killer"

fratricide /'fra-trə-ˌsīd/ *n:* act of killing (or killer of) one's brother

genocide /'jen-ə-ˌsīd/ *n:* deliberate extermination of a racial or cultural group

germicide /'jər-mə-ˌsīd/ *n:* substance that kills germs

herbicide /'(h)ər-bə-ˌsīd/ *n:* substance that kills plants

homicide /'häm-ə-ˌsīd/ *n:* killing of one human by another

infanticide /in-'fant-ə-ˌsīd/ *n:* act of killing (or killer of) an infant

insecticide /in-'sek-tə-ˌsīd/ *n:* substance that kills insects

matricide /'ma-trə-ˌsīd/ *n:* act of killing (or killer of) one's mother

patricide /'pa-trə-ˌsīd/ *n:* act of killing (or killer of) one's father

pesticide /'pes-tə-ˌsīd/ *n:* substance that kills rats, insects, bacteria, etc.

regicide /'rej-ə-ˌsīd/ *n:* act of killing (or killer of) a king

sororicide /sə-'rȯr-ə-ˌsīd/ *n:* act of killing (or killer of) one's sister

suicide /'sü-ə-ˌsīd/ *n:* act of killing (or killer of) one's self

tyrannicide /tə-'ran-ə-ˌsīd/ *n:* act of killing (or killer of) a tyrant

EXERCISE 7. On your paper, enter the most appropriate word from group 2, *cide*, for completing the sentence.

1. Friends of the victim doubted that she had taken her own life, for they could think of no reason for her committing __?__.

2. The assailant was told that he would be charged with __?__ if his victim were to die.

3. To prevent the extermination of minorities, the United Nations voted in 1948 to outlaw __?__.

4. Claudius, in Shakespeare's HAMLET, is guilty of __?__, because he has slain his brother.

5. The attempt at __?__ failed when the king's would-be assassins were arrested outside the palace.

6. One way to get rid of weeds is to spray them with a (an) __?__.

3. STRING (STRICT): "bind," "draw tight"

astringent /ə-'strin-jənt/ *adj*
    (1) drawing (the tissues) tightly together
    (2) stern; austere

astringent /ə-'strin-jənt/ *n:* substance that shrinks tissues and checks flow of blood by drawing together blood vessels

boa constrictor /'bō-ə-kən-'strik-tə(r)/ *n:* snake that "constricts" or crushes its prey in its coils

constrict /kən-'strikt/ *v:* draw together; bind

restrict /ri-'strikt/ *v:* keep within limits; confine

stricture /'strik-chə(r)/ *n:* adverse criticism (literally, "tightening"); censure

stringent /'strin-jənt/ *adj:* strict (literally, "binding tight"); rigid; severe

unrestricted /ˌən-ri-'strikt-əd/ *adj*
    (1) not confined within bounds; free
    (2) open to all

EXERCISE 8. On your paper, enter the most appropriate word from group 3, *string (strict)*, for completing the sentence.

1. All residents enjoy __?__ use of the pool, except children under 16, who must leave at 5 P.M.
2. Unless you __?__ your remarks to the topic on the floor, the chair will rule you "out of order."
3. Shavers use a styptic pencil or some other __?__ to check the bleeding from minor cuts.
4. Jean Valjean's sentence of five years at hard labor for stealing a loaf of bread seems an unusually __?__ punishment.
5. If you interpret a minor suggestion for improvement as a major __?__, you are being hypersensitive.

4. VOR: "eat greedily"

carnivore /ˈkär-nə-ˌvȯ(ə)r/ *n:* flesh-eating animal

carnivorous /kär-ˈniv-ə-rəs/ *adj:* flesh-eating

devour /di-ˈvaů-ə(r)/ *v:*
  (1) eat greedily or ravenously
  (2)· seize upon and destroy

herbivore /ˈ(h)ər-bə-ˌvȯ(ə)r/ *n:* plant-eating animal

herbivorous /ˌ(h)ər-ˈbiv-ə-rəs/ *adj:* dependent on ("eating") plants as food

insectivorous /ˌin-ˌsek-ˈtiv-ə-rəs/ *adj:* dependent on ("eating") insects as food

omnivore /ˈäm-ni-ˌvȯ(ə)r/ *n:* person or animal that eats everything (both flesh and plants)

omnivorous /äm-ˈniv-ə-rəs/ *adj*
  (1) eating everything, both plant and animal substances
  (2) avidly taking in everything, as an *omnivorous* reader

voracious /vȯ-ˈrā-shəs/ *adj*

   (1) greedy in eating

   (2) insatiable, as a *voracious* appetite

EXERCISE 9. On your paper, enter the most appropriate word from group 4, *vor*, for completing the sentence.

1. Spiders are __?__; their principal food is insects.
2. Have you ever watched a ravenous eater __?__ a sandwich in two or three gulps?
3. The diet of the __?__ lion includes the zebra, antelope, buffalo, and ostrich.
4. Since human beings obtain food from both plants and animals, they may be described as __?__ organisms.
5. The rabbit is __?__, eating grass, vegetables, and even the bark of trees.
6. The squirrel feeds on fruit, nuts, and seeds; it is not a (an) __?__.

5. VIV: "live," "alive"

convivial /kən-ˈviv-ē-əl/ *adj:* fond of eating and drinking with friends; jovial; hospitable

revive /ri-ˈvīv/ *v:* bring back to life; restore

survive /sər-ˈvīv/ *v:* outlive; remain alive after

vivacious /və-ˈvā-shəs/ *adj:* lively in temper or conduct

vivacity /və-ˈvas-ə-tē/ *n:* liveliness of spirit

vivid /ˈviv-əd/ *adj*

   (1) full of life

   (2) sharp and clear; graphic

vivify /ˈviv-ə-ˌfī/ *v:* enliven; make vivid

vivisection /ˌviv-ə-ˈsek-shən/ *n:* operation on a living animal for scientific investigation

EXERCISE 10. On your paper, enter the most appropriate word from group 5, *viv*, for completing the sentence.

1. A business must eliminate waste if it is to __?__ in a competitive market.
2. When fashion designers can offer no new styles, they usually __?__ old ones.
3. By using carefully chosen verbs and adjectives, you can turn a dull description into a __?__ one.
4. David Copperfield found a warm welcome in the __?__ Peggotty family.
5. A few inexpensive art reproductions, cleverly arranged, can __?__ an otherwise drab wall.
6. I admire her __?__ and zest for life.

6. TORT (TORS): "twist"

contortionist /kən-'tȯr-shə-nəst/ *n:* person who can twist his or her body into odd postures

distort /dis-'tȯrt/ *v*
   (1) twist out of shape; contort
   (2) falsify

extort /ek-'stȯrt/ *v:* wrest (money, promises, etc.) from a person by force (literally, "twist out")

retort /ri-'tȯrt/ *v:* reply quickly or sharply in kind ("twist back")

retort /ri-'tȯrt/ *n:* quick, witty, or cutting reply

torsion /'tȯr-shən/ *n:* act of twisting; twisting of a body by two equal and opposite forces

tortuous /'torch-ə-wəs/ *adj*
   (1) full of twists or curves; winding, as a *tortuous* road
   (2) tricky; crooked

torture /ˈtȯr-chə(r)/ *v*

    (1) wrench; twist

    (2) inflict severe pain upon

torture /ˈtȯr-chə(r)/ *n:* anguish of body or mind; agony

EXERCISE 11. On your paper, enter the most appropriate word from group 6, *tort* (*tors*), for completing the sentence.

1. The captured officer knew that the enemy would use clever means to __?__ military secrets from him.
2. It is very easy to __?__ an author's ideas if you quote them out of context.
3. When teenagers are asked to help with the chores, they often __?__ that they have no time.
4. The __?__ amazed us by her remarkable ability to throw her body into extraordinary postures.
5. Near its mouth, the Mississippi winds among numerous swamps in a (an) __?__ course to the Gulf of Mexico.

7. VICT (VINC): "conquer," "show conclusively"

convict /kən-ˈvikt/ *v:* prove guilty; show conclusively to be guilty

convict /ˈkän-ˌvikt/ *n:* person serving a prison sentence

convince /kən-ˈvins/ *v:* persuade or show conclusively by argument or proof

evict /ē-ˈvikt/ *v*

    (1) expel by legal process, as to *evict* a tenant

    (2) oust

evince /ē-ˈvins/ *v:* show clearly; disclose

invincible /in-ˈvin-sə-bəl/ *adj:* incapable of being conquered

vanquish /ˈvaŋ-kwish/ *v:* overcome in battle; conquer

victor /ˈvik-tə(r)/ *n:* winner; conqueror

EXERCISE 12. On your paper, enter the most appropriate word from group 7, *vict* (*vinc*), for completing the sentence.

1. Stadium police are empowered to __?__ any spectator who creates a disturbance.
2. After the match, the __?__ shook hands with the loser.
3. Students who __?__ a talent for writing should be encouraged to contribute to the school newspaper and literary magazine.
4. It is difficult to __?__ a biased person that he or she is wrong, no matter how much evidence you may present.
5. Our __?__ swimming team has been neither beaten nor tied in the past two seasons.

8. FRACT (FRAG): "break"

fraction /'frak-shən/ *n:* one or more of the equal parts of a whole; fragment

fractious /'frak-shəs/ *adj:* apt to break out into a passion; cross; irritable

fracture /'frak-chə(r)/ *n*
  (1) break or crack
  (2) breaking of a bone

fragile /'fraj-əl/ *adj:* easily broken; frail; delicate

fragment /'frag-mənt/ *n:* part broken off

infraction /in-'frak-shən/ *n:* act of breaking; breach; violation, as an *infraction* of a law

refract /ri-'frakt/ *v:* bend (literally, "break back") a ray of light, a heat or sound wave, etc., from a straight course

refractory /ri-'frak-tə-rē/ *adj:* resisting; intractable; hard to manage, as a *refractory* mule

EXERCISE 13. On your paper, enter the most appropriate word from group 8, *fract* (*frag*), for completing the sentence.

1. Glassware and other __?__ materials require special packaging to prevent breakage.
2. Though the motorist protested that she had committed no __?__, she was charged with failure to stop at a "Full Stop" sign.
3. X-ray diagnosis disclosed that the child had sustained no __?__ in his fall.
4. If I could find the one missing __?__, I would be able to restore the broken vase.
5. I was criticized for not reducing the __?__ 3/12 to 1/4.

9. OMNI: "all," "every," "everywhere"

omnibus /'äm-ni-bəs/ *adj:* covering many things at once, as an *omnibus* bill

omnibus /'äm-ni-bəs/ *n*

(1) bus
(2) book containing a variety of works by one author, as a Hemingway *omnibus*

omnifarious /ˌäm-nə-'far-ē-əs/ *adj:* of all varieties, forms, or kinds

omnific /äm-'nif-ik/ *adj:* all-creating

omnipotent /äm-'nip-ət-ənt/ *adj:* unlimited in power; almighty

omnipresent /ˌäm-ni-'prez-ᵊnt/ *adj:* present everywhere at the same time

omniscient /äm-'nish-ənt/ *adj:* knowing everything

omnivorous /äm-'niv-ə-rəs/ *adj*

(1) eating everything, both plant and animal substances
(2) avidly taking in everything, as an *omnivorous* reader

EXERCISE 14. On your paper, enter the most appropriate word from group 9, *omni*, for completing the sentence.

1. I cannot answer all questions, since I am not __?__.
2. With his magic lamp, Aladdin was __?__, for no feat was beyond his power.
3. Because of its __?__ uses, a scout knife is indispensable equipment for a camping trip.
4. With several desirable invitations for the same evening, I regretted that I could not be __?__.
5. To the ancient Egyptians, the sun god Ra was __?__, having created all that exists or will exist.

10. FLECT (FLEX): "bend"

deflect /di-'flekt/ *v:* turn ("bend") aside

flex /'fleks/ *v:* bend, as to *flex* a limb

flexible /'flek-sə-bəl/ *adj:* pliable ("capable of being bent"); not rigid; tractable

flexor /'flek-sə(r)/ *n:* muscle that serves to bend a limb

genuflect /'jen-yə-ˌflekt/ *v:* bend the knee; touch the right knee to the ground, as in worship

inflection /in-'flek-shən/ *n:* change ("bend") in the pitch or tone of a person's voice

inflexibility /in-ˌflek-sə-'bil-ət-ē/ *n:* rigidity; firmness

reflect /ri-'flekt/ *v*
   (1) throw ("bend") back light, heat, sound, etc.
   (2) think

reflex /'rē-ˌfleks/ *n:* involuntary response ("bending back") to a stimulus; for example, sneezing is a *reflex*

EXERCISE 15. On your paper, enter the most appropriate word from group 10, *flect* (*flex*), for completing the sentence.

1. The secretion of tears, as when a cinder enters the eye, is a (an) __?__, since it is beyond our control.
2. Copper tubing is easy to shape but much less __?__ than rubber hose.
3. Unable to catch the line drive, I managed to __?__ the ball toward the infield, holding the batter to a single.
4. Obedient subjects were expected to __?__ when admitted to the presence of an absolute monarch.
5. The __?__ of both sides makes an early settlement unlikely.

11. TEN (TIN, TENT): "hold," "keep"

detention /di-'ten-shən/ *n:* act of keeping back or detaining

impertinent /im-'pərt-ᵊn-ənt/ *adj*

   (1) not pertinent; inappropriate

   (2) rude

pertinacious /ˌpert-ᵊn-'ā-shəs/ *adj:* adhering ("holding") firmly to a purpose or opinion; very persistent

pertinent /'pərt-ᵊn-ənt/ *adj:* having to do with ("holding to") the matter at hand

retentive /ri-'tent-iv/ *adj:* tenacious; able to retain or remember

retinue /'ret-ᵊn-ˌyü/ *n:* group of followers accompanying a distinguished person

tenacity /tə-'nas-ət-ē/ *n:* firmness in holding fast; persistence

tenancy /'ten-ən-sē/ *n:* period of a tenant's temporary holding of real estate

tenet /'ten-ət/ *n:* principle, belief, or doctrine generally held to be true

tenure /'ten-yə(r)/ *n*

   (1) period for which an office or position is held, as: "U.S. Supreme Court Justices enjoy life *tenure*."

(2) status assuring an employee of permanence in his or her position

untenable /ˌən-'ten-ə-bəl/ *adj:* incapable of being held or defended

EXERCISE 16. On your paper, enter the most appropriate word from group 11, *ten* (*tin, tent*), for completing the sentence.

1. The __?__ of a member of the House of Representatives is only two years.
2. Retreating from their __?__ coastal positions, the rebels sought a more defensible foothold in the hills.
3. Your remark about yesterday's weather is not __?__; it has nothing to do with the matter we are discussing.
4. Though she can't recall names, Sylvia has a (an) __?__ memory for faces.
5. The basketball star was accompanied by a (an) __?__ of admirers.
6. Freedom of speech is one of the __?__s of democracy.

12. MON (MONIT): "warn"

admonish /ad-'män-ish/ *v:* warn of a fault; reprove

admonition /ˌad-mə-'nish-ən/ *n:* gentle reproof ("warning"); counseling against a fault or error

admonitory /ad-'män-ə-ˌtòr-ē/ *adj:* conveying a gentle reproof

monitor /'män-ət-ə(r)/ *n:* one who admonishes

monument /'män-yə-mənt/ *n:* a means of reminding us of a person or event; for example, a statue or a tomb

premonition /ˌprē-mə-'nish-ən/ *n:* forewarning; intuitive anticipation of a coming event

premonitory /prē-'män-ə-ˌtòr-ē/ *adj:* conveying a forewarning

EXERCISE 17. On your paper, enter the most appropriate word from group 12, *mon* (*monit*), for completing the sentence.

1. Had I heeded your __?__ to fill the gas tank, I would not have been stranded on the road.

2. I must __?__ you that you will be unable to vote if you do not register.
3. Some think that an early autumn snowstorm is a (an) __?__ of a severe winter, but you really can't tell in advance.
4. A (An) __?__ stands in the village square in memory of those who served in World War II.
5. The approach of the storm was signaled by a low, __?__ rumbling from the distant hills.

13. MAND (MANDAT): "order," "command," "commit"

countermand /'kaunt-ər-ˌmand/ *v:* issue a contrary order

mandate /'man-ˌdāt/ *n*

   (1) authoritative command

   (2) territory administered by a trustee (supervisory nation)

mandatory /'man-də-ˌtȯr-ē/ *adj:* obligatory; required by command

remand /ri-'mand/ *v:* send ("order") back; recommit, as to a prison

writ of mandamus /'ritəvman-'dā-məs/ *n:* written order from a court to enforce the performance of some public duty

   EXERCISE 18. On your paper, enter the most appropriate word from group 13, *mand (mandat)*, for completing the sentence.

1. The reelected candidate regarded his huge popular vote as a __?__ from the people to continue the policies of his first term in office.
2. When the captain heard of the lieutenant's ill-advised order to retreat to the hills, he hastened to __?__ it.
3. Several prominent citizens have applied for a __?__ to compel the Mayor to publish the budget, as required by law.
4. The coach regards attendance at today's practice session as __?__; no one may be excused.
5. Since the prisoner's retrial resulted in a verdict of "guilty," the judge was obliged to __?__ her to the state penitentiary.

14. CRED (CREDIT): "believe"

accredit /ə-ˈkred-ət/ v
  (1) accept as worthy of belief
  (2) provide with credentials

credence /ˈkrēd-ᵊns/ n: belief

credentials /kri-ˈden-shəlz/ n pl: documents, letters, references, etc., that inspire belief or trust

credible /ˈkred-ə-bəl/ adj: believable

credit /ˈkred-ət/ n: belief; faith; trust

credulous /ˈkrej-ə-ləs/ adj: too ready to believe; easily deceived

creed /ˈkrēd/ n: summary of principles believed in or adhered to— or **credo** /ˈkrēd-ō/

discredit /dis-ˈkred-ət/ v
  (1) cast doubt on; refuse to believe
  (2) disgrace

incredible /in-ˈkred-ə-bəl/ adj: not believable

incredulity /ˌin-kri-ˈd(y)ü-lət-ē/ n: disbelief

EXERCISE 19. On your paper, enter the most appropriate word from group 14, *cred* (*credit*), for completing the sentence.

1. His rude behavior brought __?__ not only upon himself, but also upon his team.
2. I showed __?__ negligence in not removing the pot from the burner when the timer rang.
3. When applying for admission to college, you are likely to be asked for such __?__ as your high school transcript, standardized test scores, and letters of recommendation.
4. Gerald is too __?__; he will believe anything a salesperson may tell him.
5. Olga greeted the announcement of her winning the door prize with a look of baffled __?__.

15. FID: "faith," "trust"

affidavit /ˌaf-ə-'dā-vət/ *n:* sworn written statement made before an authorized official

bona fide /'bō-nə-ˌfīd/ *adj:* made or carried out in good faith; genuine

confidant /'kän-fə-ˌdant/ *n:* (*confidante*, if a woman) one to whom secrets are entrusted

confident /'kän-fəd-ənt/ *adj:* having faith in oneself; self-reliant; sure

confidential /ˌkän-fə-'den-shəl/ *adj:* communicated in trust; secret; private

diffident /'dif-əd-ənt/ *adj:* lacking faith in oneself; timid; shy

fidelity /fə-'del-ət-ē/ *n*
(1) faithfulness to a trust or vow, (2) accuracy, as of a recording

fiduciary /fə-'d(y)ü-shē-ˌer-ē/ *adj:* held in trust; confidential

infidel /'in-fəd-ᵊl/ *n:* one who does not accept a particular faith; unbeliever

perfidious /pər-'fid-ē-əs/ *adj:* false to a trust; faithless

perfidy /'pər-fəd-ē/ *n:* violation of a trust; treachery; faithlessness

EXERCISE 20. On your paper, enter the most appropriate word from group 15, *fid*, for completing the sentence.

1. Your disclosure of secrets you were sworn to keep is unforgivable __?__.
2. Marie looks upon her cousin Nancy as a (an) __?__ with whom she can freely discuss her personal problems.
3. At first, new motorists are usually nervous, but with experience they become more __?__.
4. Our teacher recommends a particular translation of the ODYSSEY because of its __?__ to the original.
5. Steve was very __?__ as he mounted the platform, even though he knew his speech by heart.
6. The witness agreed to sign a (an) __?__ and to testify in person.

Review Exercises

EXERCISE 21. On your paper, copy each Latin root from column I, and next to it enter the *letter* of its correct meaning from column II.

COLUMN I	COLUMN II
1. CIDE	*a.* live; alive
2. VOR	*b.* break; burst
3. FLECT (FLEX)	*c.* order; command; commit
4. TORT (TORS)	*d.* bind; draw tight
5. OMNI	*e.* faith; trust
6. VICT (VINC)	*f.* warn
7. TEN (TIN, TENT)	*g.* killing; killer
8. MAND (MANDAT)	*h.* believe
9. FID	*i.* conquer; show conclusively
10. FRACT (FRAG)	*j.* bend
11. VIV	*k.* eat greedily
12. MON (MONIT)	*l.* twist
13. CRED (CREDIT)	*m.* hold; keep
14. STRING (STRICT)	*n.* all; every; everywhere

EXERCISE 22. As clues to each mystery word below, you are given some of its letters, the number of its missing letters, and its definition. On your paper, enter the complete word.

DEFINITION	WORD
1. break asunder	____3____RUPT
2. germ-killing substance	G____4____CIDE
3. part broken off	FRAG____4____
4. faithfulness to a trust	FID____5____
5. one who conquers	VICT____2____
6. flesh-eating	____5____VOR____3____
7. issue a contrary order	____7____MAND

8. forewarning	___3___ MONIT ___3___
9. muscle that serves to bend a limb	FLEX ___2___
10. readiness to believe on slight evidence	CRED ___5___
11. snake that crushes (constricts) its prey	___3___ ___3___ STRICT ___2___
12. bring back to life	___2___ VIV ___1___
13. adhering firmly to a purpose or opinion	___3___ TIN ___6___
14. present everywhere at the same time	OMNI ___7___
15. throw (bend) back heat, light, sound, etc.	___2___ FLECT
16. greedy in eating	VOR ___6___
17. breaking of a bone	FRACT ___3___
18. show conclusively by proof	___3___ VINC ___1___
19. killing of a human by another	___4___ CIDE
20. documents inspiring trust	CRED ___7___

EXERCISE 23. On your paper, enter the *letter* of the word (or set of words) that best completes the sentence.

1. Circus elephants are usually __?__, but occasionally they are refractory.
   a. unmanageable   *b.* stubborn   *c.* tractable   *d.* uncooperative
   e. resisting

2. Harvey believes he is omniscient, but we are not particularly impressed by his __?__.
   a. power   *b.* knowledge   *c.* manners   *d.* personality
   e. appearance

3. The promise had been extorted and, like all promises growing out of __?__, it was __?__.

    a. ignorance . . . perfidious *b.* haste . . . untenable
    c. rumor . . . false *d.* compulsion . . . unreliable
    e. friendship . . . dependable

4. An act of regicide always has a __?__ as its victim.

    a. rebel *b.* general *c.* president *d.* prime minister
    e. monarch

5. I usually admonished my brother for distorting facts, but Mother seldom __?__ him.

    a. reproved *b.* encouraged *c.* remanded *d.* praised
    e. supported

6. An omnibus bill deals with proposed legislation on __?__ problems.

    a. economic *b.* many *c.* minor *d.* transportation *e.* few

7. The rapid withdrawal of your hand from the flame was a reflex, not a (an) __?__ reaction.

    a. protective *b.* dangerous *c.* involuntary *d.* natural
    e. voluntary

8. The author read the critics' __?__ with incredulity; they were too laudatory to be __?__.

    a. censures . . . heeded *b.* strictures . . . ignored
    c. admonitions . . . challenged *d.* encomiums . . . believed
    e. rebukes . . . answered

9. It is advisable to take along plenty of sandwiches because hungry picnickers are __?__ eaters.

    a. admonitory *b.* abstemious *c.* omnifarious *d.* heterogeneous
    e. voracious

10. No one would dare to offer a bribe to an official who is known to be thoroughly __?__.

    a. incorruptible *b.* invincible *c.* credulous *d.* retentive
    e. convivial

EXERCISE 24. Each word or expression in column I has an ANTONYM (opposite) in column II. On your paper, enter the *letter* of the correct ANTONYM.

COLUMN I	COLUMN II
1. clear of guilt	*a.* survive
2. victorious	*b.* evince
3. not required	*c.* convict
4. perish	*d.* constrict
5. of one kind	*e.* infidel
6. believer	*f.* omniscient
7. extremely ignorant	*g.* vanquished
8. conceal	*h.* omnifarious
9. loosen	*i.* perfidious
10. true to a trust	*j.* mandatory

EXERCISE 25. On your paper, enter the *letter* of the word NOT RELATED in meaning to the other words in each group.

1. *a.* controllable   *b.* tractable   *c.* refractory   *d.* obedient   *e.* manageable
2. *a.* gay   *b.* convivial   *c.* festive   *d.* inhospitable   *e.* jovial
3. *a.* inhuman   *b.* tortuous   *c.* winding   *d.* curving   *e.* bending
4. *a.* hasty   *b.* abrupt   *c.* restricted   *d.* unexpected   *e.* sudden
5. *a.* delicate   *b.* weak   *c.* feeble   *d.* fragile   *e.* fractious
6. *a.* trustworthy   *b.* accredited   *c.* credible   *d.* believable   *e.* incredulous
7. *a.* disclosed   *b.* revealed   *c.* shone   *d.* evinced   *e.* displayed
8. *a.* satiable   *b.* ravenous   *c.* voracious   *d.* devouring   *e.* greedy
9. *a.* stringent   *b.* inflexible   *c.* pliable   *d.* rigid   *e.* firm
10. *a.* distorted   *b.* corrupted   *c.* admonished   *d.* contorted   *e.* falsified

EXERCISE 26. On your paper, enter the *letter* of the word that has most nearly the SAME MEANING as the italicized word.

1. *fragile* flower   *a.* fragrant   *b.* broken   *c.* colorful   *d.* frail
2. cling *tenaciously*   *a.* stubbornly   *b.* dangerously   *c.* hopefully   *d.* timidly

3. beyond *credence*   *a.* detention   *b.* doubt   *c.* belief   *d.* recall
4. *omnipotent* ruler   *a.* almighty   *b.* wise   *c.* cruel   *d.* greedy
5. *mandatory* increase   *a.* deserved   *b.* required   *c.* temporary
   d. substantial
6. surprising *impertinence*   *a.* firmness   *b.* unreliability
   c. impatience   *d.* rudeness
7. *breach* of trust   *a.* atmosphere   *b.* testing   *c.* breaking
   d. abundance
8. *unvanquished* foe   *a.* defeated   *b.* exhausted   *c.* treacherous
   d. unbeaten
9. in a *fiduciary* capacity   *a.* confidential   *b.* special
   c. professional   *d.* important
10. refused to *genuflect*   *a.* admit   *b.* kneel   *c.* cooperate
    d. disclose

EXERCISE 27.   Which word, selected from the vocabulary list below, will correctly complete the sentence? Enter the appropriate word on your paper. (Hint: For a clue to the missing word, study the italicized expression.)

VOCABULARY LIST

evict	fratricide	omnivorous
tortuous	mandate	confidential
regicide	fractious	vivisection
tenure	evince	genocide
omnipotent	infraction	extort

1. Tyrants who consider themselves *unlimited in power* will learn sooner or later that they are not __?__ .
2. To prevent *the deliberate extermination of racial or cultural groups,* the United Nations has made __?__ an international crime.
3. When you send a letter of a *private* nature to an executive, it is advisable to write the word "__?__" on the envelope.
4. The teacher decided to *oust* one of the unruly pupils as an example to the rest, so that she would not have to __?__ anyone else.
5. Helen is *apt to break into a passion* if she disagrees with you; her __?__ disposition makes her hard to get along with.
6. In some communities, persons opposed to *the performance of research operations on living animals* have joined anti-__?__ leagues.

7. Since you dislike driving on *winding* roads, avoid the Interborough Parkway, which is extremely __?__ .

8. Cain's *slaying of* his *brother* Abel is widely regarded as the first instance of __?__ .

9. *The period for which office is held* is not the same for all members of Congress: Senators serve for six years, but Representatives have a two-year __?__ .

10. Have you ever received a summons for a serious traffic *violation* such as speeding, passing a red light, or a similar __?__ ?

EXERCISE 28. Answer each question in a sentence or two.

1. Should the death penalty be mandatory for persons convicted of homicide? Explain.

2. Why should we not put too much credence in the opinions of those who claim to be omniscient?

3. Is it possible for the driver of a subcompact to survive an abrupt collision with a heavy truck? Why, or why not?

4. Would you take it upon yourself to admonish someone about to commit an infraction? Explain.

5. Are you in favor of the unrestricted use of pesticides to save crops and trees? Why, or why not?

EXERCISE 29. On your paper, enter the *letter* of the word that best completes the analogy.

1. *Matricide* is to *mother* as *genocide* is to __?__ .
   a. uncle   *b.* country   *c.* race   *d.* tyrant   *e.* general

2. *Flesh* is to *carnivorous* as *grass* is to __?__ .
   a. omnivorous   *b.* insectivorous   *c.* vegetarian   *d.* herbivorous
   e. agricultural

3. *Fraction* is to *whole* as *follower* is to __?__ .
   a. creed   *b.* retinue   *c.* tenure   *d.* fragment   *e.* torsion

4. *Reservation* is to *cancel* as *directive* is to __?__ .
   a. command   *b.* proclaim   *c.* flex   *d.* demand   *e.* countermand

5. *Orphan* is to *guardian* as *mandate* is to __?__ .
   a. victor   *b.* monitor   *c.* trustee   *d.* confidant   *e.* commission

Words Derived From Latin   155

16. GRAT: "pleasant," "thank," "favor"

congratulate /kən-'grach-ə-,lāt/ v: express pleasure at another's success; felicitate

gracious /'grā-shəs/ adj: pleasant; courteous; kindly

grateful /'grāt-fəl/ adj: thankful

gratify /'grat-ə-,fī/ v: give or be a source of pleasure or satisfaction

gratis /'grāt-əs/ adv
- (1) out of kindness or favor
- (2) free; without recompense

gratitude /'grat-ə-,t(y)üd/ n: thankfulness

gratuitous /grə-'t(y)ü-ət-əs/ adj
- (1) given freely; gratis
- (2) unwarranted, as a *gratuitous* remark

gratuity /grə-'t(y)ü-ət-ē/ n: present of money in return for a favor or service; tip

ingrate /'in-,grāt/ n: ungrateful ("not thankful") person

ingratiate /in-'grā-shē-,āt/ v: work (oneself) into another's favor

EXERCISE 30.   On your paper, enter the most appropriate word from group 16, *grat*, for completing the sentence.

1. I would consider myself a (an) __?__ if I did not express my gratitude to those who have helped me.
2. Some restaurants charge for a second cup of coffee, but others provide it __?__.
3. We were so pleased with the service that we left a generous __?__.
4. Shouting out answers without waiting to be recognized is no way to __?__ yourself with your teacher or your classmates.
5. I am sorry I was so discourteous. I shall try to be more __?__.
6. The compliment I paid her failed to __?__ her; she was displeased.

17. MOR (MORT): "death"

immortality /ˌim-ȯr-'tal-ət-ē/ *n*
- (1) eternal life
- (2) lasting fame

moribund /'mȯr-ə-bənd/ *adj:* dying; near death

mortal /'mȯrt-ᵊl/ *adj*
- (1) destined to die
- (2) human
- (3) causing death; fatal, as a *mortal* blow

mortality /mȯr-'tal-ət-ē/ *n*
- (1) death rate
- (2) mortal nature

mortician /mȯr-'tish-ən/ *n:* undertaker

mortification /ˌmȯrt-ə-fə-'kā-shən/ *n:* shame; humiliation; embarrassment

mortuary /'mȯr-chə-ˌwer-ē/ *n:* morgue

EXERCISE 31. On your paper, enter the most appropriate word from group 17, *mor (mort)*, for completing the sentence.

1. Patrick Henry's __?__ rests on a speech ending "Give me liberty, or give me death!"
2. Infant __?__ is relatively high in nations that have few physicians and hospitals.
3. The proprietor did not realize what __?__ she caused her assistant when she scolded him in the presence of the entire staff.
4. Though the mountain climber's injury is critical, it may not be __?__; he has a chance of recovery.
5. As a result of the reopening of two large factories, the __?__ community has received a new lease on life.

18. CORP: "body"

corporal /'kȯr-p(ə-)rəl/ *adj:* bodily, as *corporal* punishment

corporation /ˌkȯr-pə-'rā-shən/ *n:* body authorized by law to carry on an activity with the rights and duties of a single person

corps /'kȯ(ə)r/ *n*
   (1) organized body of persons, (2) branch of the military

corpse /'kȯrps/ *n:* dead body

corpulent /'kȯr-pyə-lənt/ *adj:* bulky; obese; very fat

corpus /'kȯr-pəs/ *n:* general collection of writings, laws, etc.

corpuscle /'kȯr-pəs-əl/ *n*
   (1) blood cell (literally, a "little body"), (2) minute particle

corpus delicti /ˌkȯr-pəs-di-'lik-ˌtī/ *n:* facts proving a crime has been committed (literally, "body of the crime")

esprit de corps /es-ˌprēd-ə-'kȯ(ə)r/ *n:* spirit of a body of persons; group spirit

incorporate /in-'kȯr-pə-ˌrāt/ *v:* combine so as to form one body

EXERCISE 32.   On your paper, enter the most appropriate word from group 18, *corp*, for completing the sentence.

1. The executive in charge of administration has a (an) __?__ of able assistants.
2. Criminals were flogged or put in the stocks in olden times, but such __?__ punishment is rare today.
3. The __?__ patient was advised by his physician to get rid of his excess weight.
4. Publishers often __?__ two or more works of an author into one volume.
5. Until the __?__ is produced, it cannot be established that a crime has been committed.
6. The members of the board are proud of their corporation and loyal to it; they have a fine __?__.

19. DUC (DUCT): "lead," "conduct," "draw"

aqueduct /'ak-wǝ-ˌdǝkt/ *n:* artificial channel for conducting water from a distance

conducive /kǝn-'d(y)ü-siv/ *adj:* tending to lead to; contributive; helpful

conduct /kǝn-'dǝkt/ *v:* lead; guide; escort

deduction /di-'dǝk-shǝn/ *n*
   (1) taking away; subtraction
   (2) reasoning from the general to the particular

duct /'dǝkt/ *n:* tube or channel for conducting a liquid, air, etc.

ductile /'dǝk-tᵊl/ *adj*
   (1) able to be drawn out or hammered thin (said of metal)
   (2) easily led; docile

induce /in-'d(y)üs/ *v:* lead on; move by persuasion

induction /in-'dǝk-shǝn/ *n:* reasoning from the particular to the general

seduction /si-'dǝk-shǝn/ *n:* act of leading astray into wrongdoing

traduce /trǝ-'d(y)üs/ *v:* slander (literally "lead across" or parade in public by way of disgrace); vilify; calumniate

viaduct /'vī-ǝ-ˌdǝkt/ *n:* bridge for conducting a road or railroad over a valley, river, etc.

EXERCISE 33. On your paper, enter the most appropriate word from group 19, *duc* (*duct*), for completing the sentence.

1. A (An) __?__ conducts water from a source of supply to a point of distribution.
2. How much of a (an) __?__ is made from your weekly salary for taxes?
3. Though John had said that he wouldn't join, I was able to __?__ him to become a member.
4. As the train passed over the __?__, we had an excellent view of the valley below.
5. Films that exaggerate the luxury and idleness of American life __?__ our good name when shown abroad.

20. SECUT (SEQU): "follow"

consecutive /kən-'sek-yət-iv/ *adj:* following in regular order; successive

consequence /'kän-sə-ˌkwens/ *n*
   (1) that which follows logically; result
   (2) importance, as a person of *consequence*

execute /'ek-sə-ˌkyüt/ *v*
   (1) follow through to completion; carry out
   (2) put to death

inconsequential /in-ˌkän-sə-'kwen-shəl/ *adj:* unimportant

prosecute /'präs-i-ˌkyüt/ *v*
   (1) follow to the end or until finished
   (2) conduct legal proceedings against; sue

sequel /'sē-kwəl/ *n:* something that follows; continuation; consequence; outcome

sequence /'sē-kwəns/ *n:* the following of one thing after another; succession; orderly series

EXERCISE 34.   On your paper, enter the most appropriate word from group 20, *secut (sequ)*, for completing the sentence.

1. If the vandals refuse to pay for the damage they have caused, I shall __?__ them.
2. After a string of seven __?__ victories, we suffered our first loss.
3. The book about the clever detective proved so popular that the author was induced to write a (an) __?__.
4. The cards in the card catalog are arranged in strict alphabetical __?__.
5. The shortage of water during dry spells is a matter of serious __?__ in affected communities.

21. CUR (CURR, CURS): "run"

concur /kən-'kə(r)/ *v*
- (1) agree; be of the same opinion (literally, "run together")
- (2) happen together; coincide

concurrent /kən-'kər-ənt/ *adj:* running together; occurring at the same time

current /'kər-ənt/ *adj*
- (1) running or flowing (said of water or electricity)
- (2) now in progress, prevailing

curriculum /kə-'rik-yə-ləm/ *n:* specific course of study in a school or college

cursive /'kər-siv/ *adj:* running or flowing (said of handwriting in which the letters are joined)

cursory /'kərs-ə-rē/ *adj:* running over hastily; superficially done, as a *cursory* glance

discursive /dis-'kər-siv/ *adj:* wandering ("running") from one topic to another; rambling; digressive

excursion /ik-'skər-zhən/ *n:* going ("running") out or forth; expedition

incur /in-'kə(r)/ *v*
- (1) meet with ("run into") something undesirable
- (2) bring upon oneself

incursion /in-'kər-zhən/ *n*
- (1) a rushing into
- (2) hostile invasion; raid

precursor /pri-'kər-sə(r)/ *n:* forerunner; predecessor

recur /ri-'kə(r)/ *v:* happen again (literally, "run again")

EXERCISE 35. On your paper, enter the most appropriate word from group 21, *cur (curr, curs)*, for completing the sentence.

1. If you are habitually late, you will __?__ the displeasure of your employer.
2. Does your school __?__ include a course in driver training?
3. The __?__ film at the Bijou is a western; the war drama is no longer playing there.
4. A difficult passage requires much more than a (an) __?__ reading if it is to be fully understood.
5. Our conversation, as usual, was __?__, ranging from the latest dance step to irregular French verbs.

22. GRESS (GRAD): "step," "walk," "go"

aggressive /ə-'gres-iv/ *adj:* disposed to attack (literally "step toward"); militant; assertive; pushing

egress /'ē-ˌgres/ *n:* a going out, or a way out; an exit

gradation /grā-'dā-shən/ *n*
    (1) a change by steps or stages
    (2) act of grading

grade /'grād/ *n:* step; stage; degree; rating

gradient /'grād-ē-ənt/ *n*
    (1) rate at which a road, railroad track, etc., rises ("steps" up)
    (2) slope

gradual /'graj-ə-wəl/ *adj:* by steps or degrees; bit by bit

graduate /'graj-ə-ˌwāt/ *v:* complete all the steps of a course and receive a diploma or degree

graduated /'graj-ə-ˌwāt-əd/ *adj:* arranged in regular steps, stages, or degrees

progressive /prə-'gres-iv/ *adj:* going forward to something better

regressive /ri-'gres-iv/ *adj:* disposed to move ("step") backward; retrogressive

retrograde /'re-trə-ˌgrād/ *adj*

(1) going backward

(2) becoming worse

retrogression /ˌre-trə-'gresh-ən/ *n:* act of going from a better to a worse state

transgress /trans-'gres/ *v:* step beyond the limits; go beyond; break a law

EXERCISE 36. On your paper, enter the most appropriate word from group 22, *gress* (*grad*), for completing the sentence.

1. Learning to play an instrument is a (an) __?__ process; it cannot be achieved overnight.
2. The offender knows that he will be dealt with severely if he should __?__ again.
3. When the game ended, hordes of spectators jammed the stadium exits, making __?__ painfully slow.
4. The medical report showed __?__ rather than progress, for the patient's blood pressure had gone up.
5. In a string of __?__ pearls, the individual pearls are arranged in the order of increasing size on both halves of the string.

23. PED: "foot"

biped /'bī-ˌped/ *n:* two-footed animal

centipede /'sent-ə-ˌpēd/ *n:* small, wormlike animal with many (literally, "a hundred") pairs of legs

expedite /'ek-spə-ˌdīt/ *v*

(1) facilitate (literally, "free one caught by the foot")

(2) accelerate or speed up

impede /im-'pēd/ *v:* hinder (literally, "entangle the feet"); obstruct

impediment /im-'ped-ə-mənt/ *n*

(1) hindrance; obstacle (literally, "something entangling the feet")

(2) defect

pedal /'ped-ᵊl/ *n:* lever acted on by the foot

pedestal /'ped-əst-ᵊl/ *n*
    (1) support or foot of a column or statue
    (2) foundation

pedestrian /pə-'des-tre-ən/ *n:* person traveling on foot

pedestrian /pə-'des-tre-ən/ *adj:* commonplace or dull, as a *pedestrian* performance

velocipede /və-'läs-ə-₁pēd/ *n*
    (1) child's tricycle (literally, "swift foot")
    (2) early form of bicycle

EXERCISE 37. On your paper, enter the most appropriate word from group 23, *ped*, for completing the sentence.

1. A supervisor is expected to __?__, not impede, production.
2. It is foolhardy for a (an) __?__ to cross a busy thoroughfare against the light.
3. For a smooth stop, apply foot pressure to the brake __?__ gradually, not abruptly.
4. Demosthenes, the famous orator, is said to have suffered from a speech __?__.
5. At the age of six, Judy abandoned her __?__ and learned to ride a bicycle.

24. TACT (TANG): "touch"

contact /'kän-₁takt/ *n:* touching or meeting; association; connection

contiguous /kən-'tig-yə-wəs/ *adj:* touching; in contact; adjoining

contingent /kən-'tin-jənt/ *adj*
    (1) dependent on something else (literally, "touching together")
    (2) accidental

intact /in-'takt/ *adj:* untouched or uninjured; kept or left whole

intangible /in-'tan-jə-bəl/ *adj:* not capable of being touched

tact /'takt/ *n:* sensitive mental perception of what is appropriate on a given occasion (literally, "sense of touch")

tactful /'takt-fəl/ *adj:* having or showing tact—ANT **tactless**

tactile /'tak-tᵊl/ *adj*
  (1) pertaining to the sense of touch
  (2) tangible

tangent /'tan-jənt/ *adj:* touching

tangent /'tan-jənt/ *n:* line or surface meeting a curved line or surface at one point, but not intersecting it

tangential /tan-'jen-chəl/ *adj:* merely touching; slightly connected; digressive

EXERCISE 38. On your paper, enter the most appropriate word from group 24, *tact* (*tang*), for completing the sentence.

1. To discuss your admission to college in the presence of someone who has just received a rejection notice is __?__.
2. The missing sum was found __?__; not a penny had been spent.
3. The Federal grant is __?__ on our raising a matching sum; if we fail to raise it, we will not get the grant.
4. A firm's goodwill with its clients is a most valuable, though __?__, asset.
5. If you wish to maintain __?__ with your classmates after graduation, join the Alumni Association.

25. PREHEND (PREHENS):
"seize," "grasp"

apprehend /ˌap-ri-'hend/ *v*
  (1) seize or take into custody
  (2) understand

apprehensive /ˌap-ri-ˈhen-siv/ *adj*

    (1) quick to understand or grasp

    (2) fearful of what may come; anxious

comprehensible /ˌkäm-pri-ˈhen-sə-bəl/ *adj*: able to be grasped mentally; understandable

comprehensive /ˌkäm-pri-ˈhen-siv/ *adj*: including ("seizing") very much; extensive

prehensile /prē-ˈhen-səl/ *adj*: adapted for seizing, as a *prehensile* claw

reprehensible /ˌrep-ri-ˈhen-sə-bəl/ *adj*: deserving of censure; culpable

    EXERCISE 39. On your paper, enter the most appropriate word from group 25, *prehend* (*prehens*), for completing the sentence.

1. Ignorance can be forgiven, but stealing is utterly __?__ .
2. From the observation deck at the top of the south tower of the World Trade Center, you can get a (an) __?__ view of New York City and its environs.
3. A coded message is __?__ only to those who know the code.
4. Had you attended regularly and done the assigned reading, you would have no reason to be __?__ about your grade.
5. Law enforcement officials are doing their best to __?__ the escaped convict.

26. JECT: "throw"

abject /ˈab-ˌjekt/ *adj*: sunk to a low condition; deserving contempt

conjecture /kən-ˈjek-chə(r)/ *n*: a guess; supposition; inference

dejected /di-ˈjek-təd/ *adj*: downcast ("thrown down"); discouraged; depressed

eject /ē-ˈjekt/ *v*: throw out or expel; evict

inject /in-ˈjekt/ *v*: force or introduce (literally, "throw in") a liquid, a remark, etc.

interject /ˌint-ər-ˈjekt/ *v*: throw in between; insert; interpose

projectile /prə-'jek-t^əl/ *n*

(1) object (bullet, shell, etc.) designed to be shot forward

(2) anything thrown forward

reject /ri-'jekt/ *v:* refuse to take; discard (literally, "throw back")

EXERCISE 40. On your paper, enter the most appropriate word from group 26, *ject*, for completing the sentence.

1. My friend is __?__ over the damage to her new car.
2. A wise policy in buying shares of stock is to be guided by fact rather than __?__ .
3. The umpire was obliged to __?__ a player who refused to accept his decision.
4. A hypodermic syringe is used to __?__ a dose of medicine beneath the skin.
5. The mob hurled stones, bricks, bottles, eggs, and anything else that could serve as a (an) __?__ .

27. VERT (VERS): "turn"

avert /ə-'vərt/ *v*

(1) turn away

(2) prevent; avoid

controversy /'kän-trə-ˌvər-sē/ *n:* dispute (literally, a "turning against"); debate; quarrel

divert /də-'vərt/ *v*

(1) turn aside

(2) amuse; entertain

extrovert /'ek-strə-ˌvərt/ *n:* person more interested in matters outside the self than in own thoughts and feelings

incontrovertible /in-ˌkän-trə-'vərt-ə-bəl/ *adj:* not able to be "turned opposite" or disputed; not open to question

introvert /'in-trə-ˌvərt/ *n:* person more interested in own thoughts and feelings than in matters outside the self

introvert /'in-trə-ˌvərt/ *v:* turn inward

invert /in-'vərt/ *v:* turn upside down

obverse /'äb-ˌvərs/ *n:* side turned toward the observer; therefore, the front of a coin, medal, etc.—ANT **reverse**

perverse /pər-'vərs/ *adj:* turned away from what is right or good; corrupt; wrongheaded

pervert /pər-'vərt/ *v:* turn away from right or truth; give a wrong meaning to

revert /ri-'vərt/ *v:* return; go back, as: "The property will *revert* to the owner when the lease is up."

versatile /'vər-sət-ᵊl/ *adj:* able to turn with ease from one thing to another

verse /'vərs/ *n:* line of poetry (literally, "a turning around." After a fixed number of syllables, the poet has to "turn around" to begin a new line.)

vertigo /'vərt-i-ˌgō/ *n:* condition in which one feels that one's surroundings are turning about; dizziness

EXERCISE 41. On your paper, enter the most appropriate word from group 27, *vert (vers)*, for completing the sentence.

1. Between Thanksgiving and Christmas most department store employees work overtime; then they __?__ to their normal hours.
2. The words "In God We Trust" appear above Lincoln's image on the __?__ of a cent.
3. Occasionally there is a quarrel in the student cafeteria, but as a rule there is little __?__.
4. The first __?__ of Katherine Lee Bates' "America, the Beautiful" begins "O beautiful for spacious skies."
5. A (An) __?__ musician can play several instruments.
6. The proof of his guilt was so __?__ that the defendant confessed to the crime.

28. MIS (MISS, MIT, MITT): "send"

commitment /kə-'mit-mənt/ *n*
  (1) consignment ("sending") to prison or a mental institution
  (2) pledge

demise /di-'mīz/ *n:* death (literally, "sending or putting down")

emissary /'em-ə-ˌser-ē/ *n:* person sent on a mission

emit /ē-'mit/ *v:* send out; give off

intermittent /ˌint-ər-'mit-ᵊnt/ *adj:* coming and going at intervals, as an *intermittent* fever (literally, "sending between")

missile /'mis-əl/ *n:* weapon (spear, bullet, rocket, etc.) capable of being propelled ("sent") to hit a distant object

missive /'mis-iv/ *n:* written message sent; a letter

remiss /ri-'mis/ *adj:* negligent (literally, "sent back"); careless; lax

remit /ri-'mit/ *v*
  (1) send money due
  (2) forgive, as to have one's sins *remitted*

EXERCISE 42. On your paper, enter the most appropriate word from group 28, *mis (miss, mit, mitt)*, for completing the sentence.

1. This morning's rain was __?__, starting and stopping several times.
2. It was my fault. I was __?__ in not writing sooner.
3. The President chose a distinguished veteran diplomat as his __?__ to the international conference.
4. Unless you __?__ the mortgage payment by the tenth of the month, you must pay a late fee.
5. My large searchlight can __?__ a powerful beam.
6. We gave you our word; we will not go back on our __?__.

29. LOCUT (LOQU): "speak," "talk"

circumlocution /ˌsər-kəm-lō-ˈkyü-shən/ *n:* roundabout way of speaking

colloquy /ˈkäl-ə-kwē/ *n:* a talking together; conference; conversation

elocution /ˈel-ə-ˈkyü-shən/ *n:* art of speaking or reading effectively in public

eloquent /ˈel-ə-kwənt/ *adj:* speaking with force and fluency; movingly expressive

grandiloquent /gran-ˈdil-ə-kwənt/ *adj:* using lofty or pompous words; bombastic

interlocutor /ˌint-ə(r)-ˈläk-yət-ə(r)/ *n*
   (1) questioner
   (2) one who participates in a conversation

loquacious /lō-ˈkwā-shəs/ *adj:* talkative; garrulous

obloquy /ˈäb-lə-kwē/ *n*
   (1) a speaking against; censure
   (2) public reproach

EXERCISE 43. On your paper, enter the most appropriate word from group 29, *locut (loqu)*, for completing the sentence.

1. "Your services will be terminated if you persist in disregarding our requirement of punctuality" is a (an) __?__. It would be more direct to say, "You will be dismissed if you come late again."
2. __?__ students who carry on noisy conversations in the library prevent others from concentrating.
3. A course in __?__ will help you to be an effective public speaker.
4. The referee held a short __?__ with the judges before announcing the winner.
5. Witnesses appearing before the investigating committee found that its chairman was the principal __?__; the other committee members asked very few questions.

30. FER(ous): "bearing," "producing," "yielding"

coniferous /kō-'nif-ə-rəs/ *adj:* bearing cones, as the pine tree

odoriferous /ˌōd-ə-'rif-ə-rəs/ *adj:* yielding an odor, usually fragrant

pestiferous /pe-'stif-ə-rəs/ *adj*
    (1) infected with or bearing disease; pestilential
    (2) evil

somniferous /säm-'nif-ə-rəs/ *adj:* bearing or inducing sleep

vociferous /vō-'sif-ə-rəs/ *adj:* producing a loud outcry; clamorous; noisy

EXERCISE 44. On your paper, enter the most appropriate word from group 30, *fer(ous)*, for completing the sentence.

1. The infant emitted so __?__ a protest when placed in the crib that his mother took him up at once.

2. A bunch of __?__ lilacs in a vase on the table gave the room an inviting fragrance.

3. Some people who have difficulty falling asleep have found that a glass of warm milk taken before retiring has a (an) __?__ effect.

4. The settlers were heartbroken to see their fields of corn and wheat devastated by swarms of __?__ locusts.

5. The seed-bearing part of pines, cedars, firs, and other __?__ trees is known as a cone.

Review Exercises

EXERCISE 45. As clues to each mystery word below, you are given some of its letters, the number of its missing letters, and its definition. On your paper, enter the complete word.

DEFINITION	WORD
1. moved forward to something better	_3_GRESS_2_
2. person traveling on foot	PED_7_
3. combine so as to form one body	_2_CORP_5_
4. something that follows; continuation	SEQU_2_
5. artificial channel for conducting water	_4_DUCT
6. undertaker	MORT_5_
7. gift of money in return for a favor	GRAT_4_
8. producing a loud outcry	_4_FEROUS
9. turning away; avoiding	_1_VERT_3_
10. pertaining to the sense of touch	TACT_3_
11. a speaking against; censure	_2_LOQU_1_
12. running or flowing (handwriting)	CURS_3_
13. by steps or degrees	GRAD_3_
14. a written message	MISS_3_
15. talkative	LOQU_6_
16. throw in between; interpose	_5_JECT
17. tending to lead to; contributive	_3_DUC_3_
18. person sent on a mission	_1_MISS_3_
19. running together; occurring simultaneously	_3_CURR_3_
20. turning easily from one thing to another	VERS_5_

EXERCISE 46. On your paper, copy each Latin root from column I, and next to it enter the *letter* of its correct meaning from column II.

COLUMN I	COLUMN II
1. MOR (MORT)	*a.* body
2. TACT (TANG)	*b.* step; walk; go
3. LOCUT (LOQU)	*c.* run
4. GRAT	*d.* bearing; producing; yielding
5. SECUT (SEQU)	*e.* speak; talk
6. CORP	*f.* throw
7. CUR (CURR, CURS)	*g.* touch
8. PED	*h.* pleasant; thank; favor
9. PREHEND (PREHENS)	*i.* lead; conduct; draw
10. JECT	*j.* death
11. VERT (VERS)	*k.* send
12. FER(ous)	*l.* turn
13. GRESS (GRAD)	*m.* seize; grasp
14. MIS (MISS, MIT, MITT)	*n.* foot
15. DUC (DUCT)	*o.* follow

EXERCISE 47. On your paper, copy each word or expression from column I, and next to it enter the *letter* of its correct meaning from column II.

COLUMN I	COLUMN II
1. death rate	*a.* invert
2. turn upside down	*b.* grandiloquent
3. felicitate	*c.* retrograde
4. adapted for seizing	*d.* congratulate
5. give a wrong meaning to	*e.* mortality
6. bombastic	*f.* pervert
7. interpose	*g.* ductile
8. going backward	*h.* corpuscle
9. minute particle	*i.* interject
10. able to be hammered thin	*j.* prehensile

EXERCISE 48. On your paper, enter the word that means the OPPOSITE of each word defined below.

1. *consequential* (important)
2. *incredible* (unbelievable)
3. *tactless* (having no tact)
4. *ungracious* (discourteous, rude)
5. *regressive* (disposed to move backward)
6. *injected* (thrown in)
7. *odorless* (yielding no odor)
8. *untenable* (indefensible)
9. *confident* (having faith in oneself)
10. *impertinent* (unrelated to the matter in hand)
11. *obverse* (front of a coin)
12. *corruptible* (capable of being corrupted)
13. *excursion* (a going, "running," out)
14. *tangible* (touchable)
15. *induction* (reasoning from particular to general)
16. *comprehensible* (understandable)
17. *credit* (trust in the truth of)
18. *fidelity* (faithfulness to a trust)
19. *unvanquished* (unconquered)
20. *introvert* (person more interested in own thoughts than in outside matters)

EXERCISE 49. Which of the two terms makes the sentence correct? Enter the *letter* of your answer on your paper.

1. The __?__ speaker moved the audience deeply in his brief address.
   a. loquacious   *b.* eloquent

2. Andrew is too much of an __?__; he doesn't show enough interest in what is going on around him.
   a. extrovert   *b.* introvert

3. The authorities know the identity of the __?__ and expect to apprehend him soon.
   a. transgressor   *b.* precursor

4. Larry's diverting account of his experiment __?__ the class.
   a. confused   *b.* amused

5. The entire foreign diplomatic __?__ was present at the funeral rites for the distinguished leader.
a. corpse *b.* corps

6. For all the kindness you have shown us, we are extremely __?__.
a. grateful *b.* gratuitous

7. Since Emily's motion was adopted by a 12-to-2 vote, it was clear that most of the members __?__.
a. incurred *b.* concurred

8. If you had used fewer technical terms, your explanation would have been more __?__.
a. comprehensible *b.* comprehensive

9. The employer explained that salary increases are not automatic but __?__ on satisfactory service.
a. contiguous *b.* contingent

10. The following is an example of __?__: "Swimmers come to the surface within seconds after a dive; when Dee didn't come up immediately, we knew she was in trouble."
a. induction *b.* deduction

EXERCISE 50. On your paper, enter the *letter* of the word NOT RELATED in meaning to the other words in each group.

1. *a.* transgression *b.* breach *c.* overstepping *d.* retrogression
2. *a.* commonplace *b.* dull *c.* pedestrian *d.* diverting
3. *a.* dejection *b.* conjecture *c.* sadness *d.* depression
4. *a.* vilify *b.* slander *c.* induce *d.* calumniate
5. *a.* deathless *b.* moribund *c.* everlasting *d.* immortal
6. *a.* block *b.* impede *c.* obstruct *d.* expedite
7. *a.* dependent *b.* conditional *c.* abject *d.* contingent
8. *a.* diffidently *b.* aggressively *c.* fearfully *d.* apprehensively
9. *a.* perfumed *b.* rank *c.* fragrant *d.* aromatic
10. *a.* ancestor *b.* forerunner *c.* precursor *d.* emissary

EXERCISE 51. Which word, selected from the vocabulary list below, will correctly complete the sentence? Enter the appropriate word on your paper.

VOCABULARY LIST

mortal	inconsequential	incurred
versatile	expedited	reprehensible
diverted	induced	intermittently
ingrate	moribund	gratis
comprehensive	discursive	apprehensive

1. He __?__ (*brought upon himself*) the teacher's displeasure by the cursory manner in which he had done his reading assignments.

2. Don't have anything to do with that __?__ (*unthankful person*); he never appreciates a favor.

3. Many businesses have __?__ (*increased the speed of*) delivery by extensive use of messenger service.

4. Nelson incurred a (an) __?__ (*causing death*) wound in the Battle of Trafalgar.

5. Forgetting to bring my lunch turned out to be __?__ (*of no importance*), since I was able to buy a sandwich in the cafeteria.

6. Gail is the most __?__ (*equipped with many aptitudes*) player on our team; she can play any position except first base.

7. Residents may borrow books from the library __?__ (*without charge*).

8. Some of the passengers were nervous because Sam, a newly licensed driver, was at the wheel, but I was not __?__ (*fearful of what might come*).

9. The strikers were __?__ (*moved by persuasion*) to return to their jobs with the promise of a new contract.

10. Dr. Green realized that she would not finish her lesson if she permitted the discussion to become too __?__ (*wandering from one topic to another*).

EXERCISE 52. Answer each question in a sentence or two.

1. If you were Mayor, how might you expedite the settlement of a labor-management controversy in your town?

2. Would you be remiss if you made an important decision on the basis of conjecture? Explain.

3. Is the gradual loss of population to the suburbs a mortal blow to a city? Why, or why not?

4. Would a gratuitous remark that a friend made about you incur your displeasure? Explain.

5. Why is the world apprehensive about the expanding production of nuclear missiles?

EXERCISE 53. On your paper, enter the *letter* of the word that best completes the analogy.

1. *River* is to *bridge* as *valley* is to __?__.
   a. viaduct *b.* mountain *c.* pontoon *d.* projectile *e.* road

2. *Olfactory* is to *smell* as *tactile* is to __?__.
   a. see *b.* grasp *c.* touch *d.* hear *e.* taste

3. *Birth* is to *demise* as *preface* is to __?__.
   a. foreword *b.* conclusion *c.* footnote *d.* introduction
   e. outline

4. *Corpse* is to *life* as *ingrate* is to __?__.
   a. fear *b.* ingratitude *c.* unkindness *d.* dejection
   e. gratitude

5. *Plan* is to *execution* as *outline* is to __?__.
   a. summary *b.* organization *c.* killing *d.* composition *e.* topic

cHAPTER vi **Words From Classical Mythology aNd History**

This chapter will teach you to use important words taken from classical (ancient Greek and Roman) mythology. The beautiful and profoundly significant myths created by the Greeks and adopted by the Romans have contributed words that an educated person is expected to know. All the words discussed below originate from myths, except the following, which are based on historical fact: *Draconian, laconic, Lucullan, philippic, Pyrrhic, solon,* and *thespian.*

Study Your New Words

Adonis /ə-ˈdän-əs/ *n:* very handsome young man (from *Adonis,* a handsome youth loved by Aphrodite, goddess of love)

Joanna's former boyfriend was not exactly handsome, but her new one is quite an *Adonis.*

aegis /ˈē-jəs/ *n:* shield or protection; auspices; sponsorship (from *aegis,* the protective shield of Zeus)

An international force under the *aegis* of the United Nations has been dispatched to the troubled area.

amazon /ˈam-ə-ˌzän/ *n:* tall, strong, masculine woman (from the *Amazons,* a mythological race of women warriors)

Pioneer women were veritable *amazons,* performing heavy household chores in addition to toiling in the fields beside their menfolk.

ambrosial /am-'brō-zhəl/ *adj:* exceptionally pleasing to taste or smell; extremely delicious; excellent (from *ambrosia*, the food of the gods)

The *ambrosial* aroma of the roast whetted our appetites.

atlas /'at-ləs/ *n:* book of maps (from *Atlas*, a giant who supported the heavens on his shoulders. The figure of Atlas supporting the world was prefaced to early map collections; hence the name *atlas*.)

For reliable information about present national boundaries, consult an up-to-date *atlas*.

auroral /ə-'rȯr-əl/ *adj:* pertaining to or resembling the dawn; rosy (from *Aurora*, goddess of the dawn)

The darkness waned and a faint *auroral* glow began to appear in the east.

bacchanalian /ˌbak-ə-'nāl-yən/ *adj:* jovial or wild with drunkenness (from *Bacchus*, the god of wine)—or **bacchic**

At 2 A.M. the neighbors called the police to quell the *bacchanalian* revelry in the upstairs apartment.

chimerical /kī-'mer-i-kəl/ *adj:* fantastic; unreal; impossible; absurd (from the *Chimera*, a fire-breathing monster with a lion's head, goat's body, and serpent's tail)

At first, Robert Fulton's plans for his steamboat were derided as *chimerical* nonsense.

Draconian /drə-'kō-nē-ən/ *adj:* cruel; harsh; severe (from *Draco*, an Athenian lawmaker who drew up a harsh code of laws)—or **draconian**

The dictator took *Draconian* measures against those he suspected of plotting a rebellion.

Elysian /i-'lizh-ən/ *adj:* delightful; blissful; heavenly (from *Elysium*, the mythological paradise where the brave and good live after death)

Students preparing for final examinations yearn for the *Elysian* idleness of the summer vacation.

hector /'hek-tər/ *v:* bully; intimidate with threats; bluster (from *Hector*, bravest of the Trojans)

The pickets did not allow themselves to be provoked, despite the unruly crowds that gathered to *hector* them.

herculean /ˌhər-kyə-ˈlē-ən/ *adj*: very difficult; requiring the strength of *Hercules* (a hero of superhuman strength)

Among the *herculean* tasks confronting large cities are slum clearance and traffic control.

hermetic /hər-ˈmet-ik/ *adj*: airtight (from *Hermes*, who, among his other attributes, was god of magic)

To get a vitamin pill from a new bottle, unscrew the cap and break the *hermetic* seal.

iridescent /ˌir-ə-ˈdes-ᵊnt/ *adj*: having colors like the rainbow (from *Iris*, goddess of the rainbow)

Children enjoy blowing *iridescent* soap bubbles.

jovial /ˈjo-vē-əl/ *adj*: jolly; merry; good-humored (from *Jove*, or Jupiter. The planet Jupiter was believed to make persons born under its influence cheerful or *jovial*.)

Our *jovial* host entertained us with several amusing anecdotes about his employer.

labyrinthine /lab-ə-ˈrin-thən/ *adj*: full of confusing passageways; intricate; complicated, like the *Labyrinth* (a fabled maze in Crete)

Out-of-towners may easily lose their way in New York City's *labyrinthine* subway passages.

laconic /lə-ˈkän-ik/ *adj*: using words sparingly; terse; concise (from *Lakonikos*, meaning "Spartan." The Spartans were known for their terseness.)

All I received in response to my request was the *laconic* reply "Wait."

lethargic /li-ˈthär-jik/ *adj*: unnaturally drowsy; sluggish; dull (from *Lethe*, river in Hades whose water, when drunk, caused forgetfulness of the past)

For several hours after the operation, the patient was *lethargic* because of the anesthetic.

Lucullan /lü-ˈkəl-ən/ *adj*: sumptuous; luxurious (from *Lucullus*, a Roman who gave lavish banquets)

Thanksgiving dinner is almost a *Lucullan* feast.

martial /ˈmär-shəl/ *adj:* pertaining to war; warlike (from *Mars,* god of war)

The Helvetians were a *martial* people who tried to conquer southern Gaul.

mentor /ˈmen-ˌtȯ(r)/ *n*

(1) wise and trusted adviser (from *Mentor,* to whom Odysseus entrusted the education of his son)

The retiring supervisor was persuaded to stay on for a month as *mentor* to her successor.

(2) athletic coach

Our basketball *mentor* says that our team is the best he has ever coached.

mercurial /mər-ˈkyu̇r-ē-əl/ *adj:* quick; vivacious; active; lively (from *Mercury,* the messenger of the gods, who was also god of commerce, magic, and eloquence, as well as the patron of travelers, rogues, and thieves. His name designates a planet as well as a metal.)—ANT **saturnine**

The older partner is rather dull and morose, but the younger has a *mercurial* temperament that appeals to customers.

myrmidon /ˈmər-mə-ˌdän/ *n:* obedient and unquestioning follower (from the *Myrmidons,* a martial tribe who accompanied Achilles to the Trojan War)

The dictator surrounded himself with *myrmidons* who would loyally and pitilessly execute all orders.

nemesis /ˈnem-ə-səs/ *n*

(1) due punishment for evil deeds (from *Nemesis,* goddess of vengeance)

The racketeer was acquitted on all counts accept tax evasion. That turned out to be his *nemesis.*

(2) one who inflicts such punishment

Napoleon crushed many opponents, but Wellington proved to be his *nemesis.*

odyssey /ˈäd-ə-sē/ *n:* any long series of wanderings or travels (from the *Odyssey*, the poem dealing with Odysseus' ten years of wandering on his way home from the Trojan War)

Your travel agent will gladly plan a year's *odyssey* to places of interest around the world.

paean /ˈpē-ən/ *n:* song or hymn of praise, joy, or triumph (A *paean* was a hymn in praise of Apollo, the god of deliverance.)

When the crisis was resolved, people danced in the streets and sang *paeans* of joy.

palladium /pə-ˈlād-ē-əm/ *n:* safeguard or protection (from *Palladium*, the statue of Pallas Athena, which was thought to protect the city of Troy)

The little girl habitually fell asleep clutching a battered doll, her *palladium*.

panic /ˈpan-ik/ *n:* unreasoning, sudden fright that grips a multitude (from *Pan*, a god believed to cause fear)

A *panic* ensued when someone in the crowded auditorium yelled "Fire!"

philippic /fə-ˈlip-ik/ *n:* bitter denunciation (from the *Philippics*, orations by Demosthenes denouncing King Philip of Macedon)

In an hour-long *philippic*, the legislator denounced the lobbyists opposing her bill.

plutocratic /ˌplüt-ə-ˈkrat-ik/ *adj:* having great influence because of one's wealth (from *Plutus*, god of wealth)

A handful of *plutocratic* investors, each owning several thousand shares, determined the policies of the corporation.

procrustean /prə-ˈkrəs-tē-ən/ *adj:* cruel or inflexible in enforcing conformity (from *Procrustes*, a robber who made his victims fit the length of his bed, either stretching them if they were too short, or cutting off their legs if they were too tall)—or **Procrustean**

The magistrate dispensed a *procrustean* kind of justice; he fined everyone summoned to his court $100, regardless of the circumstances.

protean /ˈprōt-ē-ən/ *adj:* exceedingly variable; readily assuming different forms or shapes (from *Proteus,* a sea god who could readily change his shape to elude capture)

The witness' *protean* tactics under cross-examination gave the impression that she was untrustworthy.

Pyrrhic /ˈpir-ik/ *adj:* ruinous; gained at too great a cost (from *Pyrrhus,* who suffered enormous losses in a "victory" over the Romans)

Our winning the opening game was a *Pyrrhic* victory, as our leading scorer was injured and put out of action for the balance of the season.

saturnine /ˈsat-ər-ˌnīn/ *adj:* heavy; dull; gloomy; morose (from *Saturn,* father of Jupiter. Though Saturn's reign was supposedly a golden age, he has become a symbol of heaviness and dullness because the alchemists and astrologers associated his name with the metal lead.)
—ANT **mercurial**

The research assistant was a *saturnine* scholar who said very little and smiled rarely.

siren /ˈsī-rən/ *n*
  (1) dangerous, attractive woman (from the *Sirens,* creatures half woman and half bird, whose sweet singing lured sailors to destruction on the rocks)

The enemy employed a redhaired *siren* as a spy.

  (2) a woman who sings sweetly

One of the entertainers was a nightclub *siren* with a melodious voice.

  (3) apparatus for sounding loud warnings

Emergency vehicles raced to the scene with *sirens* screaming.

solon /ˈsō-lən/ *n:* legislator; wise lawgiver (from *Solon,* noted Athenian lawgiver)

Next week the *solons* will return to the capital for the opening of the legislative session.

stentorian /sten-ˈtȯr-ē-ən/ *adj:* very loud (from *Stentor,* a legendary herald whose voice was as loud as fifty voices)

Speak softly; you don't need a *stentorian* voice to be heard in this small room.

Stygian /ˈstij-ē-ən/ *adj:* infernal; dark; gloomy (from *Styx*, a river of the lower world leading into Hades, or Hell)

A power failure at 11:30 P.M. plunged the city into *Stygian* blackness.

tantalize /ˈtant-ᵊl-ˌīz/ *v:* excite a hope but prevent its fulfillment; tease (from *Tantalus*, who was kept hungry and thirsty in the lower world with food and water very near but just beyond his reach)

The considerate hostess removed the strawberry shortcake from the table so as not to *tantalize* her weight-conscious guest.

terpsichorean /ˌtərp-sik-ə-ˈrē-ən/ *adj:* pertaining to dancing (from *Terpsichore*, the muse of dancing)

The reviewers lauded the ballet troupe for its *terpsichorean* artistry.

thespian /ˈthes-pē-ən/ *adj:* pertaining to the drama or acting (from *Thespis*, reputed father of Greek drama)—or **Thespian**

If you enjoy acting in plays, join a *thespian* club.

titanic /tī-ˈtan-ik/ *adj:* of enormous strength, size, or power (from the *Titans*, lawless, powerful giants defeated by Zeus)

By a *titanic* effort, our football team halted an onrush at our one-yard line.

Do not write in this book. Enter all answers on separate paper.

Apply What You Have Learned

EXERCISE 1. If the italicized word is *correctly* used in the sentence, enter *C* on your paper. If *incorrectly* used, enter *X*.

1. Our new track *mentor* has had years of coaching experience.
2. I was grateful for my sunglasses as we drove through the desert in the glaring *auroral* light of midday.
3. A *laconic* person habitually uses more words than necessary.
4. The Egyptian pyramids are structures of *titanic* dimensions.
5. A *saturnine* expression on a person's face may be taken as a sign of cheerfulness.

6. The refugee told of his *odyssey* from country to country in search of a new homeland.

7. By imposing *Draconian* fines, the judge acquired a reputation for leniency.

8. The notorious bank robber finally met his *nemesis* in the person of a courageous teller who set off the burglar alarm.

9. Do not *tantalize* the child by promising her a new toy and failing to keep that promise.

10. A practical person does not offer *chimerical* suggestions.

EXERCISE 2. On your paper, enter the *letter* of the word (or set of words) that best completes the sentence.

1. Photographs of __?__ celebrities decorated the walls of the dance studio.

    a. operatic *b.* modern *c.* thespian *d.* famous
    e. terpsichorean

2. The wrestler's __?__ maneuvers made it difficult for his opponent to obtain a hold.

    a. hermetic *b.* protean *c.* titanic *d.* procrustean *e.* philippic

3. In a locker-room speech between halves, the __?__ reaffirmed his confidence in his __?__.

    a. conductor . . . myrmidons *b.* amazon . . . team
    c. myrmidon . . . adherents *d.* mentor . . . squad
    e. conductor . . . mentors

4. Many literatures describe a paradise where the __?__ dwell in __?__ repose.

    a. heroic . . . Stygian *b.* unvanquished . . . bacchanalian
    c. sirens . . . abject *d.* perfidious . . . ambrosial
    e. brave . . . Elysian

5. When people become __?__, their ability to reason gives way to fear.

    a. lethargic *b.* saturnine *c.* panicky *d.* Draconian
    e. plutocratic

6. The audience laughed to see the corpulent actor __?__ by his puny companion's hectoring.

    a. convinced *b.* betrayed *c.* tripped *d.* intimidated
    e. encouraged

7. The Pyrrhic victory was cause for widespread __?__.

   a. dejection   b. optimism   c. paeans   d. satisfaction
   e. promotions

8. Only a person with a __?__ voice could have been heard above the din of the angry crowd.

   a. herculean   b. stentorian   c. jovial   d. laconic   e. titanic

9. Our __?__ host always enjoys having friends to share his Lucullan suppers.

   a. cursive   b. martial   c. fractious   d. convivial   e. sanguine

10. Psychoanalysis can help patients recall long-forgotten experiences lost in the __?__ recesses of their minds.

    a. labyrinthine   b. chimerical   c. iridescent   d. auroral
    e. mercurial

EXERCISE 3.   On your paper, enter the *letter* of the word or expression that has most nearly the SAME MEANING as the italicized word.

1. *ambrosial* fare   a. expensive   b. cut-rate   c. railroad
   d. delicious

2. unemployed *thespians*   a. musicians   b. actors   c. dancers
   d. loafers

3. *martial* airs   a. matrimonial   b. tuneful   c. military   d. soothing

4. impassioned *philippic*   a. plea   b. message   c. praise
   d. denunciation

5. *plutocratic* associates   a. loyal and wealthy   b. jovial   c. carefree
   d. rich and influential

6. *Draconian* laws   a. democratic   b. severe   c. unpopular
   d. unenforced

7. *hermetic* compartments   a. rigid   b. tiny   c. airtight
   d. labyrinthine

8. road *atlas*   a. traveler   b. map collection   c. network
   d. surface

9. endless *odyssey*   a. story   b. wanderings   c. sufferings
   d. errands

10. a new *Adonis*   a. lover   b. movie actor   c. myrmidon
    d. handsome youth

EXERCISE 4. As clues to each mystery word below, you are given its first letter and the number of its missing letters. On your paper, enter the complete word.

1. I found it difficult to study, since a heavy dinner had made me l___8___.

2. Jean Valjean's h___8___ strength enabled him to lift the heaviest of objects with ease.

3. You may see an i___9___ arc, known as a rainbow, when you look at the sky just after a summer shower.

4. A glass jar is airtight if it is h___7___ally sealed

5. The band concerts, formerly under private sponsorship, will be given under the a___4___ of our city from now on.

EXERCISE 5. Answer each question in a sentence or two.

1. Would you be in a jovial mood after achieving a Pyrrhic victory? Why, or why not?

2. Why is it normal for someone exploring a labyrinthine cave to be gripped with panic?

3. Is it possible to have ambrosial food in a simple meal, or do we need a Lucullan feast? Explain.

4. Are Draconian penalties an effective palladium against crime?

5. Would you withdraw from an election campaign if your rival's myrmidons hectored you at every place you tried to speak? Explain.

EXERCISE 6. On your paper, enter the *letter* of the word-pair that best expresses a relationship similar to that existing between the capitalized word-pair.

1. SOLON : LAWS

   a. atlas : maps
   b. ruler : subjects
   c. philosopher : credentials
   d. artisan : trade
   e. composer : operas

2. SIREN : BEAUTY

   a. victim : trap
   b. temptress : prey
   c. hunter : bait
   d. alarm : confidence
   e. worm : fish

3. TANTALIZE : SATISFY

    a. pester : annoy
    b. worry : harass
    c. harry : plague

    d. convict : acquit
    e. delay : postpone

4. NEMESIS : EVILDOER

    a. avenger : victim
    b. retribution : culprit
    c. punishment : benefactor

    d. justice : misdeed
    e. penalty : evil

5. AMAZON : STRENGTH

    a. comedienne : humor
    b. river : jungle
    c. nurse : invalid

    d. warrior : civilian
    e. servant : indifference

6. PALLADIUM : DANGER

    a. rumor : panic
    b. arena : excitement
    c. investigation : truth

    d. experience : skill
    e. vaccination : smallpox

7. MERCURIAL : VIVACITY

    a. procrustean : rigidity
    b. protean : uniformity
    c. ethereal : earth

    d. saturnine : hilarity
    e. ambrosial : dawn

8. PAEAN : ECSTASY

    a. anthem : nation
    b. suffering : rejoicing
    c. lament : sorrow

    d. sadness : joy
    e. hymn : congregation

9. THESPIAN : TERPSICHOREAN

    a. painter : dancer
    b. orator : musician
    c. comedian : sculptor

    d. actress : ballerina
    e. composer : singer

10. AURORAL : DAWN

    a. fragile : care
    b. autumnal : fall
    c. visual : ear

    d. annual : season
    e. juvenile : delinquency

Chapter vii French Words in English

English has never hesitated to adopt useful French words. Any French expression that describes an idea better than the corresponding English expression may sooner or later be incorporated into English. The process has been going on for centuries.

This chapter will teach you how to use some of the more important French words and expressions that are today part of an educated person's English vocabulary.

1. Terms Describing Persons

au courant /ˌō-ˌku-ˈrä^n/ *adj:* well-informed; up-to-date

By reading reviews, you can keep *au courant* with new developments in literature, films, television, and the theater.

blasé /blà-ˈzā/ *adj:* tired of pleasures; bored

After a while, Edna had had her fill of mountain scenery, and when the guide pointed out some additional peaks, she reacted in a *blasé* manner.

chic /ˈshēk/ *adj:* stylish

She looked very *chic* in her new outfit.

debonair /ˌdeb-ə-ˈne(ə)r/ *adj:* courteous, gracious, and charming

The headwaiter was *debonair* with the guests but firm with the waiters.

maladroit /ˌmal-ə-ˈdroit/ *adj:* unskillful; clumsy—ANT **adroit**

Our new supervisor is clever in many matters in which his predecessor was *maladroit*.

naive /nä-ˈēv/ *adj:* simple in nature; artless; ingenuous

You are *naive* if you believe implacable foes can be reconciled easily.

nonchalant /ˌnän-shə-ˈlänt/ *adj:* without concern or enthusiasm; indifferent

I am amazed that you can be so *nonchalant* about the coming test when everyone else is so worried.

EXERCISE 1. On your paper, enter the most appropriate expression from group 1 for completing the sentence.

1. Some advertising is so exaggerated that only a (an) __?__ person would believe it.
2. If every meal were a banquet, we should soon greet even the most delicious food with a (an) __?__ expression.
3. Read a good daily newspaper to keep __?__ with what is going on in the world.
4. The cuts on Ralph's face show that he is __?__ in the use of his razor.
5. Unlike her discourteous predecessor, the new service manager is quite __?__.

2. Terms for Persons

attaché /ˌat-ə-ˈshā/ *n:* member of the diplomatic staff of an ambassador or minister

We were unable to see the ambassador, but we spoke to one of the *attachés.*

bourgeoisie /ˌbu̇rzh-wä-ˈzē/ *n:* the middle class

A strong *bourgeoisie* contributes to a nation's prosperity.

chargé d'affaires /ˈshär-ˌzhäd-ə-ˈfe(ə)r/ *n:* temporary substitute for an ambassador

Whom did the President designate as *chargé d'affaires* when he recalled the ambassador?

confrere /ˈkōⁿ-ˌfre(ə)r/ *n:* colleague; co-worker; comrade

The attorney introduced us to his *confrere*, Mr. Quinones; they share the same office.

connoisseur /ˌkän-ə-ˈsər/ *n:* expert; critical judge

To verify the gem's value, we consulted a *connoisseur* of rare diamonds.

coterie /ˈkōt-ə-rē/ *n:* set or circle of acquaintances; clique

Helen won't bowl with us; she has her own *coterie* of bowling friends.

debutante /ˈdeb-yu̇-ˌtänt/ *n:* girl who has just had her *debut* (first introduction into society)

The *debutante's* photograph was at the head of the society page.

devotee /ˌdev-ə-ˈtē/ *n:* ardent adherent; partisan

Samuel Adams was a passionate *devotee* of American independence.

elite /ā-ˈlēt/ *n:* group of superior individuals; aristocracy; choice part

Fred likes to consider himself a member of the intellectual *elite*.

émigré /ˈem-i-ˌgrā/ *m. n:* refugee; person who has fled (*emigrated*) from his or her native land because of political conditions—**émigrée**, *f.*

A committee was formed to find housing and employment for the anxious *émigrés*.

entrepreneur /ˌän-trə-prə-ˈnər/ *n:* one who assumes the risks and management of a business

What *entrepreneur* will invest capital unless there is some prospect of a profit?

envoy /ˈen-ˌvȯi/ *n:* diplomatic agent or messenger

The President's *envoy* to the conference has not yet been chosen.

fiancé /ˌfē-än-ˈsä/ *m. n:* person engaged to be married—**fiancée**, *f.*

Madeline introduced Mr. Cole as her *fiancé*.

gendarme /ˈzhän-ˌdärm/ *n:* armed police officer, especially in France and other European countries

The charge d'affaires requested that extra *gendarmes* be posted outside the embassy.

gourmand /ˈgu̇(ə)r-ˌmänd/ *n:* person excessively fond of eating and drinking; glutton

The food was so good that I ate more than I should have. I behaved like a *gourmand*.

gourmet /'gu̇(ə)r-ˌmā/ *n:* connoisseur in eating and drinking

Valerie can recommend a good restaurant; she is a *gourmet.*

ingenue /'an-jə-ˌnü/ *n:* actress playing the role of a naive young woman; naive young woman

She was as simple and pretty as a film *ingenue.*

maître d'hôtel /ˌmä-trə-dō-'tel/ *n:* headwaiter—or **maître d'** /mä-trə-'dē/

The *maître d'hôtel* supervises the waiters.

martinet /ˌmärt-ᵊn-'et/ *n:* person who enforces very strict discipline

Our dean is an understanding counselor, not a *martinet.*

nouveaux riches /ˌnü-vō-'rēsh/ *n pl:* persons newly rich

An unexpected inheritance lifted him into the ranks of the *nouveaux riches.*

parvenu /'pär-və-ˌn(y)ü/ *m. n:* person suddenly risen to wealth or power who lacks the proper social qualifications; upstart—**parvenue,** *f.*

When the businessman first moved into the exclusive area, his aristocratic neighbors regarded him as a *parvenu.*

protégé /'prōt-ə-ˌzhā/ *m. n:* person under the care and protection of another—**protégée,** *f.*

The veteran first baseman passed on numerous fielding hints to his young *protégé.*

raconteur /ˌrak-än-'tər/ *n:* person who excels in telling stories, anecdotes, etc.

Mark Twain was an excellent *raconteur.*

valet /'val-ət/ *n:* manservant who attends to the personal needs of his employer, as by taking care of his employer's clothes

That morning, the old gentleman got dressed without the help of his *valet.*

EXERCISE 2. On your paper, enter the most appropriate expression from group 2 for completing the sentence.

1. After a particularly unpleasant quarrel with her __?__, Rita considered breaking their engagement.

2. Between the nobles on one extreme and the peasants on the other, a middle class known as the __?__ emerged.
3. The __?__ brushed his employer's clothes.
4. Sherlock Holmes collaborated on the case with his __?__, Dr. Watson.
5. Louise can relate an anecdote better than I; she is a fine __?__.
6. Though the food was delicious, Karen refused a second helping; she is no __?__.
7. If I were a (an) __?__, I would be able to tell whether the cheese in this salad is imported or domestic.
8. When the young attorney was elected to a seat on the board of directors, some of the veteran members considered her a (an) __?__.
9. A man who flees his native land to escape political oppression is a (an) __?__.
10. Though the Allens are friendly with everyone, they have rarely visited with anyone outside their tightly knit __?__.

3. Terms for Traits or Feelings of Persons

éclat /ā-ˈklä/ *n:* brilliancy of achievement
The violinist performed with rare *éclat*.

élan /ā-ˈlän/ *n:* enthusiasm; eagerness for action
Because the cast had rehearsed with such *elan*, the director had few apprehensions about the opening-night performance.

ennui /än-ˈwē/ *n:* feeling of weariness and discontent; boredom; tedium
You too would suffer from *ennui* if you had to spend months in a hospital bed.

esprit de corps /es-ˌprēd-ə-ˈkȯ(ə)r/ *n:* feeling of union and common interest pervading a group; devotion to a group or to its ideals
The employees showed extraordinary *esprit de corps* when they volunteered to work Saturdays for the duration of the crisis.

finesse /fə-'nes/ *n:* skill

The adroit prosecutor arranged his questions with admirable *finesse.*

legerdemain /ˌlej-ərd-ə-'mān/ *n:* sleight of hand; artful trick

By a feat of *legerdemain*, the magician produced a rabbit from her hat.

malaise /ma-'lāz/ *n:* vague feeling of bodily discomfort or illness

After the late, heavy supper, he experienced a feeling of *malaise.*

noblesse oblige /nō-ˌbles-ə-'blēzh/ *n:* principle that persons of high rank or birth are obliged to act nobly

In the olden days, kings and other nobles, observing the principle of *noblesse oblige*, fought at the head of their troops.

rapport /ra-'pȯ(ə)r/ *n:* relationship characterized by harmony, conformity, or affinity

A common interest in gardening brought Molly and Loretta into closer *rapport.*

sangfroid /'sän-'frwä/ *n:* coolness of mind or composure in difficult circumstances; equanimity

The quarterback's *sangfroid* during the last tense moments of the game enabled him to call the winning play.

savoir faire /ˌsav-ˌwär-'fe(ə)r/ *n:* knowledge of just what to do; tact

You need both capital and *savoir faire* to be a successful entrepreneur.

EXERCISE 3. On your paper, enter the most appropriate expression from group 3 for completing the sentence.

1. Joel is tactful; he has plenty of __?__.
2. Your physician may help you obtain some relief from the __?__ that accompanies a severe cold.
3. Instead of reducing their subordinates' salaries, the executives cut their own compensation substantially, in accordance with the principle of __?__.
4. To do card tricks, you have to be good at __?__.
5. If you get tired and bored on long train trips, try reading detective stories; they help to overcome __?__.

4. Terms Dealing With Conversation and Writing

adieu /ə-'d(y)ü/ *n:* good-by; farewell

On commencement day we shall bid *adieu* to our alma mater.

au revoir /ˌȯr-əv-'wär/ *n:* good-by till we meet again

Since I hope to see you again, I'll say *au revoir* rather than adieu.

billet-doux /ˌbil-ā-'dü/ *n:* love letter

A timely *billet-doux* can patch up a lovers' quarrel.

bon mot /bōⁿ-'mō/ *n:* clever saying; witty remark

The jester Yorick often set the table a-roaring with a well-placed *bon mot.*

brochure /brō-'shu̇(ə)r/ *n:* pamphlet; treatise

This helpful *brochure* explains social security benefits.

canard /kə-'närd/ *n:* false rumor; absurd story; hoax

It took a public appearance by the monarch to silence the *canard* that he had been assassinated.

cliché /klē-'shā/ *n:* trite or worn-out expression

Two *clichés* that we can easily do without are "first and foremost" and "last but not least."

entre nous /ˌän-trə-'nü/ *adv:* between us; confidentially

The Wildcats expect to win, but *entre nous* their chances are not too good.

mot juste /mō-zhūest/ *n:* the exactly right word

To improve your writing, try to find the *mot juste* for each idea and avoid clichés.

précis /'prā-sē/ *n:* brief summary

Include only the essential points when you write a *précis.*

repartee /ˌrep-ər-'tē/ *n:* skill of replying quickly, cleverly, and humorously; witty reply

Dorothy Parker was known for her amusing *repartee.*

résumé /ˈrez-ə-ˌmā/ *n*

(1) summary

The teacher asked us to write a *résumé* of the last act.

(2) brief account of personal, educational, and professional qualifications and experience submitted by an applicant for a position

Martha sent copies of her *résumé* to fourteen prospective employers.

riposte /ri-ˈpōst/ *n*

(1) quick retort or repartee

Surprised to see him eating the apple core, I asked, "Won't it affect you?" "Pleasurably," was his *riposte*.

(2) in fencing, a quick return thrust after a parry

The fencing instructor showed us how to defend ourselves against *ripostes*.

tête-à-tête /ˌtāt-ə-ˈtāt/ *n:* private conversation between two persons

Before answering, the witness had a *tête-à-tête* with his attorney.

EXERCISE 4. On your paper, enter the most appropriate expression from group 4 for completing the sentence.

1. There are valuable hints on safe driving in this sixteen-page __?__ .
2. The expression "old as the hills" should be avoided because it is a (an) __?__ .
3. Investigation proved that the story was unfounded; it was just a (an) __?__ .
4. The manager went out to the mound for a brief __?__ with his faltering pitcher.
5. Everyone supposes this diamond is genuine, but __?__ it's only an imitation.

5. Terms Dealing With Situations

bête noire /ˌbāt-nə-ˈwär/ *n:* object or person dreaded; bugbear

He enjoyed all his subjects except mathematics, his *bête noire*.

carte blanche /'kärt-'blän̄sh/ *n:* full discretionary power; freedom to use one's own judgment

Ms. Mauro gave her assistant *carte blanche* in managing the office while she was away.

cause célèbre /ˌkōz-sā-'lebrə/ *n:* famous case in law that arouses considerable interest; an incident or situation attracting much attention

The trial of John Peter Zenger, a *cause célèbre* in the eighteenth century, helped to establish freedom of the press in America.

cul-de-sac /ˌkəl-di-'sak/ *n:* blind alley

Painting proved to be a *cul-de-sac* for Philip Carey, because he had no real talent.

debacle /di-'bäk-əl/ *n:* collapse; overthrow; rout

The *debacle* at Waterloo signaled the end of Napoleon's power.

fait accompli /ˌfä-ta-kōn̄-'plē/ *n:* thing already done

A reconciliation between the bitter foes, once thought an impossibility, may soon become a *fait accompli*.

faux pas /(')fō-'pä/ *n:* misstep or blunder in conduct, manners, speech, etc.

One of the guests got no dessert because Dolores had committed the *faux pas* of serving herself too generous a helping.

impasse /'im-ˌpas/ *n:* deadlock; predicament affording no escape; impassable road

The foreman reported that the jury had reached an *impasse* and could deliberate no further.

liaison /'lē-ə-ˌzän/ *n:* bond; linking up; coordination of activities

By joining the alumni association, graduates can maintain their *liaison* with the school.

mélange /mā-'län̄zh/ *n:* mixture; medley; potpourri

Our last amateur show was a *mélange* of dramatic skits, acrobatics, ballet, popular tunes, and classical music.

mirage /məˈräzh/ *n:* optical illusion

The sheet of water we thought we saw on the road ahead turned out to be only a *mirage*.

EXERCISE 5. On your paper, enter the most appropriate expression from group 5 for completing the sentence.

1. Your flippant remark to Mrs. Lee about her ailing son was a (an) __?__ .

2. The inhabitants of the remote Eskimo village had practically no __?__ with the outside world.

3. Mr. Briggs never concerned himself with hiring or dismissing employees, having given his plant manager __?__ in these matters.

4. Despite seventeen hours of continuous deliberations, the weary negotiators still faced a (an) __?__ over wages.

5. Alice's position turned out to be a (an) __?__, as it offered no opportunity for advancement.

Do not write in this book. Enter all answers on separate paper.

Review Exercises

EXERCISE 6. On your paper, copy each word or expression from column I, and next to it enter the *letter* of its correct meaning from column II.

COLUMN I	COLUMN II
1. refugee	*a.* devotee
2. till we meet again	*b.* debacle
3. well-informed	*c.* bête noire
4. partisan	*d.* au courant
5. brief summary	*e.* sangfroid
6. hoax	*f.* billet-doux
7. bugbear	*g.* émigré
8. rout	*h.* précis
9. love letter	*i.* au revoir
10. equanimity	*j.* canard

EXERCISE 7. Which of the three terms makes the sentence correct? Enter the *letter* of your answer on your paper. (Hint: For a clue to the missing term, study the italicized word or expression.)

1. In serving the soup, the __?__ (*clumsy*) waitress spilled some of it on the guest of honor.
   a. chic *b.* maladroit *c.* debonair

2. Monotonous repetition usually brings on __?__ (*boredom*).
   a. ennui *b.* éclat *c.* savoir faire

3. I'll be glad to give my opinion, but you must realize I am no __?__ (*expert*).
   a. raconteur *b.* martinet *c.* connoisseur

4. A bibliophile is usually a __?__ (*ardent adherent*) of good literature.
   a. protégée *b.* devotee *c.* repartee

5. We made a right turn into the next street, but it proved to be a __?__ (*blind alley*).
   a. mélange *b.* cul-de-sac *c.* canard

6. The President was represented at the state funeral in Paris by a special __?__ (*diplomatic agent*).
   a. ingenue *b.* bourgeoisie *c.* envoy

7. We had a __?__ (*private conversation*) over a couple of ice-cream sodas.
   a. bête noire *b.* tête-à-tête *c.* mirage

8. Do not commit the __?__ (*blunder*) of seating Frank next to Rhoda because they are not on speaking terms.
   a. faux pas *b.* impasse *c.* riposte

9. Today, my biology teacher began with a __?__ (*summary*) of yesterday's lesson.
   a. rapport *b.* résumé *c.* brochure

10. Because of her excellent training, she has developed remarkable __?__ (*skill*) at the piano.
    a. sangfroid *b.* élan *c.* finesse

EXERCISE 8. As clues to each mystery word below, you are given its first letter and the number of its missing letters. On your paper, enter the complete word.

1. Albert introduced us to his f____6____ several weeks before they were to be married.

2. Try to find the m____2____ ____5____ for your idea; if a word only approximates what you wish to say, reject it.

3. Don't spoil your writing with such a c____5____ as "the fly in the ointment" or "dumb as an ox."

4. Mae watched impatiently for the letter carrier; she was eagerly expecting a long b____5____-____4____ from her fiancé.

5. The celebrity was surrounded by a c____6____ of admirers.

6. She was as nervous as a d____8____ at a coming-out party.

7. A good p____5____ should contain fewer than a third of the number of words in the original.

8. Some employees regard the manager as a m____7____, but I have found him not too strict.

9. The prosecutor, it was said, had made the trial into a c____4____ ____7____ to further her political ambitions.

10. My mispronunciation of our guest's name was an embarrassing f____3____ ____3____.

EXERCISE 9. Answer each question in a sentence or two.

1. Can a naive entrepreneur succeed in business? Why, or why not?

2. Why is it usually a faux pas to give someone else carte blanche to make decisions for you?

3. Is it normal for employees who consider themselves in a cul-de-sac to show ennui? Explain.

4. Would it hurt a professional ball club's esprit de corps to have a martinet as a manager? Why, or why not?

5. Why must you have rapport with your audience to succeed as a raconteur?

6. Terms Dealing With History and Government

coup d'etat /ˌküd-ə-ˈtä/ *n:* sudden, violent, or illegal overthrow of a government—or **coup** /ˈkü/

Napoleon seized power by a *coup d'etat.*

demarche /dā-ˈmärsh/ *n:* course of action, especially one involving a change of policy

Hitler's attack on Russia, shortly after his pact with Stalin, was a stunning *demarche.*

détente /dā-ˈtänt/ *n:* a relaxing, as of strained relations between nations

An effective world disarmament treaty should bring a *détente* in international tensions.

entente /än-ˈtänt/ *n:* understanding or agreement between governments

Canada and the United States have a long-standing *entente* on border problems.

laissez-faire /ˌles-ˌā-ˈfe(ə)r/ *n:* absence of government interference or regulation

Adam Smith believed a policy of *laissez-faire* toward business would benefit a nation.

lettre de cachet /ˌle-trə-də-ˌka-ˈshā/ *n:* sealed letter obtainable from the King of France (before the Revolution) ordering the imprisonment without trial of the person named in the letter

Dr. Manette was imprisoned through a *lettre de cachet.*

rapprochement /ˌrap-ˌrōsh-ˈmä^{n}/ *n:* establishment or state of cordial relations; coming together

The gradual *rapprochement* between these two nations, long traditional enemies, cheered all Europeans.

regime /rā-ˈzhēm/ *n:* system of government or rule

The coup d'etat brought to power a *regime* that restored civil liberties to the oppressed people.

EXERCISE 10. On your paper, enter the most appropriate expression from group 6 for completing the sentence.

1. Do you favor strict regulation of business or a policy of __?__?
2. The tyrannical ruler was eventually overthrown by a (an) __?__, engineered by a strong military group.
3. The newly elected officials will face many problems left by the outgoing __?__.
4. Before 1789, a French nobleman could have an enemy imprisoned without trial by obtaining a (an) __?__.
5. Hopes for world peace rose sharply with reports of a (an) __?__ in the strained relations between the two rulers.

7. Terms Dealing With the Arts

avant-garde /ˌäv-ˌän-ˈgärd/ *n:* experimentalists or innovators in any art
Walt Whitman was no conservative; his daring innovations in poetry place him in the *avant-garde* of nineteenth-century writers.

bas-relief /ˌbä-ri-ˈlēf/ *n:* carving or sculpture in which the figures project only slightly from the background
The ancient Greek Parthenon is famed for its beautiful sculpture in *bas-relief*.

baton /ba-ˈtän/ *n:* stick with which a conductor beats time for an orchestra or band
A downbeat is the downward stroke of the conductor's *baton*, denoting the principally accented note of a measure.

chef d'oeuvre /shā-ˈdəvrə/ *n:* masterpiece in art, literature, etc.
Many connoisseurs regard HAMLET as Shakespeare's *chef d'oeuvre*.

denouement /ˌdā-nü-ˈmäⁿ/ *n:* solution ("untying") of the plot in a play, story, or complex situation; outcome; end
In the *denouement* of GREAT EXPECTATIONS, Pip's benefactor is identified as the escaped convict whom Pip had once befriended.

encore /ˈän-ˌkȯ(ə)r/ *n:* repetition of a performance (or the rendition of an additional selection) in response to the demand from an audience

In appreciation of the enthusiastic applause, the vocalist sang an *encore*.

genre /ˈzhän-rə/ *n*

(1) kind; sort; category

The literary *genre* to which Virginia Woolf contributed most is the novel.

(2) style of painting depicting scenes from everyday life

Painters of *genre* choose scenes from everyday life as their subject matter.

musicale /ˌmyü-zi-ˈkal/ *n:* social gathering, with music as the featured entertainment

At last night's *musicale* in my cousin's house, we were entertained by a folk singer.

palette /ˈpal-ət/ *n:* thin board (with a thumb hole at one end) on which an artist lays and mixes colors

After a few strokes on the canvas, an artist reapplies the brush to the *palette* for more paint.

repertoire /ˈrep-ə(r)-ˌtwär/ *n:* list of plays, operas, roles, compositions, etc., that a company or performer is prepared to perform

The guitarist apologized for not being able to play the requested number, explaining that it was not in his *repertoire*.

vignette /vin-ˈyet/ *n:* short verbal description; small, graceful literary sketch

James Joyce's DUBLINERS offers some unforgettable *vignettes* of life in Dublin at the turn of the century.

EXERCISE 11. On your paper, enter the most appropriate expression from group 7 for completing the sentence.

1. After studying some poems, we turned our attention to another ___?___, short stories.

2. A novel with a suspenseful plot makes the reader impatient to get to the ___?___.

3. If audience reaction is favorable, Selma is prepared to play a (an) ___?___.

4. Beethoven's NINTH SYMPHONY is regarded by many as his ___?___.
5. By diligent study the young singer added several new numbers to his ___?___.

8. Terms Dealing With Food

a la carte /ˌal-ə-ˈkärt/ *adv:* according to the bill of fare; dish by dish, with a stated price for each dish

If you order *a la carte*, you select whatever you wish from the bill of fare, paying only for the dishes ordered.

aperitif /ˌap-ˌer-ə-ˈtēf/ *n:* alcoholic drink taken before a meal as an appetizer

Select a nonalcoholic appetizer, such as tomato juice, if you do not care for an *aperitif.*

bonbon /ˈbän-ˌbän/ *n:* piece of candy

For St. Valentine's Day, we gave Mother a heart-shaped box of delicious *bonbons.*

cuisine /kwi-ˈzēn/ *n:* style of cooking or preparing food

Around the corner is a restaurant specializing in French *cuisine.*

demitasse /ˈdem-ē-ˌtas/ *n:* small cup for, or of, black coffee

Aunt Dorothy always takes cream with her coffee; she is not fond of *demitasse.*

entrée /ˈän-trā/ *n:* main dish at lunch or dinner

We had a choice of the following *entrées:* roast beef, fried chicken, or baked mackerel.

filet /fi-ˈlā/ *n:* slice of meat or fish without bones or fat

Because they contain no bones or excess fat, *filets* are more expensive than ordinary cuts of meat.

hors d'oeuvres /ȯr-ˈdərvz/ *n pl:* light food served as an appetizer before the regular courses of a meal

Malcolm purchased olives, celery, and anchovies for the *hors d'oeuvres.*

pièce de résistance /pē-ˌes-də-rə-ˌzē-ˈstäns/ *n*

    (1) main dish

If you eat too much of the introductory dishes, you will have little appetite for the *pièce de résistance*.

    (2) main item of any collection, series, program, etc.

The preliminaries were followed by the *pièce de résistance*, the title fight.

table d'hôte /ˌtäb-əl-ˈdōt/ *n:* complete meal of several courses offered in a hotel or restaurant at a fixed price

If you order the *table d'hôte*, you pay the fixed price for the entire dinner, even if you do not have some of the dishes.

EXERCISE 12. On your paper, enter the most appropriate expression from group 8 for completing the sentence.

1. Before dinner, our hostess brought in a large tray of appetizing ___?___.

2. Though this chef's style of cooking is quite interesting, it cannot compare with Grandmother's ___?___.

3. When I do not care to have a complete dinner, I order a few dishes ___?___.

4. My little sister was so fond of candy that she had to be restricted to one ___?___ after each meal.

5. If you like flounder but are worried that you may accidentally swallow a fishbone, try ___?___ of flounder.

9. Terms Dealing With Dress

bouffant /bü-ˈfänt/ *adj:* puffed out; full

Corridors and stairways would have to be widened considerably if all women were to wear *bouffant* skirts.

boutique /bü-ˈtēk/ *n:* small shop specializing in fashionable clothes

Rhoda buys her clothes in a midtown *boutique*.

chemise /shə-'mēz/ *n:* loose-fitting, sacklike dress

Though more comfortable than most other dresses, the *chemise* has often been ridiculed for its shapelessness.

coiffure /kwä-'fyủ(ə)r/ *n:* style of arranging the hair; headdress

Sally's attractive new *coiffure* was arranged for her by my sister's hair stylist.

corsage /kȯr-'säzh/ *n:* small bouquet worn by a woman

At the Christmas season, women often adorn their coats with a holly *corsage*.

cravat /krə-'vat/ *n:* necktie

He wore a light blue shirt and a navy blue *cravat*.

flamboyant /flam-'bȯi-ənt/ *adj:* flamelike; very ornate; showy

To add a touch of bright color to his outfit, Jack wore a *flamboyant* scarf.

toupee /tü-'pā/ *n:* wig

The actor's baldness was cleverly concealed by a very natural-looking *toupee*.

vogue /'vōg/ *n:* fashion; accepted style

Fashions change rapidly; today's style may be out of *vogue* tomorrow.

EXERCISE 13. On your paper, enter the most appropriate expression from group 9 for completing the sentence.

1. The excessive heat made George untie his __?__ and unbutton his shirt collar.
2. After trying several elaborate hair styles, Marie has returned to a simple __?__.
3. On your visit to Mount Vernon in Virginia, you will see furniture styles that were in __?__ in George and Martha Washington's time.
4. It was easy to identify the guest of honor because of the beautiful __?__ at her shoulder.
5. The gowns in the dress salon range from sedate blacks to __?__ reds and golds.

10. Miscellaneous Terms

ambience /äⁿ-'byäns/ *n:* surrounding atmosphere; environment

We enjoyed the restaurant for its food, as well as its *ambience;* never had we dined in pleasanter surroundings.

apropos /ˌap-rə-'pō/ *adv:* by the way; incidentally

We'll meet you at the station. *Apropos,* when does your train arrive?

avoirdupois /ˌav-ərd-ə-'pȯiz/ *n:* weight; heaviness

Dieters constantly check their *avoirdupois.*

bagatelle /ˌbag-ə-'tel/ *n:* trifle

Pay attention to important matters; don't waste time on *bagatelles.*

coup de grace /ˌküd-ə-'gräs/ *n:* merciful or decisive finishing stroke

Ma Baxter had merely wounded the yearling; poor Jody himself had to administer the *coup de grace.*

facade /fə-'säd/ *n:* face or front of a building, or of anything

The patient's cheerful smile was just a *facade;* actually, she was suffering from ennui.

fete /'fāt/ *n:* festival; entertainment; party

Our block party last year was a memorable *fete.*

fete /'fāt/ *v:* honor with a fete

Retiring employees are often *feted* at a special dinner.

foyer /'foi(-ə)r/ *n:* entrance hall; lobby

Let's meet in the *foyer* of the public library.

milieu /mēl-'yə/ *n:* environment; setting

David found it much easier to make friends in his new *milieu.*

parasol /'par-ə-ˌsȯl/ *n:* umbrella for protection against the sun

In summer when you stroll on the boardwalk in the noonday sun, it is advisable to take along a *parasol.*

par excellence /ˌpär-ˌek-sə-'läⁿs/ *adj:* above all others of the same sort (follows the word it modifies)

Charles Dickens was a raconteur *par excellence.*

pince-nez /pa^{n}s-'nā/ *n:* eyeglasses clipped to the nose by a spring

Since they are held in place by a spring that pinches the nose, *pince-nez* may not be as comfortable as ordinary eyeglasses.

premiere /pri-'mye(ə)r/ *n:* first performance

The second performance was even better than the *premiere.*

queue /'kyü/ *n:* line of persons waiting their turn

The *queue* at the box office was so long that I decided to come back another time.

raison d'être /ˌrā-ˌzō^n-'detr^ə/ *n:* reason or justification for existing

Apparently, Alice lives just for dancing; it is her *raison d'être.*

rendezvous /'rän-di-ˌvü/ *n*

(1) meeting place fixed by prior agreement

We agreed to meet after the test at the handball courts, our usual *rendezvous.*

(2) appointment to meet at a fixed time and place

Our *rendezvous* with the coach and captain of the visiting team was set for 2 P.M.

silhouette /ˌsil-ə-'wet/ *n:* shadow; outline

I knew Jonah was coming to let me in because I recognized his *silhouette* behind the curtained door.

sobriquet /'sō-bri-ˌkā/ *n:* nickname—or **soubriquet**

Andrew Jackson was known by the *sobriquet* "Old Hickory."

souvenir /'sü-və-ˌni(ə)r/ *n:* reminder; keepsake; memento

The Yearbook, in time to come, will be a treasured *souvenir* of high school days.

tour de force /ˌtù(ə)rd-ə-'fȯrs/ *n:* feat of strength or skill; adroit accomplishment

George's sixty-yard touchdown run was an admirable *tour de force* that won the game for us.

vis-à-vis /ˌvē-zə-ˈvē/ *prep:* face to face; opposite

At the banquet table, I had the good fortune to sit *vis-à-vis* an old friend.

EXERCISE 14. On your paper, enter the most appropriate expression from group 10 for completing the sentence.

1. Carmela brought me a print of the Lincoln Memorial as a (an) __?__ of her visit to Washington.
2. Paul mounts the scale morning and night to check his __?__.
3. After class, my friends gather at our __?__ outside the pizza parlor.
4. Agnes is a mimic __?__; no one in our club can do impersonations as well as she.
5. Because of his flaming hair, Harvey is popularly known by the __?__ "Red."
6. The few small merchants who have survived the intense competition are fearful that the opening of another supermarket will be the __?__ for them.
7. Our club is planning a (an) __?__ in honor of the outgoing president.
8. The first day of classes places the newly arrived student in a bewildering __?__.
9. I did not recognize the hotel because its __?__ and foyer had been modernized since I was last there.
10. Winning the league pennant is an outstanding achievement, but going on to capture the World Series in four straight victories is an even greater __?__.
11. When the film had its premiere at our local theater, the __?__ stretched half way around the block.
12. Blanche, we're glad to see you. __?__, how is your brother?

Do not write in this book. Enter all answers on separate paper.

Review Exercises

EXERCISE 15. On your paper, copy each word or expression from column I, and next to it enter the *letter* of its correct meaning from column II.

COLUMN I	COLUMN II
1. piece of candy	*a.* silhouette
2. nickname	*b.* coup d'etat
3. relaxing of strained relations	*c.* bouffant
4. full; puffed out	*d.* coup de grace
5. style of cooking	*e.* détente
6. masterpiece	*f.* bonbon
7. shadow	*g.* chef d'oeuvre
8. weight	*h.* cuisine
9. decisive finishing stroke	*i.* avoirdupois
10. sudden overthrow of a regime	*j.* sobriquet

EXERCISE 16. On your paper, enter the *letter* of the expression NOT RELATED in meaning to the other expressions in each group.

1. *a.* face to face   *b.* up to date   *c.* opposite   *d.* vis-à-vis
2. *a.* setting   *b.* milieu   *c.* surroundings   *d.* mélange
3. *a.* pamphlet   *b.* treatise   *c.* brochure   *d.* silhouette
4. *a.* category   *b.* style   *c.* rate   *d.* genre
5. *a.* par excellence   *b.* exploit   *c.* tour de force   *d.* achievement
6. *a.* binoculars   *b.* spectacles   *c.* pince-nez   *d.* camera
7. *a.* engagement   *b.* rendezvous   *c.* adieu   *d.* appointment
8. *a.* précis   *b.* encore   *c.* résumé   *d.* summary
9. *a.* entente   *b.* understanding   *c.* rapprochement   *d.* regime
10. *a.* aperitif   *b.* debut   *c.* hors d'oeuvres   *d.* denouement

EXERCISE 17. On your paper, enter the *letter* of the word or expression that has most nearly the SAME MEANING as the italicized expression.

1. prosperous *bourgeoisie*   *a.* elite   *b.* entrepreneur
   c. middle class   *d.* citizenry   *e.* officialdom

2. *flamboyant* jacket *a.* debonair *b.* warm *c.* sanguinary
   d. showy *e.* stylish
3. happy *denouement* *a.* ending *b.* vignette *c.* milieu *d.* event
   e. episode
4. sudden *demarche* *a.* détente *b.* reversal *c.* entrée
   d. discovery *e.* aggression
5. attitude of *laissez-faire* *a.* boredom *b.* equanimity
   c. eagerness *d.* cordiality *e.* noninterference
6. enduring *entente* *a.* influence *b.* understanding *c.* bitterness
   d. cause célèbre *e.* entrance
7. serve *hors d'oeuvres* *a.* entrée *b.* appetizers *c.* desserts
   d. pièce de résistance *e.* table d'hôte
8. join the *avant-garde* *a.* gendarmes *b.* protégés *c.* devotees
   d. underground *e.* innovators
9. welcome *encore* *a.* cancellation *b.* delay *c.* repetition
   d. refund *e.* improvement
10. flavor *par excellence* *a.* new *b.* unsurpassed *c.* spicy
    d. mild *e.* inferior

EXERCISE 18. Which word, selected from the vocabulary list below, will correctly complete the sentence? Enter the appropriate word on your paper.

VOCABULARY LIST

coiffure	chargé d'affaires	regime
au courant	pièce de résistance	raison d'être
envoy	éclat	avant-garde
genre	bagatelle	nouveaux riches
laissez-faire	facade	souvenir

1. At one time or another, some hobby or interest becomes so important to us that it is practically our only __?__ (*reason for existence.*)
2. This piece of driftwood is a (an) __?__ (*something that serves as a reminder*) of last summer's camping trip.
3. The reason you were not ready is that you spent too much time on a mere __?__ (*unimportant, trifling matter*).
4. What __?__ (*style of arranging the hair*) is most in vogue today?
5. The __?__ (*persons who had newly become rich*) felt ill at ease in their new social milieu.

6. In her letters Susan kept me __?__ (*up to date*) about events in my old neighborhood.
7. The __?__ (*main number on the program*) of the musicale was a medley of Gilbert and Sullivan airs.
8. It is an unwise parent who follows a policy of __?__ (*absence of interference*) in bringing up children.
9. The United States has encouraged nations everywhere to install a democratic __?__ (*system of government or rule*).
10. The __?__ (*ambassador's substitute*) has had years of experience in the diplomatic service.

EXERCISE 19. If the italicized expression is *correctly* used in the sentence, enter *C* on your paper. If *incorrectly* used, write the expression that should replace it.

1. One of the piano pieces I have recently added to my *repertoire* is "Autumn Leaves."
2. My guest declined the *hors d'oeuvres*, as he does not usually take an alcoholic drink before dinner.
3. Only his closest friends know that he wears a *sobriquet* to cover his bald spot.
4. Most of Washington's political elite attended the *tête-à-tête* celebrating the President's inauguration.
5. There is an excellent *vignette* on the small-town mind in Sinclair Lewis' ARROWSMITH.
6. Recalled by tumultuous applause, the violinist played an *encore* to the delight of the audience.
7. There was a hushed silence in the auditorium as the conductor raised her *palette*.
8. By means of a *pièce de résistance*, a Frenchman in the Old Regime could be imprisoned without knowing the charges against him and without being brought to trial.
9. On her jacket she wore a fragrant *mirage* sent by her fiancé.
10. On the way out of the theater we passed through the *filet*, where a line of ticket holders are awaiting the next performance.

EXERCISE 20. Answer each question in a sentence or two.

1. Why are some gourmands likely to have trouble with their avoirdupois?
2. Are parasols in vogue? Why, or why not?

3. Suppose you are eager to attend a premiere, but when you get there you find a queue stretching around the block. What would you do? Why?

4. Why do so many émigrés from totalitarian regimes seek to settle in our country? Give one important reason.

5. Would you be able to do justice to the pièce de résistance after filling up on the hors d'oeuvres? Explain.

EXERCISE 21. On your paper, enter the *letter* of the expression that best completes the analogy.

1. *Parasol* is to *sun* as *variety* is to __?__.
   a. queue   *b.* fete   *c.* ennui   *d.* sky   *e.* souvenir

2. *Regime* is to *revolutionists* as *custom* is to __?__.
   a. elite   *b.* connoisseurs   *c.* devotees   *d.* avant-garde
   e. conservatives

3. *Scene I* is to *climax* as *hors d'oeuvres* is to __?__.
   a. entrée   *b.* cuisine   *c.* bonbon   *d.* chef d'oeuvre   *e.* bagatelle

4. *Demitasse* is to *coffee* as *drum* is to __?__.
   a. orchestra   *b.* conductor   *c.* drummer   *d.* oil   *e.* sugar

5. *Bottle* is to *neck* as *hotel* is to __?__.
   a. facade   *b.* cul-de-sac   *c.* foyer   *d.* suburb   *e.* table d'hôte

6. *Nourished* is to *food* as *au courant* is to __?__.
   a. exercise   *b.* drink   *c.* news   *d.* rest   *e.* rumor

7. *Star* is to *understudy* as *ambassador* is to __?__.
   a. coterie   *b.* valet   *c.* entrepreneur   *d.* chargé d'affaires
   e. protégé

8. *Bas-relief* is to *sculpture* as *genre* is to __?__.
   a. palette   *b.* painter   *c.* sculptor   *d.* baton   *e.* painting

9. *Faux pas* is to *embarrassment* as *détente* is to __?__.
   a. rapprochement   *b.* impasse   *c.* cul-de-sac
   d. pièce de résistance   *e.* encore

10. *Ice* is to *thaw* as *hostility* is to __?__.
    a. coup de grace   *b.* détente   *c.* coup d'etat   *d.* tour de force
    e. denouement

chapter viii **Italian Words in English**

The Italian impact on English, though not as great as the French impact, is nevertheless important. Italy's rich contributions to the arts have profoundly influenced our cultural life. In our language, this influence shows itself by the presence of useful Italian loanwords dealing mainly with music, painting, architecture, sculpture, and other arts.

1. Words for Singing Voices

(arranged in order of increasing pitch)

basso /'bas-ō/ *n:* lowest male voice; bass (pronounced bās)

baritone /'bar-ə-ˌtōn/ *n:* male voice between bass and tenor

tenor /'ten-ə(r)/ *n:* adult male voice between baritone and alto

alto /'al-tō/ *n*
    (1) highest male voice, (2) lowest female voice, the contralto

contralto /kən-'tral-tō/ *n:* lowest female voice

mezzo-soprano /ˌmet-sō-sə-'pran-ō/ *n:* female voice between contralto and soprano

soprano /sə-'pran-ō/ *n:* highest singing voice in women and boys

coloratura /ˌkəl-ə-rə-'t(y)ùr-ə/ *n*
    (1) ornamental passages (runs, trills, etc.) in vocal music
    (2) soprano who sings such passages, i.e., a *coloratura* soprano

falsetto /fòl-'set-ō/ *n*
    (1) unnaturally high-pitched male voice, (2) artificial voice

EXERCISE 1. On your paper, enter the most appropriate expression from group 1 for completing the sentence.

1. For her superb rendering of ornamental passages, the __?__ was wildly acclaimed.

2. The lowest singing voice is *contralto* for women and __?__ for men.

3. Yodeling is a form of singing that requires frequent changes from the natural voice to a (an) __?__.

4. Since Oscar's singing voice is between baritone and alto, he is classified as a (an) __?__.

5. The highest singing voice is *soprano* for women and __?__ for men.

2. Words for Tempos (Rates of Speed) of Musical Compositions

(arranged in order of increasing speed)

grave /ˈgräv-ā/ *adv* or *adj*: slow (the slowest tempo in music); serious

largo /ˈlär-gō/ *adv* or *adj*: slow and dignified; stately

adagio /ə-ˈdäj-ō/ *adv* or *adj*: slow; in an easy, graceful manner

lento /ˈlen-ˌtō/ *adv* or *adj*: slow

andante /än-ˈdän-ˌtä/ *adv* or *adj*: moderately slow, but flowing

moderato /ˌmäd-ə-ˈrät-ō/ *adv* or *adj*: in moderate time

allegro /ə-ˈleg-rō/ *adv* or *adj*: brisk; quick; lively

vivace /vē-ˈväch-ā/ *adv* or *adj*: brisk; spirited

presto /ˈpres-tō/ *adv* or *adj*: quick

prestissimo /pre-ˈstis-ə-ˌmō/ *adv* or *adj*: at a very rapid pace

EXERCISE 2. On your paper, enter the most appropriate expression from group 2 for completing the sentence.

1. A piece of music marked __?__ moves more rapidly than one marked *presto*.
2. The slowest tempo in music, __?__, is used in the opening measures of Beethoven's SONATE PATHÉTIQUE.
3. ANNIE LAURIE should be sung at a moderately slow but flowing pace, for its tempo is __?__.
4. The __?__ movement of Dvořák's NEW WORLD SYMPHONY is played in a slow and dignified manner.
5. The term __?__ over the opening notes of SWEET GEORGIA BROWN indicates that this tune should be played neither rapidly nor slowly, but in moderate time.

3. Words for Dynamics (Degrees of Loudness)

crescendo /kri-'shen-dō/ *adv, adj,* or *n:* gradually increasing (or a gradual increase) in force or loudness—ANT **decrescendo**

decrescendo /ˌdā-krə-'shen-dō/ *adv, adj,* or *n:* gradually decreasing (or a gradual decrease) in force or loudness—SYN **diminuendo,** ANT **crescendo**

dolce /'dōl-chā/ *adv* or *adj:* soft; sweet

forte /'fȯr-ˌtā/ *adv* or *adj:* loud—ANT **piano**

fortissimo /fȯr-'tis-ə-ˌmō/ *adv* or *adj:* very loud—ANT **pianissimo**

pianissimo /ˌpē-ə-'nis-ə-ˌmō/ *adv* or *adj:* very soft—ANT **fortissimo**

piano /pē-'än-ō/ *adv* or *adj:* soft—ANT **forte**

sforzando /sfȯrt-'sän-dō/ *adv* or *adj:* accented

EXERCISE 3. On your paper, enter the most appropriate expression from group 3 for completing the sentence.

1. The word __?__ designates a familiar musical instrument, as well as a musical direction meaning "soft."
2. Ravel's BOLERO rises to a dramatic climax by a gradual increase in loudness; few pieces have such an electrifying __?__.
3. When a chord is to be played with a strong accent, the composer marks it with the term __?__.
4. Mendelssohn's SCHERZO has a __?__ ending; it has to be played very softly.
5. A degree of loudness higher than *forte* is __?__.

4. Words for Musical Effects

a cappella /ˌäk-ə-ˈpel-ə/ *adv* or *adj:* (literally, "in chapel or choir style") without musical accompaniment, as to sing *a cappella*, or an *a cappella* choir

arpeggio /är-ˈpej-ō/ *n*
   (1) production of the tones of a chord in rapid succession, rather than at the same time. (Normally, the tones of a chord are played simultaneously.)
   (2) a chord thus played

legato /li-ˈgät-ō/ *adv* or *adj:* smooth and connected

pizzicato /ˌpit-si-ˈkät-ō/ *adv* or *adj:* by means of plucking the strings instead of using the bow

staccato /stə-ˈkät-ō/ *adv* or *adj:* with breaks between successive notes; disconnected; abrupt

tremolo /ˈtrem-ə-ˌlō/ *n:* rapid ("trembling") repetition of a tone or chord, without apparent breaks, to express emotion

vibrato /vē-ˈbrät-ō/ *n:* slightly throbbing or pulsating effect, adding warmth and beauty to the tone

EXERCISE 4. On your paper, enter the most appropriate expression from group 4 for completing the sentence.

1. By plucking the strings with the fingers, a violinist achieves a (an) __?__ effect.

2. In Tchaikovsky's 1812 OVERTURE, the rapid and prolonged repetition of two tones produces a "trembling," emotion-stirring effect known as __?__.

3. Some beginning piano students strike all the correct notes but fail to achieve a smooth and connected effect because they do not play them __?__.

4. It is surely much easier to play the tones of a chord simultaneously than to play them as a (an) __?__.

5. In Schubert's AVE MARIA, the notes are smoothly connected, but in his MARCHE MILITAIRE they are mainly __?__.

5. Words Dealing With Musical Compositions

aria /ˈär-ē-ə/ *n:* air, melody, or tune; especially, an elaborate, accompanied melody for a single voice in an opera

bravura /brə-ˈv(y)ủr-ə/ *n*
  (1) piece of music requiring skill and spirit in the performer
  (2) display of daring or brilliancy

cantata /kən-ˈtät-ə/ *n:* story or play set to music to be sung by a chorus, but not acted

concerto /kən-ˈchert-ō/ *n:* long musical composition for one or more principal instruments with orchestral accompaniment

duet /d(y)ü-ˈet/ *n*
  (1) piece of music for two voices or instruments
  (2) two singers or players performing together

finale /fə-ˈnal-ē/ *n:* close or termination, as the last section of a musical composition

intermezzo /ˌint-ər-ˈmet-sō/ *n*

    (1) short musical or dramatic entertainment between the acts of a play

    (2) short musical composition between the main divisions of an extended musical work

    (3) short, independent musical composition

libretto /lə-ˈbret-ō/ *n:* text or words of an opera or other long musical composition

opera /ˈäp-(ə)-rə/ *n:* play mostly sung, with costumes, scenery, action, and music

oratorio /ˌȯr-ə-ˈtȯr-ē-ˌō/ *n:* musical composition, usually on a religious theme, for solo voices, chorus, and orchestra

scherzo /ˈskert-sō/ *n:* light or playful part of a sonata or symphony

solo /ˈsō-lō/ *n*

    (1) piece of music for one voice or instrument

    (2) anything done without a partner

sonata /sə-ˈnät-ə/ *n:* piece of music (for one or two instruments) having three or four movements in contrasted rhythms but related tonality

trio /ˈtrē-ō/ *n*

    (1) piece of music for three voices or instruments

    (2) three singers or players performing together

EXERCISE 5. On your paper, enter the most appropriate expression from group 5 for completing the sentence.

1. To perform in a (an) __?__, one must be gifted both as a singer and as an actor.
2. Roberta refuses to do a solo, but she is willing to join with someone else in a (an) __?__.
3. From the opening selection to the __?__, we enjoyed the concert thoroughly.
4. Though there is orchestral accompaniment in a piano __?__, the pianist is the principal performer.
5. The selection you played is unfamiliar to me, but its light and playful character leads me to believe that it's a (an) __?__.

6. Words Dealing With Arts Other Than Music

cameo /'kam-ē-ˌō/ *n:* stone or shell on which a figure, cut in relief, appears against a background of a different color—ANT **intaglio**

campanile /ˌkam-pə-'nē-lē/ *n:* bell tower

canto /'kan-ˌtō/ *n:* one of the chief divisions of a long poem

chiaroscuro /kē-ˌär-ə-'sk(y)ù(ə)r-ō/ *n*
   (1) style of pictorial art using only light and shade
   (2) sketch in black and white

cupola /'kyü-pə-lə/ *n*
   (1) rounded roof; dome
   (2) small dome or tower on a roof

fresco /'fres-ˌkō/ *n*
   (1) art of painting with water colors on damp, fresh plaster
   (2) picture or design so painted

intaglio /in-'tal-yō/ *n:* design engraved by making cuts in a surface—ANT **cameo**

majolica /mə-'jäl-i-kə/ *n:* enameled Italian pottery richly decorated in colors

mezzanine /'mez-ᵊn-ˌēn/ *n:* intermediate story in a theater between the main floor and the first balcony

mezzotint /'met-sō-ˌtint/ *n:* picture engraved on copper or steel by polishing or scraping away parts of a roughened surface

patina /'pat-ə-nə/ *n:* film or incrustation, usually green, on the surface of old bronze or copper

portico /'pōrt-i-ˌkō/ *n:* roof supported by columns, forming a porch or a covered walk

rotunda /rō-'tən-də/ *n*
   (1) round building, especially one with a dome or cupola
   (2) large round room, as the *rotunda* of the Capitol

stucco /'stək-ō/ *n:* plaster for covering exterior walls of buildings

tempera /'tem-pə-rə/ *n:* method of painting in which the colors are mixed with white of egg or other substances, instead of oil

terra-cotta /'ter-ə-'kät-ə/ *n*
> (1) kind of hard, brownish-red earthenware, used for vases, statuettes, etc.
> (2) dull brownish-red color

torso /'tȯr-sō/ *n*
> (1) trunk or body of a statue without head, arms, or legs
> (2) human trunk

EXERCISE 6. On your paper, enter the most appropriate expression from group 6 for completing the sentence.

1. Because it is a large round room, the __?__ of the Capitol in Washington, D.C., is ideal for an impressive ceremony.
2. The __?__ my aunt wears has a carved ivory head raised on a light brown background.
3. A (An) __?__ actually becomes a part of the wall on whose damp, fresh plaster it is painted.
4. The head of the statue was discovered not far from the place where its __?__ had been found.
5. An antique increases in artistic value when its surface becomes incrusted with a fine natural __?__.
6. The white of egg or similar substance used for mixing colors in __?__ painting.
7. Read the fifth __?__ of Dante's INFERNO for a stirring account of the lovers Paolo and Francesca.
8. The __?__ applied to exterior walls of buildings is a mixture of portland cement, sand, and lime.
9. In the morning we heard the sound of bells coming from the __?__, a tall structure right next to the church.
10. The main building and the annex are connected by a (an) __?__ that facilitates traffic between the two buildings, especially in bad weather.

7. Words Dealing With Persons

cognoscente /ˌkän-yō-ˈshent-ē/ *n:* connoisseur

dilettante /ˌdil-ə-ˈtänt(-ē)/ *n:* person who follows some art or science as an amusement or in a trifling way

inamorata /in-ˌam-ə-ˈrät-ə/ *n:* woman who is loved

inamorato /in-ˌam-ə-ˈrät-ō/ *n:* male lover

maestro /mä-ˈe-strō/ *n*
 (1) eminent conductor, composer, or teacher of music
 (2) master in any art

mountebank /ˈmaủn-ti-ˌbaŋk/ *n:* boastful pretender; charlatan; quack

politico /pə-ˈlit-i-ˌkō/ *n:* politician

prima donna /ˌprim-ə-ˈdän-ə/ *n*
 (1) principal female singer, as in an opera
 (2) high-strung, vain, or extremely sensitive person

simpatico /sim-ˈpät-i-ˌkō/ *m. adj:* possessing attractive qualities; appealing; likable; congenial—**simpatica,** *f.*

virtuoso /ˌvər-chə-ˈwō-sō/ *n:* one who exhibits great technical skill in an art, especially in playing a musical instrument

EXERCISE 7. On your paper, enter the most appropriate expression from group 7 for completing the sentence.

1. All eyes were riveted on the __?__ as he raised his baton to begin the concert.
2. She hopes one day to take up the cello as a serious student rather than as a (an) __?__.
3. The versatile young musician has won fame not only as a conductor and composer, but as a (an) __?__ at the piano.
4. That attractive lady on the gentleman's arm is apparently his __?__.
5. The owner is unpleasant to deal with, but the salesman is very __?__.

8. Words for Situations Involving Persons

dolce far niente /'dol-chē-ˌfär-nē-'ent-ē/ *n:* delightful idleness

fiasco /fē-'as-kō/ *n:* crash; complete or ridiculous failure

imbroglio /im-'brōl-yō/ *n*
   (1) difficult situation
   (2) complicated disagreement

incognito /ˌin-ˌkäg-'nēt-ō/ *adv:* with one's identity concealed

incognito /ˌin-ˌkäg-'nēt-ō/ *n:* disguised state

vendetta /ven-'det-ə/ *n:* feud for blood revenge

9. Words Dealing With Food

antipasto /ˌant-i-'pas-tō/ *n:* appetizer consisting of fish, meats, etc.; hors d'oeuvres

Chianti /ke-'änt-ē/ *n:* a dry, red Italian wine

gusto /'gəs-ˌtō/ *n:* liking or taste; hearty enjoyment

pizza /'pēt-sə/ *n:* large, flat pie of bread dough spread with tomato pulp, cheese, meat, anchovies, etc.

10. Miscellaneous Common Words

gondola /'gän-də-lə/ *n*
   (1) boat used in the canals of Venice
   (2) cabin attached to the underpart of an airship

grotto /'grät-ō/ *n:* cave

piazza /pē-'az-ə/ *n*
   (1) open square in an Italian town
   (2) veranda or porch

portfolio /pȯrt-'fō-lē-ˌō/ *n*

  (1) briefcase

  (2) position or duties of a cabinet member or minister of state

salvo /'sal-vō/ *n*

  (1) simultaneous discharge of shots

  (2) burst of cheers, as a *salvo* of applause

sotto voce /ˌsät-ō-'vō-chē/ *adv* or *adj*: under the breath; in an undertone; privately, as a *sotto voce* remark

EXERCISE 8. On your paper, enter the most appropriate expression from groups 8–10 for completing the sentence.

1. My old briefcase can hold more books and papers than his new __?__.

2. The host filled his guests' wineglasses from a freshly opened bottle of __?__.

3. The complicated disagreement about this year's budget is similar to the __?__ we had about last year's budget.

4. Philip's cold prevented him from eating his dinner with his usual __?__.

5. The playwright attended the premiere __?__; he was not recognized.

6. Because of the ridiculous failure of last year's amateur show, we are determined that this year's performance will not likewise become a (an) __?__.

7. At last the feuding parties have ended their __?__.

8. I did not hear what the mother said to the daughter, for they conferred __?__.

9. The tourist relies on the taxicab in New York City and on the __?__ in Venice.

10. While in prison, Edmond Dantès learned of an immense fortune concealed in an underground __?__ on the island of Monte Cristo.

Do not write in this book. Enter all answers on separate paper.

Review Exercises

EXERCISE 9. On your paper, enter the *letter* of the word or expression in each group that means either the SAME as or the OPPOSITE of the italicized word.

1. *canto*   *a.* pace   *b.* lore   *c.* solo   *d.* division   *e.* cantata
2. *cognoscente*   *a.* politico   *b.* connoisseur   *c.* prima donna
   d. falsetto   *e.* coloratura
3. *grotto*   *a.* cave   *b.* terra-cotta   *c.* crash   *d.* trunk   *e.* veranda
4. *cameo*   *a.* patina   *b.* tempera   *c.* intaglio   *d.* campanile
   e. bagatelle
5. *imbroglio*   *a.* finale   *b.* fiasco   *c.* stucco   *d.* diminuendo
   e. agreement
6. *sforzando*   *a.* unstressed   *b.* dignified   *c.* brisk   *d.* sweet
   e. slow
7. *torso*   *a.* arm   *b.* statue   *c.* trunk   *d.* aria   *e.* leg
8. *antipasto*   *a.* Chianti   *b.* hors d'oeuvres   *c.* piazza   *d.* gusto
   e. aperitif
9. *crescendo*   *a.* salvo   *b.* cupola   *c.* applause   *d.* diminuendo
   e. soprano
10. *piazza*   *a.* pizza   *b.* square   *c.* town   *d.* rotunda   *e.* column

EXERCISE 10. Which of the two terms makes the sentence correct? Enter the *letter* of the correct answer on your paper.

1. A (An) __?__ choir performs without accompaniment.
   a. a cappella   *b.* cantata

2. A __?__ is a musical composition requiring an entire orchestra, but featuring a solo instrument such as the piano or violin.
   a. sonata   *b.* concerto

3. When Ulysses returned __?__ to his palace, he was recognized by his dog Argus.
   a. incognito   *b.* falsetto

4. The anchored fleet welcomed the chief of state with a thunderous __?__.
   a. salvo   *b.* staccato

5. An impression made from an __?__ results in an image in relief.

    a. imbroglio   *b.* intaglio

6. The overworked executive longed for the __?__ of a Caribbean cruise.

    a. sotto voce   *b.* dolce far niente

7. With the orchestra and balcony seats completely sold out, only a few __?__ tickets are available.

    a. mezzanine   *b.* mezzotint

8. To achieve a smooth and flowing effect, my teacher advised me to play the first two measures __?__.

    a. tremolo   *b.* legato

9. For an example of a crescendo from pianissimo all the way to __?__, listen to Grieg's IN THE HALL OF THE MOUNTAIN KING.

    a. prestissimo   *b.* fortissimo

10. A __?__ sketch achieves its effects solely by shadings between black and white.

    a. chiaroscuro   *b.* terra-cotta

EXERCISE 11. On your paper, enter the word of Italian origin that is equivalent to the italicized expression. The letters of each answer appear in scrambled form in the parentheses.

1. While the spaghetti was boiling, our hostess served a delicious *appetizer* (SOPATTIAN) attractively arranged on a large platter.
2. The article stated that the *cave* (TOGORT) had once been used as a hiding place for stolen treasure.
3. Have you ever heard of the *feud* (DEENVATT) between the Hatfields and the McCoys?
4. Over the years a (an) *green film* (TAPANI) had formed on the surface of the copper vessel.
5. Responding to the *gradual increase in volume* (CODSCREEN) of applause, the violinist returned for an encore.
6. After having cried his fill, the child continued to punctuate the silence with occasional *disconnected* (CATOSCAT) sobs.
7. The ill-matched challenger's bid to dethrone the heavyweight champion ended in a (an) *ridiculous failure* (ISCOFA) in the opening seconds of the first round.

8. In their reports on the pianist's performance, most of the critics lauded her finesse and *display of brilliancy* (RARAVUB).

9. My uncle paints as a (an) *trifler* (NILETATTED), not as a serious artist.

10. Verdi composed the music for the opera AÏDA, and Ghislanzoni wrote the *words* (RITTOBEL).

EXERCISE 12. Answer each question in a sentence or two.

1. Do you eat pizza with gusto? Why, or why not?

2. Would a virtuoso enjoy being called a dilettante by a music critic? Explain.

3. When you take the up elevator at the opera, which do you come to first, the first balcony or the mezzanine? Why?

4. Why is an action taken on the advice of a mountebank likely to end in a fiasco?

5. Why are there salvos of applause when the prima donna makes her entrance on the stage?

EXERCISE 13. On your paper, enter the *letter* of the word-pair that best expresses a relationship similar to that existing between the capitalized word-pair.

1. DESSERT : ANTIPASTO
   - *a.* grave : prestissimo
   - *b.* basso : soprano
   - *c.* entrée : hors d'oeuvres
   - *d.* play : denouement
   - *e.* finale : overture

2. STAR : FILM
   - *a.* composer : sonata
   - *b.* soloist : concerto
   - *c.* aria : vocalist
   - *d.* drama : protagonist
   - *e.* actor : cast

3. COGNOSCENTE : DILETTANTE
   - *a.* uncle : aunt
   - *b.* professional : amateur
   - *c.* odor : aroma
   - *d.* ignoramus : connoisseur
   - *e.* artist : patron

4. INCOGNITO : IDENTITY
   - *a.* novel : pen name
   - *b.* masquerade : disguise
   - *c.* pseudonym : authorship
   - *d.* fiction : real
   - *e.* anonymous : known

5. TORSO : STATUE

    a. trunk : tree

    b. dismember : intact

    c. shard : vase

    d. atom : nucleus

    e. violinist : orchestra

6. PATINA : AGE

    a. film : camera

    b. hair : baldness

    c. blush : embarrassment

    d. mold : cheese

    e. tarnish : silver

7. LENTO : TEMPO

    a. gondola : canal

    b. papers : portfolio

    c. Chianti : meal

    d. piano : volume

    e. allegro : loudness

8. ROTUNDA : EDIFICE

    a. gondola : canal

    b. pizza : dough

    c. sole : fish

    d. stucco : wall

    e. portico : columns

chapter ix Spanish Words in English

It should not surprise you that English has adopted many Spanish words. For centuries Spain governed many areas of this continent, including Florida and our vast Southwest. Despite the disintegration of the Spanish Empire, Spanish today is spoken in Mexico, virtually all of Central and South America (except Brazil), most of the islands in the Caribbean, the Philippines, and numerous other regions. As one of the world's principal languages, Spanish continues to exert its influence on English.

1. Words for Persons

aficionado /ə-ˌfis-ē-ə-ˈnäd-ō/ *n*
    (1) person very enthusiastic about anything
    (2) sports devotee

caballero /ˌkab-ə-ˈler-ō/ *n*
    (1) gentleman or gallant
    (2) horseman

conquistador /kȯŋ-ˈkēs-tə-ˌdȯ(r)/ *n:* conqueror

desperado /ˌdes-pə-ˈräd-ō/ *n:* bold, reckless criminal

duenna /d(y)ü-ˈen-ə/ *n:* elderly woman chaperon of a young lady; governess

gaucho /ˈgaù-chō/ *n:* Argentine cowboy of mixed Spanish and Indian descent

grandee /gran-'dē/ *n*
    (1) nobleman of the highest rank, (2) person of eminence

hidalgo /hid-'al-gō/ *n:* nobleman of the second class (not so high as a *grandee*)

junta /'hủn-tə/ *n*
    (1) council for legislation or administration, (2) junto

junto /'jənt-ō/ *n*
    (1) political faction, (2) group of plotters; clique

matador /'mat-ə-ˌdȯ(r)/ *n:* bullfighter assigned to kill the bull

mestizo /me-'stē-zō/ *n:* person of mixed (usually Spanish and Indian) blood

peon /'pē-ˌän/ *n*
    (1) common laborer
    (2) worker kept in service to repay a debt

picador /'pik-ə-ˌdȯ(r)/ *n:* rider on horseback who irritates the bull with a lance

picaro /'pē-kä-ˌrō/ *n*
    (1) rogue; knave
    (2) vagabond (A *picaresque* novel is one that has a *picaro*, a rogue or vagabond, as the hero.)

renegade /'ren-i-ˌgād/ *n*
    (1) apostate (deserter) from a religion, party, etc.
    (2) turncoat; traitor

señor /sān-ᴶyȯ(r)/ *n:* gentleman; Mr. or Sir

señora /sān-'yōr-ə/ *n:* lady; Mrs. or Madam

señorita /ˌsān-yə-'rēt-ə/ *n:* young lady; Miss

toreador /'tȯr-ē-ə-ˌdȯ(r)/ *n:* bullfighter, usually mounted

torero /tə-'rer-ō/ *n:* bullfighter on foot

vaquero /vä-'ker-ō/ *n:* herdsman; cowboy

EXERCISE 1. On your paper, enter the most appropriate word from group 1 for completing the sentence.

1. The onetime Democrat who joined the Republican Party was regarded as a (an) __?__ by some of his former Democratic colleagues.
2. In the Old West, it was common for a stagecoach to be robbed by a (an) __?__.
3. A (An) __?__ is a nobleman of higher rank than a hidalgo.
4. Without an education or a skilled trade, you may earn little more than the wages of a (an) __?__.
5. The average fan attends two or three games a season, but the __?__ goes to many more.
6. Columbus was not a (an) __?__; he engineered no military conquests, as did Cortez in Mexico and Pizzaro in Peru.
7. The __?__ was chaperoned by her duenna.
8. The ruler ordered the arrest of all members of the __?__ involved in the plot against his regime.
9. Before slaying the bull, the __?__ thrills the spectators by gracefully evading its charges.
10. The Spanish expressions for "Mr." and "Mrs." are __?__ and __?__.

2. Miscellaneous Words

adobe /ə-'dō-bē/ *n*
 (1) brick of sun-dried clay or mud
 (2) structure made of such bricks

bolero /bə-'ler-ō/ *n*
 (1) lively dance in ¾ time
 (2) the music for this dance
 (3) short, loose jacket

bonanza /bə-'nan-zə/ *n*
 (1) accidental discovery of a rich mass of ore in a mine
 (2) something yielding a rich return

bravado /brə-'väd-ō/ *n*
  (1) boastful behavior
  (2) pretense of bravery

cabana /kə-'ban-(y)ə/ *n:* beach shelter resembling a cabin

castanets /ˌkas-tə-'nets/ *n pl:* hand instruments clicked together to accompany music or dancing

fiesta /fē-'es-tə/ *n:* religious holiday; any festival or holiday

flotilla /flō-'til-ə/ *n:* small fleet; fleet of small vessels

hacienda /ˌ(h)äs-ē-'en-də/ *n*
  (1) large ranch
  (2) landed estate
  (3) country house

incommunicado /ˌin-kə-ˌmyü-nə-'käd-ō/ *adv:* deprived of communication with others, as a prisoner held *incommunicado*

mantilla /man-'tē-(y)ə/ *n*
  (1) woman's light scarf or veil
  (2) cloak or cape

olio /'ō-lē-ˌō/ *n:* mixture; hodgepodge; medley

patio /'pat-ē-ˌō/ *n:* courtyard; inner court open to the sky

peccadillo /ˌpek-ə-'dil-ō/ *n:* slight offense

pimento /pə-'ment-ō/ *n:* thick-fleshed pepper used for stuffing olives and as a source of paprika—or **pimiento**

poncho /'pän-chō/ *n:* large cloth, often waterproof, with a slit for the head

pueblo /pü-'eb-lō/ *n:* Indian village built of adobe and stone

siesta /sē-'es-tə/ *n:* short rest or nap, especially at midday

tortilla /tȯr-'tē-(y)ə/ *n:* thin, flat, round corn cake

EXERCISE 2. On your paper, enter the most appropriate word from group 2 for completing the sentence.

1. Have you ever seen graceful Spanish dancers do the bolero to the accompaniment of clicking __?__?

2. For every prospector who struck a (an) __?__, there were countless others whose finds were disappointing.

3. Taking a bribe is no __?__, but a serious infraction of ethics.

4. You may be surprised to learn that a house made of __?__ can last for more than a hundred years.

5. The ruffian's defiant challenge turned out to be mere __?__, for when I offered to fight him, he backed down.

6. Our Latin American neighbors celebrate a (an) __?__ by wearing brightly colored costumes and by singing and dancing.

7. By midafternoon, the whole __?__ of fishing vessels had returned to port with the day's catch.

8. A gaucho often carries a (an) __?__, which he uses as a blanket or wears as a cape.

9. When the afternoon heat is most intense, Elena often takes a __?__ before resuming her work.

10. Mexicans are very fond of the __?__, a thin, flat, round cake made of corn.

11. The store had no plain olives, only olives stuffed with __?__.

12. Shall we stay indoors, or would you prefer to sit on the __?__?

3. Additional Miscellaneous Words

arroyo /ə-'rȯi-ō/ *n:* watercourse; small, often dry, gully

bronco /'bräŋ-kō/ *n:* half-wild pony—or **broncho**

burro /'bər-ō/ *n:* small donkey used as a pack animal

canyon /'kan-yən/ *n:* deep valley with high, steep slopes, often with a stream flowing through it, as the Colorado River in the Grand Canyon

indigo /'in-di-ˌgō/ *n*
  (1) plant yielding a blue dye, (2) deep violet-blue color

mañana /mən-'yän-ə/ adv: tomorrow; in the indefinite future

mesa /'mā-sə/ n: flat-topped rocky hill with steeply sloping sides

mustang /'məs-ˌtaŋ/ n: bronco

pampas /'pam-pəz/ n pl: vast, treeless, grassy plains, especially in Argentina

sierra /sē-'er-ə/ n: ridge of mountains with an irregular, serrated (saw-toothed) outline

EXERCISE 3. On your paper, enter the most appropriate word from group 3 for completing the sentence.

1. A Hopi village was secure against enemy attacks because it was built on top of a steeply sloping, flat-topped __?__.
2. The blue dye formerly obtained from __?__ can now be made artificially.
3. Do today's work today; don't postpone it until __?__.
4. In desert areas of Mexico and of our own Southwest, the __?__ is used for carrying heavy loads.
5. The __?__ in Argentina are famous for their cattle, corn, and wheat.

Do not write in this book. Enter all answers on separate paper.

Review Exercises

EXERCISE 4. On your paper, enter the *letter* of the word or expression in each group that means either the SAME as or the OPPOSITE of the italicized words.

1. *duenna* a. duet b. junta c. chaperon d. twosome e. fiancé
2. *indigo* a. hill b. sugar c. clay d. native e. blue color
3. *peccadillo* a. pepper b. groundhog c. alligator d. petty officer e. serious offense
4. *olio* a. grease b. mixture c. fuel d. page e. noise
5. *grandee* a. peon b. river c. niece d. dam e. canyon
6. *aficionado* a. zeal b. connoisseur c. enthusiast d. trifler e. fictional hero

7. *conquistadors*   *a.* discoverers   *b.* conquests   *c.* explorers
   d. conquerors   *e.* bullfighters
8. *renegade*   *a.* infidel   *b.* desperado   *c.* rogue   *d.* villain
   e. turncoat
9. *arroyo*   *a.* dart   *b.* gully   *c.* mesa   *d.* waterfall   *e.* bronco
10. *siesta*   *a.* holiday   *b.* sojourn   *c.* fiesta   *d.* vigil   *e.* sierra

EXERCISE 5.   On your paper, enter the *letter* of the word (or set of words) that best completes the sentence.

1. The __?__ has become an institution in climates where the oppressive midday sun makes activity difficult.
   a. fiesta   *b.* vendetta   *c.* bourgeoisie   *d.* siesta   *e.* bolero

2. To maintain anonymity, the leader of the junto employed a __?__.
   a. lackey   *b.* grandee   *c.* pseudonym   *d.* mantilla   *e.* peon

3. __?__ are Argentine cowboys who inhabit the __?__.
   a. Gauchos . . . pampas   *b.* Caballeros . . . mesas
   c. Desperadoes . . . sierras   *d.* Vaqueros . . . pueblos
   e. Picaros . . . adobes

4. A famous painting by Murillo depicts a smiling señorita looking down from a window with her mantilla-clad __?__ by her side.
   a. protégée   *b.* aficionado   *c.* duenna   *d.* grandee   *e.* fiancé

5. Benedict Arnold was the American __?__ whose plot to surrender West Point resulted in a __?__.
   a. patriot . . . vendetta   *b.* renegade . . . coup d'etat
   c. grandee . . . junto   *d.* turncoat . . . fiasco   *e.* apostate . . . détente

EXERCISE 6.   Answer each question in a sentence or two.

1. Suppose a security guard is discovered taking a siesta while on duty. Should the matter be treated as a peccadillo? Explain.
2. Is it advisable to put on a show of bravado when confronted by an armed desperado? Why, or why not?
3. Would an offshore oil spill be a bonanza for the owners of a fishing flotilla? Explain.

4. What would be the attitude of a civil rights aficionado towards any law enforcement officer who held a prisoner incommunicado?

5. Why might the members of a junto hesitate to admit a renegade from a rival party?

EXERCISE 7. On your paper, enter the *letter* of the word-pair that best expresses a relationship similar to that existing between the capitalized word-pair.

1. MATADOR : SWORD

    a. gaucho : poncho   *d.* desperado : loot
    b. picador : lance   *e.* toreador : bull
    c. torero : horse

2. BONANZA : MINER

    a. legacy : heir   *d.* jackpot : gambler
    b. crop : farmer   *e.* bull's-eye : sharpshooter
    c. diploma : student

3. ADOBE : PUEBLO

    a. settlement : Indian   *d.* seaport : flotilla
    b. cabana : beach   *e.* concrete : turnpike
    c. terra-cotta : clay

4. OLIO : INGREDIENT

    a. concerto : instrument   *d.* entrée : dessert
    b. medley : tune   *e.* aria : opera
    c. potpourri : confusion

5. SIERRA : CANYON

    a. zenith : nadir   *d.* grandee : hidalgo
    b. arroyo : mesa   *e.* monarch : retinue
    c. indigo : red

CHAPTER X **Sample Vocabulary Questions in Pre-College Tests**

Vocabulary questions play a prominent and decisive role in pre-college tests. You will probably take one or more of these tests in high school if you expect to apply for college admission or college scholarship awards. The makers of these tests rely heavily on vocabulary because of its demonstrated correlation with intelligence. Naturally, you will want to familiarize yourself with the types of vocabulary questions you are likely to encounter on such tests. For your guidance, therefore, this chapter will present officially released sample vocabulary questions for two widely administered pre-college examinations:

1. The Preliminary Scholastic Aptitude Test/National Merit Scholarship Qualifying Test (PSAT/NMSQT)
2. The Scholastic Aptitude Test (SAT)

The PSAT/NMSQT

The sample vocabulary questions and explanations below are from the 1982 PSAT/NMSQT *Student Bulletin*, published by the College Entrance Examination Board and the Educational Testing Service, which have graciously granted permission to reprint this material. Copies of the *Student Bulletin* are supplied to schools for distribution to students planning to take the PSAT/NMSQT. For further information about the test, consult your school counselor, or write to PSAT/NMSQT, Box 589, Princeton, NJ 08541.

Questions selected from *PSAT/NMSQT Student Bulletin* and *Taking the SAT*. College Entrance Examination Board, 1982. Reprinted by permission of Educational Testing Service, the copyright owner of the sample questions.

Permission to reprint the above material does not constitute review or endorsement by Educational Testing Service or the College Board of this publication as a whole or of any testing information it may contain.

Antonyms (Opposites)

Antonym questions are designed to test the extent and depth of your vocabulary. The words used will be those met by most students in their general reading, although some will not be found frequently in everyday speech.

Each question below consists of a word in capital letters, followed by five lettered words or phrases. Choose the word or phrase that is most nearly *opposite* in meaning to the word in capital letters. Since some of the questions require you to distinguish fine shades of meaning, consider all the choices before deciding which is best.

1. AGILE: (A) humble (B) clumsy (C) useless (D) timid
   (E) ugly

Because *agile* means dexterous and easy in movement, the best opposite would be a word meaning awkward or ungainly. Choice (B), *clumsy*, meets this requirement best and is the correct answer.

2. PINNACLE: (A) buttress (B) hinge (C) abyss (D) surface
   (E) oblivion

This question requires selection of a word that is most nearly opposite rather than directly opposite to the word given. A *pinnacle* is a peak, or highest point, of anything. The opposite of *pinnacle*, then, should refer to the lowest point of anything. The correct choice, (C), abyss, refers to any deep, immeasurable space or chasm. While not an exact opposite to *pinnacle*, it is more nearly so than any of the other words listed.

Sentence Completions

Sentence completion questions measure your ability to select a word or phrase that is consistent in logic and style with other elements in the sentence. The sentences, taken from published material, cover a wide variety of topics of the sort you are likely to have encountered in your general reading. Your understanding of the sentences will not depend on specialized knowledge in science, literature, the social sciences, or other fields.

Each sentence below has one or two blanks, each blank indicating that something has been omitted. Beneath the sentence are five lettered words or sets of words. Choose the word or set of words that *best* fits the meaning of the sentence as a whole.

3. If your garden plot is small, it will not pay to grow crops that require a large amount of ---- in order to develop.

(A) moisture (B) rain (C) fertilizer (D) space (E) care

In this sentence the key word for choosing the answer is *small*. If the garden is small, then the crops cannot require a large area within which to grow. The answer, therefore, must be a word that suggests area. Only the word *space*, choice (D), does this, so (D) is the correct answer.

4. If we survey the development of dancing as an art in Europe, we recognize two streams of tradition which have sometimes ---- and yet remain essentially ----.

(A) changed . . modern (B) divided . . separate
(C) abated . . primitive (D) merged . . distinct
(E) advanced . . comparable

In this sentence there are two strong clues to the pair of words that must fill the blanks. First, the sentence focuses on the fact that the development of dancing exhibits "two streams of tradition." The missing words must further describe that dual development. The second clue is the construction: "have sometimes . . . and yet remain . . ." This suggests that the conclusion of the sentence refers to an apparent contradiction. The words that fill the blanks must express this contradiction. Of the five choices, choice (D), *merged . . distinct*, best satisfies both requirements. Merged and distinct are both appropriate words to apply to "two streams of tradition," and their contradictory meanings make them appropriate words in the construction: "have sometimes . . . and yet remain . . ." As a final test of correctness, insertion of the words in the sentence yields a meaningful English sentence.

Analogies

Analogy questions require you to analyze relationships and to recognize those that are parallel in nature. In answering analogies, it is usually helpful to establish as precisely as you can the relationship between the first two words before you examine the answer choices.

Each question below consists of a related pair of words or phrases, followed by five lettered pairs of words or phrases. Select the lettered pair that *best* expresses a relationship similar to that expressed in the original pair.

5. FOOTBALL : SPORT : : (A) frame : picture
   (B) clock : time   (C) gourmet : food
   (D) cherry : fruit   (E) intelligence : personality

Because football is one of a number of sports, the correct answer must involve something that is included in a larger category described by the second part of the answer. The choice that best fits this description is (D), *cherry : fruit.*

6. ILLEGIBLE : WRITING : : (A) obnoxious : odor
   (B) iridescent : glass   (C) soundproof : wall
   (D) transparent : sight   (E) garbled : speech

The relationship between *illegible* and *writing* can be stated as: (first term) describes incomprehensible (second term), or *illegible* describes incomprehensible *writing.* Choice (E) expresses the same relationship because *garbled* describes incomprehensible *speech.*

PSAT/NMSQT Vocabulary Questions
from Sample Test in *Student Bulletin*

For each question in this section, choose the best answer and blacken the corresponding oval on the answer sheet.

Each question below consists of a word in capital letters, followed by five lettered words or phrases. Choose the word or phrase that is most nearly *opposite* in meaning to the word in capital letters. Since some of the questions require you to distinguish fine shades of meaning, consider all the choices before deciding which is best.

Example

GOOD : (A) sour   (B) bad   (C) red   (D) hot   (E) ugly

            Ⓐ ● Ⓒ Ⓓ Ⓔ

1. PROMPTNESS : (A) excessive modesty   (B) extreme rigidity
   (C) reluctance or apathy   (D) hesitation or delay
   (E) embarrassment or shame
2. INDULGE : (A) adhere   (B) abstain   (C) divulge
   (D) exonerate   (E) expiate
3. COMMONPLACE : (A) genuine   (B) illogical
   (C) enormous   (D) intermediate   (E) extraordinary
4. DEADEN : (A) join   (B) justify   (C) stimulate
   (D) guard carefully   (E) alter significantly
5. ROVE : (A) whisper   (B) nourish   (C) close up
   (D) squeeze dry   (E) settle down
6. RELINQUISH : (A) retain   (B) conform   (C) persuade
   (D) send forward   (E) move together
7. SHREWD : (A) glum   (B) witless   (C) sinister   (D) penniless
   (E) mischievous
8. OUTCLASS : (A) initiate   (B) oppress   (C) keep secret
   (D) be inferior   (E) arrange in order
9. MONOCHROMATIC : (A) polygamous   (B) multicolored
   (C) multitudinous   (D) syndicated   (E) bilateral
10. FORESHADOWED : (A) unwanted   (B) unrecognizable
    (C) unobserved   (D) unintentional   (E) unanticipated

[Editor's note: Questions 11–20, not reprinted here, are similar to the above. Numerous additional questions dealing with opposites appear throughout this book.]

Each sentence below has one or two blanks, each blank indicating that something has been omitted. Beneath the sentence are five lettered words or sets of words. Choose the word or set of words that *best* fits the meaning of the sentence as a whole.

Example

Although its publicity has been ----, the film itself is intelligent, well-acted, handsomely produced, and altogether ----.

(A) tasteless . . respectable   (B) extensive . . moderate
(C) sophisticated . . amateur   (D) risqué . . crude
(E) perfect . . spectacular

---

21. It is particularly unfortunate that such an otherwise ---- mind is ---- hatred and suspicion.

    (A) devious . . devoid of
    (B) inventive . . free from
    (C) limited . . obsessed with
    (D) twisted . . devoted to
    (E) brilliant . . burdened with

22. The speaker acknowledged that his remarks were not ----, but had been made repeatedly by others.

    (A) brief   (B) original   (C) erroneous   (D) eclectic
    (E) speculative

23. Anderson has ---- territory that others, searching for more obvious ores, have thought worthless and left unclaimed.

    (A) disposed of   (B) passed by   (C) prospected in
    (D) warned about   (E) trespassed on

24. While spices have little food value, they ---- even bland foods that are ---- and make them enjoyable.

    (A) replace . . indigestible   (B) dilute . . organic
    (C) taint . . pungent   (D) enhance . . nutritious
    (E) resemble . . tasteless

25. Unlike most other animals, the brown rat can ---- specific knowledge; it first ---- knowledge gained from experience and then disseminates it within the rat community.

(A) transmit . . retains   (B) create . . shares
(C) intuit . . suppresses   (D) furnish . . explores
(E) assign . . forfeits

[*Editor's note: Questions 26–30, not reprinted here, are similar to the above. Numerous additional questions dealing with sentence completion appear throughout this book.*]

Each question below consists of a related pair of words or phrases, followed by five lettered pairs of words or phrases. Select the lettered pair that *best* expresses a relationship similar to that expressed in the original pair.

Example

> YAWN : BOREDOM : : (A) dream : sleep
>   (B) anger : madness (C) smile : amusement
>   (D) face : expression (E) impatience : rebellion
>   Ⓐ Ⓑ ● Ⓓ Ⓔ

31. SANDAL : STRAP : : (A) bonnet : string (B) coat : hanger
  (C) glove : wrist (D) belt : waist (E) shoe : sole
32. SHEEP : FLOCK : : (A) jaguar : feline (B) elephant : cow
  (C) pig : runt (D) goose : gosling (E) hound : pack
33. BROOK : RIVER : : (A) sleet : storm (B) dike : flood
  (C) pond : lake (D) wave : ocean (E) ditch : puddle
34. TRACK : HUNTER : : (A) implicate : partner
  (B) shop : seller (C) work : idler (D) investigate : researcher
  (E) rescue : swimmer
35. CANOE : BOAT : : (A) wagon : train (B) cabin : house
  (C) skates : skis (D) horse : carriage (E) door : arch
36. INKLING : KNOWLEDGE : : (A) umbrella : rain
  (B) glimmer : light (C) summary : speech
  (D) shadow : time (E) rust : iron
37. SKIN DIVER : SEA : : (A) jockey : racetrack
  (B) explorer : safari (C) navigator : ocean
  (D) astronaut : space (E) pilot : plane

[Editor's note: Questions 38–45, not reprinted here, are similar to the above. Numerous additional questions dealing with analogies appear throughout this book.]

Answer Key

1. D	21. E	31. A
2. B	22. B	32. E
3. E	23. C	33. C
4. C	24. D	34. D
5. E	25. A	35. B
6. A		36. B
7. B		37. D
8. D		
9. B		
10. E		

The SAT

The following vocabulary questions and explanations are reprinted with permission from *Taking the SAT*, a 1981–1982 booklet published by the College Entrance Examination Board and the Educational Testing Service. *Taking the SAT* is supplied to secondary schools for free distribution to students planning to register for the SAT. For a copy, see your school counselor. Individual copies may also be purchased from College Board Publications, Box 886, New York, NY 10101.

Antonyms (Opposites)

Antonym questions test the extent of your vocabulary. The vocabulary used in the antonym questions includes words that high school students come across in their general reading, although some words may not be the kind that you use in everyday speech.

Each question below consists of a word in capital letters, followed by five lettered words or phrases. Choose the word or phrase that is most nearly *opposite* in meaning to the word in capital letters. Since some of the questions require you to distinguish fine shades of meaning, consider all the choices before deciding which is best.

Example

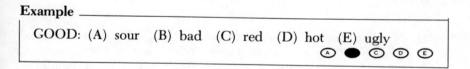

GOOD: (A) sour (B) bad (C) red (D) hot (E) ugly

You can probably answer this example without carefully considering all of the choices. However, most of the antonyms in the verbal section require more careful analysis. When you work on antonym questions, remember that:

1. Among the five choices offered, you are looking for the word that means the *opposite* of the given word. No words that have the same meaning as the given word are included among the five choices.

2. You are looking for the *best* answer. Read all of the choices before deciding which one is best, even if you feel sure you know the answer. For example:

SUBSEQUENT: (A) primary (B) recent (C) contemporary
  (D) prior (E) simultaneous

Someone working quickly might choose (B) *recent* because it refers to a past action and *subsequent* refers to a future action. However, choice (D) *prior* is the best answer.

3. Few words have exact opposites, that is, words that are opposite in all of their meanings. You should find the word that is *most nearly* opposite. For example:

FERMENTING: (A) improvising (B) stagnating (C) wavering
  (D) plunging deeply (E) dissolving

Even though *fermenting* is normally associated with chemical reactions, whereas *stagnating* is normally associated with water, *fermenting* means being agitated and *stagnating* means being motionless. Therefore, choice (B) *stagnating* is the best antonym of *fermenting*.

4. You need to be flexible. A word can have several meanings. For example:

DEPRESS: (A) force (B) allow (C) clarify (D) elate
  (E) loosen

The word *depress* can mean "to push down." However, no word meaning "to lift up" is included among the choices. Therefore, you must consider another meaning of *depress*, "to sadden or discourage." Option (D) *elate* means to fill with joy or pride. The best answer is (D) *elate*.

5. You could try to put the word in a sentence. If you don't know the dictionary meaning of a word but have a feeling for how the word should be used, try to make up a short phrase or sentence using the word. This may give you a clue as to which choice is an opposite, even though you may not be able to define the word precisely.

INCUMBENT: (A) conscious (B) effortless (C) optional
  (D) improper (E) irrelevant

One of the meanings of *incumbent*, and the one you may know best, is "the holder of an office" as in the sentence, "The incumbent president usually has a better chance of winning an election than the challenger." However, an opposite of that meaning is not included in the choices. Try to think of another use of *incumbent*, such as in the sentence, "It is incumbent upon me to finish this." If you can think of such a phrase, you realize that *incumbent* means "imposed as a duty" or "obligatory."

Of the five choices, (A), (B), and (D) are in no way opposites of *incumbent* and you can easily eliminate them. Choice (E) means "not pertinent" and choice (C) means "not compulsory." Although choice (E) may look attractive, choice (C) *optional* is more nearly an exact opposite to *incumbent*. Choice (C), therefore, is the answer.

6. Because answering antonyms depends on knowing the meanings and uses of words, memorizing word lists is probably of little use. Anything that helps you to think about words and how they are used improves your verbal ability and is likely to improve your performance on antonyms and other kinds of verbal questions. Read carefully some moderately complex books or some good magazines on topics with which you are not familiar. If you come across unfamiliar words that you can't understand from the context, use a dictionary. Do crossword puzzles or play word games with your friends or family. These exercises should be at least as helpful as studying word lists and certainly more interesting.

Analogies

Analogy questions test your ability to see a relationship in a pair of words, to understand the ideas expressed in the relationship, and to recognize a similar or parallel relationship.

Each question below consists of a related pair of words or phrases, followed by five lettered pairs of words or phrases. Select the lettered pair that *best* expresses a relationship similar to that expressed in the original pair.

Example

YAWN : BOREDOM : : (A) dream : sleep
(B) anger : madness   (C) smile : amusement
(D) face : expression   (E) impatience : rebellion

Ⓐ Ⓑ ● Ⓓ Ⓔ

When you answer analogy questions,

1. Try to establish a precise relationship between the first two words
before examining the answer choices. State this relationship as clearly
as you can in a sentence or phrase. Next, find the choice with a pair
of words that have the same relationship, and that express the same
idea as the original pair of words. In the example above, a yawn is a
sign of boredom in the same way that a smile is a sign of amusement.
Another example is the following:

SUBMISSIVE : LED : : (A) wealthy : employed
  (B) intolerant : indulged (C) humble : humiliated
  (D) incorrigible : taught (E) inconspicuous : overlooked

The relationship between *submissive* and *led* could be expressed as
"to be submissive is to be easily led." Only choice (E) has the same
relationship as *submissive* and *led;* "to be inconspicuous is to be easily
overlooked" parallels "to be submissive is to be easily led."

Although the wealthy may find it easier to get employment than
do the poor, the statement "to be wealthy is to be easily employed"
is an expression of opinion and not an expression of the relationship
between the words according to their dictionary meanings. Remember that the relationship that is to be established between the two
words should take into account either the dictionary or implied
meanings of the words.

2. Practice recognizing relationships. Below are three examples of the
relationships that could be used.

SONG : REPERTOIRE : : (A) score : melody
  (B) instrument : artist (C) solo : chorus
  (D) benediction : church (E) suit : wardrobe

The best answer is choice (E). The relationship between the words
can be expressed as "several (first word) make up a (second word)."
Several (songs) make up a (repertoire) as several (suits) make up a
(wardrobe).

REQUEST : ENTREAT : : (A) control : explode
  (B) admire : idolize (C) borrow : steal
  (D) repeat : plead (E) cancel : invalidate

The best answer is choice (B). Although both words have similar meanings, they express different degrees of feeling. To (entreat) is to (request) with strong feeling as to (idolize) is to (admire) with strong feeling.

To answer analogy questions, you must think carefully about the precise meanings of words. For instance, if you thought the word "entreat" meant only "to ask" instead of "to ask urgently," you would have trouble establishing the correct relationship between *request* and *entreat*.

FAMINE : STARVATION : : (A) deluge : flood
  (B) drought : vegetation   (C) war : treaty
  (D) success : achievement   (E) seed : mutation

The best answer is choice (A). (Famine) results in (starvation) as a (deluge) results in a (flood).

3. Don't be misled by relationships that are close to but not parallel to the relationship in the original pair. All of the pairs of words listed in the choices have relationships that can be stated; however, the correct answer has most nearly the same relationship as the original pair. Look at the following example.

KNIFE : INCISION : : (A) bulldozer : excavation
  (B) tool : operation   (C) pencil : calculation
  (D) hose : irrigation   (E) plow : agriculture

On the most general level, the relationship between *knife* and *incision* is that the object indicated by the first word is used to perform the action indicated by the second word. Since "a knife is used to make an (incision)," "a bulldozer is used to make an (excavation)," and "a hose is used for (irrigation)," there appear to be two correct answers. You need to go back and state the relationship more precisely. Some aspect of the relationship between the original pair exists in only one of the choices. A more precise relationship between *knife* and *incision* could be expressed as: "a knife cuts into something to make an incision" and "a bulldozer cuts into something to make an excavation." This relationship eliminates *hose : irrigation* as a possible answer, and no other relationship between *hose : irrigation* parallels the relationship to *knife : incision* as well. The best answer is choice (A).

4. Remember that words can have more than one relationship. For example:

PRIDE : LION :: (A) snake : python (B) pack : wolf
  (C) rat : mouse (D) bird : starling (E) dog : canine

A possible relationship between *pride* and *lion* might be that "the first term describes a characteristic of the second (especially in mythology)." Using this reasoning, you might look for an answer such as *wisdom : owl*, but none of the given choices has that kind of relationship. Another relationship between *pride* and *lion* is "a group of lions is called a pride"; therefore, the answer is (B) *pack : wolf;* "a group of wolves is called a pack."

Sentence Completion Questions

Sentence completion questions test your ability to recognize the relationships among parts of a sentence. You are given a sentence from which one or two words have been removed and asked to complete the sentence by choosing the word or words that are consistent with other parts. Sentence completion questions ask you to know the words listed as choices and their proper use in the context of a sentence. The sentences, taken from published material, cover a variety of topics. Each sentence provides enough information so that you can find the correct answer without any information beyond what is contained in the sentence itself.

Each sentence below has one or two blanks, each blank indicating that something has been omitted. Beneath the sentence are five lettered words or sets of words. Choose the word or set of words that *best* fits the meaning of the sentence as a whole.

Example _____

Although its publicity has been ----, the film itself is intelligent, well-acted, handsomely produced, and altogether ----.

  (A) tasteless . . respectable (B) extensive . . moderate
  (C) sophisticated . . amateur (D) risqué . . crude
  (E) perfect . . spectacular

The word *although* suggests that the publicity gave the wrong impression of the movie, so look for two words that are more or less opposite in meaning. Also, the second word has to fit in with "intelligent, well-acted, handsomely produced." Choices (B), (D), and (E) are not opposites. Choice (C) can't be the correct answer even though *sophisticated* and *amateur* are nearly opposites, because an "intelligent, well-acted, handsomely produced" film isn't amateurish. Only choice (A), when inserted in the sentence, gives a logical statement.

Here are some suggestions to keep in mind when you answer sentence completion questions:

1. Read the entire sentence carefully; make sure you understand the ideas being expressed.
2. Don't select an answer simply because it is a popular cliché or "sounds good."
3. Look for grammatical clues within the sentence. For example:

The excitement does not ---- but ---- his senses, giving him a keener perception of a thousand details.

   (A) slow . . diverts   (B) blur . . sharpens
   (C) overrule . . constricts   (D) heighten . . aggravates
   (E) forewarn . . quickens

The word *but* implies that the answer will involve two words that are more or less opposite in meaning. If you keep this in mind, you can eliminate all of the choices except for (B) *blur . . sharpens*. Only the words in choice (B) imply opposition. Also, "sharpens his senses" is consistent with the notion that he had a "keener perception of a thousand details."

4. If the sentence has two blanks to be filled, make sure that *both* words make sense in the sentence. For example:

They argue that the author was determined to ---- his own conclusion, so he ---- any information that did not support it.

   (A) uphold . . ignored   (B) revise . . destroyed
   (C) advance . . devised   (D) disprove . . distorted
   (E) reverse . . confiscated

The first words in choices (A) *uphold* . . *ignored* and (C) *advance* . .
devised seem all right. However, the second word in choice (C)
advance . . *devised* does not make sense in the sentence; why would
an author who wished to advance his theory devise information that
did not support it? Only choice (A) makes a logically consistent
sentence.

Mr. Dillon is a skeptic, - - - - to believe that the accepted opinion of
the majority is generally - - - -.

(A) prone . . infallible   (B) afraid . . misleading
(C) inclined . . justifiable   (D) quick . . significant
(E) disposed . . erroneous

The words to be inserted in the blank spaces in the question above
must result in a statement that is consistent with the definition of a
skeptic. Since a skeptic would hardly consider the accepted opinion
of the majority as *infallible, justifiable,* or *significant,* you can eliminate choices (A), (C), and (D). A skeptic would not be *afraid* that
the accepted opinion of the majority is *misleading;* he would believe
that it was. Therefore, choice (B) is not correct. Only choice (E)
disposed . . *erroneous* yields a logical sentence.

5. After choosing an answer, read the entire sentence to yourself. Make
   sure that the sentence is logical.

SAT Vocabulary Questions from Sample Test in *Taking the SAT*

SECTION 1

For each question in this section, choose the best answer and blacken the corresponding space on the answer sheet.

Each question below consists of a word in capital letters, followed by five lettered words or phrases. Choose the word or phrase that is most nearly *opposite* in meaning to the word in capital letters. Since some of the questions require you to distinguish fine shades of meaning, consider all the choices before deciding which is best.

Example

GOOD: (A) sour (B) bad (C) red (D) hot (E) ugly

Ⓐ ● Ⓒ Ⓓ Ⓔ

1. BAN: (A) borrow (B) regret (C) permit (D) conquer (E) exaggerate
2. COMPRESSION: (A) equality (B) expansion (C) exposure (D) endurance (E) excitement
3. FRAUDULENT: (A) dynamic (B) masterly (C) possible (D) genuine (E) abundant
4. PARASITE: (A) expert (B) imposter (C) instigator (D) self-assured snob (E) self-sufficient individual
5. SPARSE: (A) thick (B) tidy (C) wealthy (D) round (E) sticky
6. DENOUNCE: (A) overstate (B) acclaim (C) destroy (D) refuse (E) hasten
7. FLY-BY-NIGHT: (A) unbalanced (B) moderate (C) permanent (D) incredible (E) modern

[*Editor's note: Questions 8–15, not reprinted here, are similar to the above. Numerous additional questions dealing with opposites appear throughout this book.*]

Each sentence below has one or two blanks, each blank indicating that something has been omitted. Beneath the sentence are five lettered words or sets of words. Choose the word or set of words that *best* fits the meaning of the sentence as a whole.

Example

Although its publicity has been ----, the film itself is intelligent, well-acted, handsomely produced, and altogether ----.

  (A) tasteless . . respectable (B) extensive . . moderate
  (C) sophisticated . . amateur (D) risqué . . crude
  (E) perfect . . spectacular

16. Rather than ---- wagon trains and ---- the pioneer's movement westward, many American Indians acted as guides and companions.

  (A) encountering . . helping
  (B) seeking . . encouraging
  (C) attacking . . hindering
  (D) welcoming . . allowing
  (E) repulsing . . following

17. Although Ricardo looked tired, he was enormously ---- by Maria's election, a victory they had both labored so hard for.

  (A) elated (B) baffled (C) fatigued (D) surprised
  (E) exasperated

[*Editor's note: Questions 18–20, not reprinted here, are similar to the above. Numerous additional questions dealing with sentence completion appear throughout this book.*]

Each question below consists of a related pair of words or phrases, followed by five lettered pairs of words or phrases. Select the lettered pair that *best* expresses a relationship similar to that expressed in the original pair.

Example

YAWN : BOREDOM : : (A) dream : sleep
  (B) anger : madness (C) smile : amusement
  (D) face : expression (E) impatience : rebellion

36. FOOD : STARVATION : : (A) liquor : inebriation
(B) water : saturation   (C) heat : inflammation
(D) privacy : isolation   (E) air : suffocation

37. TAPE RECORDER : EAR : : (A) radio : antenna
(B) camera : eye   (C) phonograph : volume
(D) journal : hand   (E) telephone : speech

38. SUMMONS : ATTENDANCE : : (A) allowance : money
(B) bill : payment   (C) purchase : article
(D) question : examination   (E) continuation : action

39. HOPE : DESPAIRING : : (A) confidence : friendly
(B) respect : governing   (C) wittiness : humorous
(D) jollity : gloomy   (E) unconcern : poised

40. ACT : TRAGEDY : : (A) stanza : poem   (B) palette : artist
(C) inventor : machine   (D) gate : fence   (E) cover : book

[*Editor's note: Questions 41–45, not reprinted here, are similar to the above. Numerous additional questions dealing with analogies appear throughout this book.*]

SECTION 3

For each question in this section, choose the best answer and blacken the corresponding space on the answer sheet.

Each question below consists of a word in capital letters, followed by five lettered words or phrases. Choose the word or phrase that is most nearly *opposite* in meaning to the word in capital letters. Since some of the questions require you to distinguish fine shades of meaning, consider all the choices before deciding which is best.

Example

GOOD: (A) sour   (B) bad   (C) red   (D) hot   (E) ugly

Ⓐ ● Ⓒ Ⓓ Ⓔ

---

1. ORDINARY: (A) numerical   (B) rational   (C) impolite
   (D) staunch   (E) abnormal
2. ATHEIST: (A) believer   (B) scholar   (C) recluse
   (D) expatriate   (E) pauper
3. FLICKER: (A) rise slowly   (B) burn steadily
   (C) warm completely   (D) fume   (E) collide
4. SERRATED: (A) undervalued   (B) aggressive
   (C) smooth and even   (D) loose and flexible
   (E) supremely confident
5. COSMOPOLITAN: (A) indecisive   (B) ineffectual
   (C) antagonistic   (D) parochial   (E) deferential

[Editor's note: Questions 6–10, not reprinted here, are similar to the above. Numerous additional questions dealing with opposites appear throughout this book.]

Each sentence below has one or two blanks, each blank indicating that something has been omitted. Beneath the sentence are five lettered words or sets of words. Choose the word or set of words that *best* fits the meaning of the sentence as a whole.

Example

Although its publicity has been ----, the film itself is intelligent, well-acted, handsomely produced, and altogether ----.

(A) tasteless . . respectable   (B) extensive . . moderate
(C) sophisticated . . amateur   (D) risqué . . crude
(E) perfect . . spectacular

11. As tourism and industry develop along the shores of the Gulf of California, it is possible that the increased human ---- may drive the gray whales from their ---- calving sites.

(A) access . . forsaken
(B) knowledge . . impending
(C) activity . . preferred
(D) indifference . . destined
(E) concern . . despoiled

12. Because of its immense scope, critics have rightly referred to the book as the most ---- examination of minority concerns in the United States ever written.

(A) deficient   (B) intuitive   (C) obscure   (D) unaspiring
(E) comprehensive

[*Editor's note: Questions 13–15, not reprinted here, are similar to the above. Numerous additional questions dealing with sentence completion appear throughout this book.*]

Each question below consists of a related pair of words or phrases, followed by five lettered pairs of words or phrases. Select the lettered pair that *best* expresses a relationship similar to that expressed in the original pair.

Example

YAWN : BOREDOM : : (A) dream : sleep
(B) anger : madness   (C) smile : amusement
(D) face : expression   (E) impatience : rebellion

16. SANDBOX : PLAY : : (A) picture : see (B) office : work
(C) library : publish (D) restaurant : guide
(E) kindergarten : manipulate

17. TENANT : RENT : : (A) salesperson : commission
(B) performer : ticket (C) investor : interest
(D) client : fee (E) professor : tuition

18. DAWN : DAY : : (A) moon : night (B) star : sun
(C) week : year (D) birth : life (E) beginning : end

19. MALLET : POLO : : (A) putter : club (B) bat : baseball
(C) field : football (D) puck : hockey (E) lane : bowling

20. TERRESTRIAL : LUNG : : (A) marsupial : pouch
(B) floral : root (C) aquatic : gill (D) perennial : seed
(E) canine : mouth

[*Editor's note: Questions 21–25, not reprinted here, are similar to the
above. Numerous additional questions dealing with analogies appear
throughout this book.*]

Answer Key					
Section 1			**Section 3**		
1. C	16. C	36. E	1. E	11. C	16. B
2. B	17. A	37. B	2. A	12. E	17. D
3. D		38. B	3. B		18. D
4. E		39. D	4. C		19. B
5. A		40. A	5. D		20. C
6. B					
7. C					

CHAPTER XI Dictionary of Words Taught in This Text

The following pages contain a partial listing of the words presented in this book. The words included are those likely to offer some degree of difficulty. The definitions given have in many cases been condensed.

The numeral following a definition indicates the page on which the word appears. Roman type (e.g., abrupt, 135) is used when the word appears as a main entry. Italic type (e.g., abase, *64*) is used when the word appears as a subentry, such as a definition or a synonym of the main entry.

Use this dictionary as a tool of reference and review. It is a convenient means of restudying the meanings of words that you may have missed in the exercises. It is also a useful device for a general review before an important vocabulary test. Bear in mind, however, that you will get a fuller understanding of these words from the explanations and exercises of the foregoing chapters.

abase: lower *64*

abhorrent: loathsome, repugnant 23

abiogenesis: spontaneous generation 109

abject: deserving contempt; sunk to a low condition 63, 166

abrupt: broken off; sudden 135

abstemious: sparing in eating and drinking 76

abstinent: sparing in eating and drinking 76

absurd: ridiculous 87

abyss: bottomless, immeasurably deep space 63

a cappella: without musical accompaniment 218

acclaim: welcome with approval 52

acclivity: upward slope 60

accredit: accept as worthy of belief; provide with credentials 148

acme: highest point 61

acquit: pronounce not guilty 31

acrid: sharp in smell or taste *66*

acrophobia: fear of being at a great height 96

adagio: slow; in an easy, graceful manner 216

adherent: supporter; follower *191*

adieu: good-by 195

adjacent: lying near or next to 80

admonish: warn of a fault 23, 146

admonition: counseling against a fault or error 146

admonitory: conveying a gentle rebuke 146

adobe: brick of sun-dried clay or mud; structure made of such bricks 232

adolescent: growing from childhood to adulthood   72

adolescent: teenager   72

Adonis: very handsome young man   178

adulation: excessive praise   42

aegis: shield or protection; sponsorship   178

affidavit: sworn written statement made before an authorized official   149

aficionado: person very enthusiastic about anything; sports devotee   230

aggressive: disposed to attack   162

agoraphobia: fear of open spaces   96

à la carte: dish by dish, with a stated price for each dish   204

alacrity: cheerful willingness   60

allegro: quick   216

alto: highest male voice; lowest female voice (contralto)   215

amazon: tall, strong, masculine woman   178

ambience: surrounding atmosphere   207

ambrosia: food of the gods   24, 179

ambrosial: exceptionally pleasing to taste or smell   24, 179

ameliorate: become better; improve   8

amoral: without sense of moral responsibility   102

amorphous: without definite form or shape   88, 102, 121

amphibious: able to live both on land and in water   109

analogy: likeness in some respects between things otherwise different   85

anarchy: total absence of rule or government; confusion   118

anatomy: dissection of plants or animals for the purpose of studying their structure; structure of a plant or animal   111

andante: moderately slow, but flowing   216

anemia: lack of a normal number of red blood cells   102

anesthesia: loss of feeling or sensation resulting from ether, chloroform, novocaine, etc.   102

Anglophile: supporter of England or the English   98

Anglophobe: one who dislikes England or the English   97

Anglophobia: dislike of England or the English   96

anguish: extreme pain   *41*

anhydrous: destitute of water   102

anomaly: deviation from the common rule   102

anonymous: nameless; of unknown or unnamed origin   102

anoxia: deprivation of oxygen   102

antediluvian: antiquated; belonging to the time before the Biblical Flood   72

anthropology: science dealing with the origin, races, customs, and beliefs of man   108

anthropomorphic: attributing human form or characteristics to beings not human, especially gods   121

antibiotic: antibacterial substance produced by a living organism   109

anticlimax: abrupt decline in dignity or importance at the end   63

antidote: remedy for a poison or evil   50

antipasto: appetizer consisting of fish, meats, etc.; hors d'oeuvres   224

antipathy: strong dislike   *60*, 120

antipodes: parts of the earth (or their inhabitants) diametrically opposite   112

anxious: fearful of what may come   *166*

apathy: lack of feeling, emotion, interest, or excitement   120

apéritif: alcoholic drink taken before a meal as an appetizer   204

apex: farthest point opposite the base, as in a triangle or pyramid   *62*

apiary: place where bees are kept   49

apogee: farthest point from the earth in the orbit of a man-made satellite or heavenly body; highest point   61, 119

apostate: one who has forsaken the faith, principles, or party he supported earlier   *231*

appendectomy: surgical removal of the appendix   111

apprehend: seize or take into custody; understand   165

apprehensive: fearful of what may come   166

approximate: nearly correct   80

apropos: by the way; incidentally   207

aqueduct: artificial channel for conducting water from a distance   159

arbiter: a person having power to decide a dispute   85

arbitrary: proceeding from a whim or fancy   85

arbitrate: decide a dispute, acting as arbiter (judge); submit a dispute to an arbiter   85

archaic: no longer used, except in a special context; old-fashioned   72

aria: melody; an elaborate, accompanied melody for a single voice in an opera   219

aristocracy: class regarded as superior in some respect   *191*

aroma: pleasant odor   66

arpeggio: production of the tones of a chord in rapid succession and not simultaneously; a chord thus played   218

arrogant: haughty   *91*

arroyo: watercourse; small, often dry, gully   234

arthropod: any invertebrate (animal having no backbone) with jointed legs   112

ascetic: self-denying; person who shuns pleasures   39

aseptic: free from disease-causing micro-organisms   102

assertive: acting and speaking boldly   *162*

astringent: drawing (the tissues) tightly together; stern; substance that shrinks tissues and checks flow of blood by contracting blood vessels   50, 137

atheism: godlessness   102

atlas: book of maps   179

atom: smallest particle of an element   111

atomizer: instrument for reducing to minute particles or a fine spray   111

atrophy: lack of growth from want of nourishment or from disuse   102

attaché: member of the diplomatic staff of an ambassador or minister   190

attenuate: make thin; weaken   42

atypical: unlike the typical   102

au courant: well-informed; up-to-date   189

au revoir: good-by till we meet again   195

auroral: pertaining to or resembling the dawn; rosy   179

auspices: patronage and care   *178*

austere: stern   *137*

autarchy: rule by an absolute sovereign   118

autobiography: story of a person's life written by the person himself   109

avant-garde: experimentalists or innovators in any art   202

averse: disinclined   *60*

aversion: strong dislike   60, 97

avert: turn away; prevent   167

aviary: place where birds are kept   49

avoirdupois: weight   207

axiomatic: self-evident   85

bacchanalian: jovial or wild with drunkenness   179

bacchic: jovial or wild with drunkenness   179

bacteriology: science dealing with the study of bacteria   108

badger: nag   49
baffle: bewilder   15
bagatelle: trifle   207
banter: playful teasing   54
baritone: male voice between bass and tenor   215
bas-relief: carving or sculpture in which the figures project only slightly from the background   202
bass: lowest male voice   215
basso: lowest male voice   215
bathos: abrupt decline in dignity or importance at the end   *63*
baton: stick with which a conductor beats time for an orchestra or band   202
benign: not dangerous; gentle   50
besmirch: soil   *79*
bête noire: object or person dreaded   196
bias: opinion formed before there are grounds for it; unthinking preference   85
bibliophile: lover of books   98
bigoted: narrow-minded   85
billet-doux: love letter   195
biochemistry: chemistry dealing with chemical compounds and processes in living plants and animals   110
biogenesis: development of life from pre-existing life   110
biography: story of a person's life written by another person   110
biology: science dealing with the study of living organisms   108
biometry: calculation of the probable duration of human life   110
biopsy: diagnostic examination of a piece of tissue from the living body   110
biota: the living plants (flora) and living animals (fauna) of a region   110
biped: two-footed animal   *163*
blandishment: word or deed of mild flattery   42

blasé: tired of pleasures; bored   189
bliss: perfect happiness   38
blithe: cheerful   38
bluster: talk or act with noisy violence   *179*
boa constrictor: snake that crushes its prey in its coils   137
bolero: lively dance in ¾ time; the music for this dance; short, loose jacket   232
bombastic: using pompous language   *170*
bona fide: made or carried out in good faith   149
bonanza: accidental discovery of a rich mass of ore in a mine   232
bonbon: piece of candy   204
bon mot: clever saying   195
bouffant: full; puffed out   205
bouquet: pleasant odor   *66*
bourgeoisie: the middle class   190
boutique: small shop specializing in fashionable clothes   205
bow: forward part of a ship   77
bowdlerize: remove objectionable material from a book   *79*
bravado: boastful behavior; pretense of bravery   233
bravura: piece of music requiring skill and spirit in the performer; display of daring or brilliancy   219
brazen: shameless; made of brass or bronze; harsh-sounding   90–91
breach: a breaking gap; violation   *142*
brine: salty water; ocean   77
brisk: lively   *216*
brochure: pamphlet   195
broncho: half-wild pony   234
bronco: half-wild pony   234
bugbear: object of dread   *196*
buoyant: cheerful; able to float   38
burly: stout   41
burro: small donkey used as a pack animal   234
buxom: plump and attractive   41

caballero: gentleman or gallant; horseman 230

cabana: beach shelter resembling a cabin 233

cajole: persuade by pleasing words 42

callow: young and inexperienced 72

calumnious: falsely and maliciously accusing 53

calumny: false and malicious accusation 53

cameo: stone or shell on which a figure, cut in relief, appears against a background of a different color 221

campanile: bell tower 221

canard: false rumor 195

cantata: story or play set to music to be sung by a chorus, but not acted 219

canto: one of the chief divisions of a long poem; book 221

canyon: deep valley with high, steep slopes, often with a stream flowing through it 234

capricious: proceeding from a whim or fancy 85

cardiology: science dealing with the action and diseases of the heart 108

caricature: drawing, imitation, or description that ridiculously exaggerates peculiarities or defects 54

carnivore: flesh-eating animal 138

carnivorous: flesh-eating 138

carousal: drinking party 76

carrion: decaying flesh of a carcass 78

carte blanche: freedom to use one's own judgment 197

castanets: hand instruments clicked together to accompany music or dancing 232

castigated: denounced 233

cause célèbre: famous case in law that arouses considerable interest 197

celestial: of the heavens 61

censure: adverse criticism 137

centipede: small wormlike animal with many pairs of legs 163

chagrin: embarrassment; disappointment 39

chargé d'affaires: temporary substitute for an ambassador 190

chasm: wide gap 63

chef d'oeuvre: masterpiece in art, literature, etc. 202

chemise: loose-fitting, sacklike dress 206

cherub: angel in the form of a baby or child 41

cherubic: chubby and innocent-looking 41

Chianti: a dry, red Italian wine 224

chiaroscuro: style of pictorial art using only light and shade; sketch in black and white 221

chic: stylish 189

childish: of or like a child in a bad sense 75

childlike: of or like a child in a good sense 73

chimerical: fantastic 179

chiropodist: one who specializes in the care of the feet 112

cinema: motion picture 16

circumlocution: roundabout way of speaking 170

clamorous: noisy 171

claustrophobia: fear of confined spaces 96

cliché: trite or worn-out expression 195

climactic: arranged in order of increasing force and interest; of or constituting a climax 61

clique: small and exclusive set of persons 191, 231

cogitate: consider with care 85

cognoscente: connoisseur 223

coiffure: style of arranging the hair; headdress 206

coincide: happen together   *161*
colloquy: conversation; conference   170
coloratura: ornamental passages (runs, trills, etc.) in vocal music; soprano who sings such passages   215
commendable: praiseworthy   *52*
commitment: consignment ("sending") to prison, etc.; pledge   169
complacent: self-satisfied   38
complex: complicated; intricate   31
comprehensible: understandable   166
comprehensive: including very much   166
compunction: regret; misgiving   39
concave: curved inward, creating a hollow space   88
concerto: long musical composition for one or more principal instruments   219
concise: expressing much in a few words   *180*
concur: agree; happen together   161
concurrent: running together; occurring at the same time   161
conducive: tending to lead to   159
conduct: lead; guide   159
confidant(e): one to whom secrets are entrusted   149
confident: having faith in oneself   149
confidential: communicated in trust   149
confine: imprison   24
confrere: colleague; co-worker   190
congratulate: express pleasure at another's success   156
coniferous: bearing cones   171
conjectural: of the nature of a guess or assumption   *115*
conjecture: a guess   *88*, 166
connoisseur: expert   191, *192*
conquistador: conqueror   230
consecutive: following in order   160
consequence: result; importance   160
conserve: keep from waste; save   8

consign: hand over   31
constrict: bind   137
consummate: perfect   61
contact: touching or meeting; connection   164
contaminate: make impure by mixture   78
contemporary: of the same period   72
contemporary: person living at same time as another   72
contiguous: touching; near   80, 164
contingent: dependent on something else; accidental   164
contort: twist out of shape   *140*
contortionist: person who can twist or bend his body into odd postures   140
contour: outline of a figure   88
contralto: lowest female voice   215
contrite: showing regret for wrongdoing   39
controversy: dispute   167
convalesce: recover health after illness   50
conventional: generally accepted   *87*
convict: prove guilty; person serving a prison sentence   141
convince: persuade or show conclusively by argument or proof   141
convivial: fond of dining with friends; jovial   38, 139
corporal: bodily   158
corporation: body authorized by law to carry on an activity   158
corps: organized body of persons; branch of the military   158
corpse: dead body   158
corpulent: very fat   *41*, 158
corpus: general collection of writings, laws, etc.   158
corpuscle: blood cell; minute particle   158
corpus delicti: facts proving a crime has been committed   158

corrupt: change from good to bad   67, 135

corsage: small bouquet worn by a woman   206

coterie: set or circle of acquaintances   191

countermand: issue a contrary order   147

coup de grâce: merciful or decisive finishing stroke   207

coup d'état: sudden, violent, or illegal overthrow of a government   201

coy: pretending to be shy   90

cravat: necktie   206

credence: belief   148

credentials: documents, letters, references, etc., that inspire belief or trust   148

credible: believable   148

credit: trust   148

credulous: too ready to believe   24, 148

creed: summary of principles believed in or adhered to   148

crescendo: gradually increasing (or a gradual increase) in force or loudness   217

criminology: scientific study of crimes and criminals   108

criterion: standard   85

crone: withered old woman   72

crux: essential part   86

cuisine: style of cooking   204

cul-de-sac: blind alley   197

culmination: highest point   62

culpable: blamable   166

cupola: rounded roof; small dome or tower on a roof   221

current: now in progress; a running or flowing, as of water   161

curriculum: specific course of study in a school or college   161

curry favor: seek to gain favor by flattery   42

cursive: running or flowing   161

cursory: running over hastily   161

deadlock: stoppage produced by the opposition of equally powerful persons or groups   197

debacle: collapse   197

debonair: affable and courteous   189

debut: formal entrance into society; first public appearance   191

debutante: girl who has just made her debut   191

decade: period of ten years   24

deceased: dead   73

deceptive: misleading   86

declivity: downward slope   63

decrepit: weakened by old age   73

decrescendo: gradually decreasing (or a gradual decrease) in force or loudness   217

deduce: derive by reasoning   86

deduction: subtraction; reasoning from the general to the particular   159

defamatory: harming or destroying a reputation   53

defile: make filthy   79

deflect: turn aside   144

defunct: dead; extinct   73

degrade: lower   64

dejected: in low spirits   39, 166

delectable: very pleasing   38

démarche: course of action, especially one involving a change of policy   201

demise: death, especially of a monarch or other important person   169

demitasse: small cup for, or of, black coffee   204

demure: falsely modest or serious; grave   90

denouement: solution of the plot in a play, story, or complex situation   202

denunciation: public condemnation   182

dermatology: science dealing with the skin and its diseases   108

derogatory: expressing low esteem   53

desperado: bold, reckless criminal   230

despise: loathe   16

despotic: unjustly severe   85

détente: a relaxing, as of strained relations between nations   201

detention: act of keeping back or detaining   145

detonate: explode; cause to explode   24

detriment: damage; disadvantage   8

devotee: ardent adherent   191, *230*

devour: eat greedily or ravenously; seize upon and destroy   138

dichotomy: cutting or division into two   111

diffident: lacking self-confidence   90, 149

digressive: rambling   *161, 165*

dilemma: situation requiring a choice between two equally bad alternatives   86

dilettante: person who follows some art or science as an amusement or in a trifling way   223

dimeter: line of poetry consisting of two feet   *112*

dimorphous: occurring under two distinct forms   121

dipody: verse (line of poetry) consisting of two feet   112

dipsomania: abnormal, uncontrollable craving for alcohol   76

disconsolate: cheerless   39

discredit: cast doubt on; disgrace   148

discursive: wandering from one topic to another   161

disgruntled: in bad humor   40

disrupt: break apart   135

distort: twist out of shape; change from the true meaning   88–89, 140

divert: turn aside; amuse   167

docile: easily led   *10, 159*

dogmatic: asserting opinions as if they were facts   86

dolce: soft; sweet   217

dolce far niente: delightful idleness   224

doldrums: calm, windless part of the ocean near the equator; listlessness   77–78

doleful: full of sorrow   40

dolorous: full of sorrow   *40*

dour: gloomy   *40*

Draconian: harsh   179

dregs: most worthless part; sediment at the bottom of a liquid   63

droll: odd and laughter-provoking   54

dross: waste; scum on the surface of melting metals   79

duct: tube or channel for conducting a liquid, air, etc.   159

ductile: able to be drawn out or hammered thin (said of a metal); easily led   159

duenna: elderly woman chaperon of a young lady; governess   230

duet: piece of music for two voices or instruments; two singers or players performing together   219

dysentery: inflammation of the large intestine   99

dysfunction: abnormal functioning, as of an organ of the body   99

dyslexia: impairment of ability to read   99

dyspepsia: difficult digestion; indigestion   99

dysphagia: difficulty in swallowing   99

dysphasia: speech difficulty resulting from brain disease   99

dystrophy: faulty nutrition   99

earthy: coarse; worldly   63

ebullient: overflowing with enthusiasm   16

éclat: brilliancy of achievement   193

eclectic: choosing (ideas, methods, etc.) from various sources   86

ecology: science dealing with the relation

of living things to their environment and to each other   108

ecstasy: state of overwhelming joy   38

effrontery: shameless boldness   31

egoism: conceit   91

egress: exit   162

eject: throw out   166

élan: enthusiasm   193

elate: lift up with joy   *61*

elated: in high spirits   38

elite: group of superior individuals   191

elocution: art of speaking or reading effectively in public   170

eloquent: speaking with force and fluency   170

Elysian: blissful; heavenly   179

emaciated: made unnaturally thin   42

émigré: refugee   191

eminence: high rank; lofty hill   61

emissary: person sent on a mission   169

emit: send out; give off   169

empathy: the complete understanding of another's feelings, motives, etc.   120

encomium: speech or writing of high praise   52

encore: repetition of a performance; rendition of an additional selection   202

endocarditis: inflammation of the lining of the heart   117

endocrine: secreting internally   116

endoderm: membranelike tissue lining the greater part of the digestive tract   117

endogamy: marriage within the tribe, caste, or social group   116

endogenous: produced from within; due to internal causes   116

endomorphic: occurring within   121

endoparasite: parasite living in the internal organs of an animal   117

endophyte: plant growing within another plant   117

endoskeleton: internal skeleton or supporting framework in an animal   116

endosmosis: osmosis inward   116

ennui: boredom   193

entente: understanding or agreement between governments   201

entrée: main dish at lunch or dinner   204

entre nous: between us   195

entrepreneur: one who assumes the risks and management of a business   191

environs: districts surrounding a place; suburbs   80

envoy: diplomatic agent; messenger   191

ephemeral: fleeting; short-lived   24

equanimity: evenness of mind   *194*

erupt: burst or break out   135

esprit de corps: feeling of union and common interest pervading a group   158, 193

ethereal: of the heavens; delicate   61

ethnology: science dealing with the races of mankind, their origin, distribution, culture, etc.   108

eugenics: science dealing with improving the hereditary qualities of the human race   100

eulogistic: expressing praise   *53*

eulogize: write or speak in praise of someone   52, 100

eupepsia: good digestion   100

euphemism: substitution of a "good" expression for an unpleasant one   100

euphonious: pleasing in sound   100

euphoria: sense of well-being   100

euthanasia: illegal practice of painlessly putting to death a person suffering from an incurable, painfully distressing disease   100

euthenics: science dealing with improving living conditions   100

evict: expel   141

evince: show clearly   141

exaggerate: overstate 16
exalt: lift up with joy, pride, etc.; raise in rank, dignity, etc. 61
excruciating: unbearably painful 31
exculpate: acquit *31*
excursion: going out or forth, expedition 161
execute: follow through to completion; put to death 160
exhort: urge 16
exocrine: secreting externally 116
exogamy: marriage outside the tribe, caste, or social group 116
exogenous: produced from without; due to external causes 116
exoskeleton: hard protective structure developed outside the body 116
exosmosis: osmosis outward 116
exoteric: external, readily understandable 117
exotic: introduced from a foreign country; excitingly strange 8, 117
expedite: accelerate or speed up; make easy 163
expertise: expertness 16
expurgate: remove objectionable material from a book; purify 79
extinct: no longer in existence 73
extol: praise 52, *61*
extort: wrest (money, promises, etc.) from a person by force 140
extrovert: person more interested in what is going on around him than in his own thoughts and feelings 167

facade: face or front of a building, or of anything 207
facetious: in the habit of joking; said in jest without serious intent 54
facilitate: make easy *163*
fait accompli: thing accomplished and presumably irrevocable 197
fallacious: based on an erroneous idea 86
fallacy: erroneous idea *86*

fallible: liable to be mistaken 86
falsetto: unnaturally high-pitched male voice; artificial voice 215
farcical: exciting laughter 55
fatal: causing death 157
fathom: get to the bottom of; ascertain the depth of *64*
faux pas: misstep or blunder in conduct, manners, speech, etc. 197
fawning: slavishly attentive *43*
felicitate: wish one joy or happiness *156*
fester: form pus; rot 50
fête: to honor with a party; festival 207
fetid: ill-smelling *66*
fiancé(e): person engaged to be married 191
fiasco: crash; complete or ridiculous failure 224
fidelity: faithfulness to a trust or vow; accuracy 149
fiduciary: held in trust; confidential 149
fiesta: religious holiday; any festival or holiday 233
filet: slice of meat or fish without bones or fat 204
filial: of or like a son or daughter 64
finale: close or termination, as the last section of a musical composition 219
finesse: skill 194
finicky: hard to please 16
flamboyant: flamelike; showy 206
flex: bend 144
flexible: capable of being bent 144
flexor: muscle that serves to bend a limb 144
flippant: treating serious matters lightly 54
flotilla: small fleet; fleet of small vessels 233
flotsam: wreckage of a ship or its cargo found floating on the sea; driftage 78

folly: lack of good sense   8

forbearance: leniency; patience   31

forebear: ancestor   73

forefather: ancestor   *65, 73*

formerly: previously   9

forte: loud   217

fortissimo: very loud   217

foyer: lobby; entrance hall   207

fraction: one or more of the equal parts of a whole   142

fractious: apt to break out into a passion   142

fracture: break or crack; breaking of a bone   142

fragile: easily broken   142

fragment: part broken off   142

fragrant: having a pleasant odor   66

Francophile: supporter of France or the French   98

Francophobe: one who dislikes France or the French   97

fraternal: brotherly; having to do with a fraternal society   64

fratricide: act of killing (or killer of) one's own brother   136

fresco: art of painting with water colors on damp, fresh plaster; picture or design so painted   221

frivolity: trifling gaiety   *55*

frolicsome: full of gaiety   38

frustrate: baffle   *15*

fulsome: offensive because of excessive display or insincerity   43

fusty: stale-smelling; old-fashioned   66

gala: characterized by festivity   39

gall: irritate mentally; vex   16, *31*

gallant: man of fashion; lover   *230*

garrulous: talkative   *170*

gastrectomy: surgical removal of part or all of the stomach   111

gaucho: Argentine cowboy of mixed Spanish and Indian descent   230

gaunt: excessively thin   *42*

gendarme: policeman with military training   191

genealogy: account of the descent of a person or family from an ancestor   65, 108

genocide: deliberate extermination of a racial or cultural group   136

genre: kind; style   203

gentility: good manners; membership in the upper class   65

genuflect: bend the knee; touch the right knee to the ground, as in worship   144

geocentric: measured from the earth's center   119

geodesy: mathematics dealing with the earth's shape and dimensions   *119*

geodetic: pertaining to geodesy   119

geography: study of the earth's surface, etc.   119

geology: science dealing with the earth's history as recorded in rocks   108, 119

geometry: mathematics dealing with lines, angles, surfaces, and solids   119

geomorphic: pertaining to the shape of the earth or the form of its surface   119

geophysics: science treating of the forces that modify the earth   119

geopolitics: study of government and its policies as affected by physical geography   119

geoponics: art or science of agriculture   119

georgic: agricultural; poem on husbandry (farming)   119

geotropism: response to earth's gravity, as the growing of roots downward in the ground   119

Germanophobe: one who dislikes Germany or the Germans   97

Germanophobia: dislike of Germany or the Germans   96

germicide: substance that kills germs   136

gigantic: prodigious   32
glee: joy   54
glum: gloomy   40
gondola: boat used in the canals of Venice; cabin attached to the under part of an airship   224
gourmand: person excessively fond of eating and drinking   191
gourmet: connoisseur in eating and drinking   192
gracious: courteous   156
gradation: a change by steps or stages 162
grade: step; stage   162
gradient: rate at which a road, railroad track, etc., rises; slope   162
gradual: by steps or degrees   162
graduate: complete all the steps of a course and receive a diploma or degree   162
graduated: arranged in regular steps, stages, or degrees   162
grandee: nobleman of the highest rank; person of eminence   231
grandiloquent: using lofty or pompous words   170
graphic: clear-cut and lifelike   139
grateful: thankful   156
gratify: give or be a source of pleasure or satisfaction   156
gratis: out of kindness or favor; free 156
gratitude: thankfulness   156
gratuitous: given freely; unwarranted 156
gratuity: present of money in return for a favor or service   156
grave: deserving serious attention   89
grave: slow (the slowest tempo in music); serious   216
grotto: cave   224
gruesome: horrifying and repulsive   51
gullible: easily deceived   24
gully: gorge excavated by running water 234

gusto: liking or taste; hearty enjoyment 224
hacienda: large ranch; landed estate; country house   233
haggard: careworn   42
haggle: argue over a price   24
halcyon: calm   49
hamper: interfere with   31
harlequin: clown   54
harmony: peaceable relations   9
hector: to bully; to bluster   179
herbicide: substance that kills plants 136
herbivore: plant-eating animal   138
herbivorous: dependent on plants as food   138
Herculean: very difficult; having or requiring the strength of Hercules 180
herdsman: one who owns, keeps, or tends a herd   231
heretical: rejecting regularly accepted beliefs or doctrines   86
hermetic: airtight   180
heterochromatic: having different colors 113
heteroclite: deviating from the common rule; person or thing deviating from the common rule   113
heterodox: rejecting regularly accepted beliefs or doctrines   86, 113
heterogeneous: dissimilar   113
heterology: lack of correspondence between parts   113
heteromorphic: exhibiting diversity of form   113, 122
heteronym: word spelled like another, but differing in sound and meaning 113
hidalgo: nobleman of the second class 231
hierarchy: body of rulers or officials grouped in ranks, each being subordinate to the rank above it   118

hilarity: noisy gaiety   54

hoary: white or gray with age; ancient   73

hoax: deception; joke   *195*

hodgepodge: mixture   *233*

homeopathy: system of medical practice that treats disease by administering minute doses of a remedy which, if given to healthy persons, would produce symptoms of the disease treated   121

homicide: killing of one human by another   136

homocentric: having the same center   113

homochromatic: having the same color   113

homogeneous: similar   113

homology: fundamental similarity of structure   113

homomorphic: exhibiting similarity of form   113

homonym: word that sounds like another but differs in meaning   113

homophonic: having the same sound   113

hors d'oeuvres: light food served as an appetizer before the regular courses of a meal   204, *224*

humble: of low position or condition; modest   63, *90*

humiliate: lower the pride, position, or dignity of   64

humility: freedom from pride   64

hydrophobia: rabies   96

hyperacidity: excessive acidity   114

hyperactive: overactive   115

hyperbole: extravagant exaggeration of statement   115

hypercritical: overcritical   115

hyperemia: superabundance of blood   115

hyperglycemia: excess of sugar in the blood   114

hyperopia: farsightedness   115

hypersensitive: excessively sensitive   115

hypertension: abnormally high blood pressure   114

hyperthyroid: marked by excessive activity of the thyroid gland   115

hypertrophy: enlargement of a part or organ, as from excessive use   115

hypoacidity: weak acidity   114

hypochondriac: person morbidly anxious about his health or suffering from imagined illness   50

hypodermic: injected under the skin   115

hypoglycemia: abnormally low level of sugar in the blood   114

hypotension: low blood pressure   114

hypothesis: theory or supposition assumed as a basis for reasoning   *86*, 115

hypothetical: pertaining to a supposition made as a basis for reasoning or research   86, 115

hypothyroid: marked by deficient activity of the thyroid gland   115

ignore: disregard   9

illusion: false impression   87

imbroglio: difficult situation, complicated disagreement   224

immaculate: absolutely clean   79

immerse: plunge into a liquid   24

immortality: eternal life; lasting fame   157

immunity: resistance to a disease; freedom from an obligation   50

impasse: predicament affording no escape; impassable road   197

impede: hinder   *31*, 163

impediment: hindrance; defect   9, 163

impertinent: inappropriate, rude   *91*, 145

impudent: insolent   *90*

imputation: insinuation; accusation   53

inamorata: woman who is loved   *223*

inamorato: male lover 223
inane: silly; pointless 16
incense: substance yielding a pleasant odor when burned 66
incognito: with one's identity concealed; disguised state 224
incommunicado: deprived of communication with others; in solitary confinement 233
inconsequential: unimportant 160
incontrovertible: certain 87, 167
incorporate: combine so as to form one body 158
incorruptible: incapable of being corrupted or bribed 135
incredible: not believable 148
incredulity: disbelief 148
incrustation: crust or coating *221*
incur: meet with something undesirable; bring upon oneself 161
incursion: a rushing into; raid 161
indemnify: reimburse 17
indigo: plant yielding a blue dye; deep violet blue 234
indisputable: too evident for doubt 87
indolent: lazy 9
indubitable: certain 87
induce: move by persuasion 159
induction: reasoning from the particular to the general 159
inebriated: drunk 77
infanticide: act of killing (or killer of) an infant 136
infantile: of or like a very young child; babyish 73
infer: derive by reasoning *86*
inference: conclusion *166*
infernal: pertaining to the realm of the dead; hellish *184*
infidel: one who does not accept a particular faith 149
inflection: change in the pitch or tone of a person's voice 144
inflexibility: rigidity 144
infraction: violation 142

ingénue: naive young woman; actress playing such a role 192
ingenuous: artlessly frank *190*
ingrate: ungrateful person 156
ingratiate: work (oneself) into another's favor 43, 156
inject: force or introduce a liquid, a remark, etc. 166
insatiable: incapable of being satisfied *139*
insecticide: preparation for killing insects 136
insectivorous: dependent on insects as food 138
insomnia: inability to sleep 24
intact: kept or left whole 9, 164
intaglio: design engraved by making cuts in a surface 221
intangible: not capable of being touched *61*, 165
interject: throw in between 166
interlocutor: one who participates in a conversation; questioner 170
intermezzo: short musical or dramatic entertainment between the acts of a play; short musical composition between the main divisions of an extended musical work; a short, independent musical composition 220
intermittent: coming and going at intervals 169
interpose: place between *166*
interrupt: break into or between 135
intimidate: make fearful *179*
intolerant: narrow-minded 85
intoxicated: drunk 77
intractable: hard to manage *142*
intricate: complicated *31*
introvert: person more interested in his own thoughts than in what is going on around him 168
invalid: having no force; void 9
invert: turn upside down 168
inveterate: firmly established by age; habitual 73

invincible: incapable of being conquered 141

iridescent: having colors like the rainbow 180

irony: type of humor whose intended meaning is the opposite of the words used 54–55

irrational: senseless 87

jetsam: goods cast overboard to lighten a ship in distress 78

jettison: throw (goods) overboard to lighten a ship or plane; discard 78

jocose: given to jesting; playfully humorous 55

jocular: given to jesting; done as a joke 55

jocund: merry 39

jovial: jolly 38, 139, 180

jubilation: rejoicing 39

junta: council for legislation or administration 231

junto: political faction; group of plotters 231

juvenile: of or for youth; immature 73

juxtaposition: close or side-by-side position 80

kith and kin: friends and relatives 65

knave: tricky, deceitful fellow 231

labyrinthine: full of confusing passageways; complicated like the Labyrinth 180

lackey: slavish follower 43

laconic: using words sparingly 180

laissez-faire: absence of government interference or regulation 201

lamentable: pitiable 40

lank: long and thin 42

lapse: accidental mistake 25

largo: slow and dignified 216

laudatory: expressing praise 53

lax: careless 169

leeward: in the direction away from the wind 78

legato: smooth and connected 218

legerdemain: sleight of hand 194

lento: slow 216

lesion: injury 50

lethargic: unnaturally drowsy; sluggish 180

lettre de cachet: sealed letter obtainable from the King of France (before the Revolution) ordering the imprisonment without trial of the person named in the letter 201

levity: lack of proper seriousness 55

liaison: bond; coordination of activities 197

libel: false and defamatory written or printed statement 53

libretto: text or words of an opera or other long musical composition 220

lineage: descent in a line from a common ancestor 65

lionize: treat as highly important 49

lithe: slender and agile 42

loath: disinclined 60

lobotomy: type of brain surgery 111

longevity: long life; length of life 74

loquacious: talkative 170

Lucullan: luxurious 180

ludicrous: exciting laughter 55

macrocosm: great world; universe 101

macron: horizontal mark indicating that the vowel over which it is placed is long 101

macroscopic: large enough to be visible to the naked eye 101

maestro: eminent conductor, composer, or teacher of music; master in any art 223

maître d'hôtel: headwaiter 192

majolica: variety of enameled Italian pottery richly decorated in colors 221

maladroit: unskillful; clumsy 189

malaise: vague feeling of bodily discomfort or illness   194

malign: speak evil of   53

malignant: threatening to cause death; very evil   51

malleable: capable of being shaped by hammering; adaptable   89

malodorous: ill-smelling   66

mañana: tomorrow   235

mandate: authoritative command; a territory administered by a trustee (supervisory nation)   147

mandatory: required by command   147

mantilla: woman's light scarf or veil; cloak or cape   233

marine: of the sea or shipping   78

maritime: of the sea or shipping   78

martial: pertaining to war; warlike   181

martinet: person who enforces very strict discipline   192

matador: bullfighter appointed to kill the bull   231

maternal: motherly; inherited from or related to the mother's side   65

matriarchy: form of social organization in which the mother rules the family or tribe, descent being traced through the mother   118

matricide: act of killing (or killer of) one's own mother   136

mature: full-grown; carefully thought out   74

maudlin: weakly sentimental and tearful   40

mean: without distinction   *64*

medley: mixture   *197, 233*

melancholy: sad   *40*

mélange: mixture   197

memento: keepsake; reminder   *208*

menial: low   64

mentor: wise and trusted advisor; athletic coach   181

mercurial: vivacious; changeable; crafty; eloquent   181

mesa: flat-topped rocky hill with steeply sloping sides   235

mestizo: person of mixed (usually Spanish and American Indian) blood   231

metamorphosis: change of form   121

meteorology: science dealing with the atmosphere and weather   108

mezzanine: intermediate story in a theater between the main floor and the first balcony   221

mezzo-soprano: female voice between contralto and soprano   215

mezzotint: picture engraved on copper or steel by polishing or scraping away parts of a roughened surface   221

microbe: very minute organism; microorganism   101, 110

microbicide: agent that destroys microbes   101

microcosm: little world   101

microdont: having small teeth   101

microfilm: film of very small size   101

micrometer: instrument for measuring very short distances   101

microscopic: invisible to the naked eye   101

microsecond: millionth of a second   101

microwave: very short electromagnetic wave   101

milieu: environment   207

militant: given to fighting   *162*

mirage: optical illusion   198

mirth: merriment   *54*

misandry: hatred of males   98

misanthrope: hater of mankind   98

misanthropy: hatred of mankind   98

misconception: erroneous belief   87

misogamy: hatred of marriage   98

misogyny: hatred of women   98

misology: hatred of argument or discussion   98

misoneism: hatred of anything new   98

missile: weapon propelled to hit a distant object   169

missive: letter 169
mocking: ridiculing 55
moderato: in moderate time 216
modest: humble; decent 63
modesty: humbleness 64
molt: shed feathers, skin, hair, etc. 49
momentous: very important 89
monarchy: state ruled over by a single person, as a king or queen 103, 118
monitor: one who admonishes 146
monochromatic: of one color 103
monocle: eyeglass for one eye 103
monogamy: marriage with but one mate at a time 103
monogram: two or more letters interwoven to represent a name 103
monograph: written account of a single thing or class of things 103
monolith: single stone of large size 103
monolog(ue): long speech by one person in a group 104
monomania: derangement of mind on one subject only 104
monomorphic: having a single form 103
monophobia: fear of being alone 97
monosyllabic: having but one syllable 103
monotheism: belief that there is but one God 103
monotonous: continuing in an unchanging tone; wearying 104
monument: a means of reminding us of a person or event; for example, a statue or tomb 146
morbid: having to do with disease; gruesome 51
moribund: near death 157
morose: ill-humoredly silent 41
morphology: branch of biology dealing with the form and structure of animals and plants 108, 122
mortal: destined to die; human; causing death 157
mortality: death rate; mortal nature 157
mortician: undertaker 157

mortification: embarrassment 39, 157
mortify: humiliate; embarrass 64
mortuary: morgue 157
mot juste: the exactly right word 195
mountebank: quack; boastful pretender 223
mournful: full of sorrow 40
musicale: social gathering, with music as the featured entertainment 203
mustang: bronco 235
musty: moldy or stale 66
myrmidon: obedient and unquestioning follower 181
mythology: account or study of myths 108

nadir: lowest point 64
naive: simple; unsophisticated 190
nautical: of the sea or shipping 78
necrology: register of persons who have died 108
nemesis: due punishment for evil deeds; one who inflicts such punishment 181
nepotism: favoritism to relatives by those in power 65
nettlesome: irritating 31
neurology: scientific study of the nervous system and its diseases 108
noblesse oblige: principle that person of high rank or birth are obliged to act nobly 194
noisome: offensive to the sense of smell; unwholesome 66
nonage: legal minority; period before maturity 74
nonagenarian: person in his 90's 74
noncarcinogenic: not cancer-producing 9
nonchalant: without concern or enthusiasm 190
nostalgia: homesickness; yearning for the past 40
nouveaux riches: persons newly rich 192
noxious: harmful 66
nugatory: worthless 89

obese: very fat   41, *158*

obligatory: required   *147*

oblivious: forgetful   32

obloquy: a speaking against; public reproach   170

obsequious: slavishly attentive   43

obsolescent: going out of use   74

obsolete: no longer in use   74

obverse: front of a coin, medal, etc. 168

Occident: West   17

octogenarian: person in his 80's   74

odoriferous: yielding an odor, usually fragrant   *66*, 171

odorous: having an odor, especially a sweet odor   *66*

odyssey: any long series of wanderings or travels   182

offal: waste parts of a butchered animal; refuse   79

olfactory: pertaining to the sense of smell   66

oligarchy: form of government in which a few people have the power   118

olio: mixture   233

omnibus: bus; book containing a variety of works by one author; covering many things at once   143

omnifarious: of all varieties, forms, or kinds   143

omnific: all-creating   143

omnipotent: unlimited in power   143

omnipresent: present everywhere at the same time   143

omniscient: knowing everything   143

omnivore: person or animal that eats everything   138

omnivorous: eating everything; fond of all kinds   138, 143

opera: play mostly sung, with costumes, scenery, action, and music   219

opinionated: unduly attached to one's own opinion   *86*

oratorio: musical composition, usually on a religious theme, for solo voices, chorus, and orchestra   220

ornate: elaborate   *206*

ornithology: study of birds   49

orthodox: generally accepted, especially in religion   87

ostentatious: done to impress others   91

osteopath: practitioner of osteopathy 121

osteopathy: treatment of diseases by manipulation of bones, muscles, nerves, etc.   *121*

oust: expel   *141*

overweening: thinking too highly of oneself   91

paean: song or hymn of praise, joy, or triumph   182

paleontology: science dealing with life in the remote past as recorded in fossils   108

palette: thin board on which an artist lays and mixes colors   203

palladium: safeguard or protection   182

paltry: practically worthless   89

pampas: vast, treeless, grassy plains, especially in Argentina   235

panic: unreasoning, sudden fright that grips a multitude   182

paradox: self-contradictory statement which may nevertheless be true   87

paradoxical: self-contradictory, yet possibly true   87

paramount: chief   90

parasite: animal, plant, or person living on others   49

parasol: umbrella for protection against the sun   207

par excellence: above all others of the same sort   207

parody: humorous imitation of a serious writing   55

parrot: repeat mechanically   49

parsimonious: stingy   9

partiality: special taste or liking 85

partisan: supporter; follower *191*

parvenu: person suddenly risen to wealth or power who lacks the proper social qualifications 192

paternal: fatherly; inherited from or related to the father's side 65

pathetic: arousing pity 40, 120

pathogenic: causing disease 121

pathological: due to disease 121

pathology: science dealing with the nature and causes of disease 109

pathos: quality in speech, writing, music, events, etc., that arouses a feeling of pity or sadness 40, 120

patina: film or incrustation, usually green, on the surface of old bronze or copper 221

patio: courtyard 232

patriarch: venerable old man; father and ruler of a family or tribe; founder 74–75

patriarchy: form of social organization in which the father rules the family or tribe, descent being traced through the father 118

patricide: act of killing (or killer of) one's own father 136

peccadillo: slight offense 233

pedal: lever acted on by the foot 164

pedestal: support or foot of a column or statue; foundation 164

pedestrian: foot traveler; commonplace 164

pedigree: an ancestral line *65*

penitent: feeling regret for wrongdoing 39

pensive: thoughtful in a sad way 40

peon: common laborer; worker kept in service to repay a debt 231

perfidious: false to a trust; faithless 149

perfidy: violation of a trust 149

pericardium: membranous sac enclosing the heart 122

perigee: nearest point to the earth in the orbit of a man-made satellite or heavenly body 119, 122

perihelion: nearest point to the sun in the orbit of a planet or comet 122

perimeter: the whole outer boundary or measurement of a surface or figure 122

periphery: outside boundary 122

periphrastic: expressed in a roundabout way 123

periscope: instrument permitting those in a submarine a view of the surface 123

peristalsis: wavelike contraction of the intestines which propels contents onward 123

peristyle: row of columns around a building or court; the space so enclosed 123

peritoneum: membrane lining the abdominal cavity and covering the organs 123

peritonitis: inflammation of the peritoneum 123

persistence: perseverance *145*

pert: saucy 91

pertinacious: adhering firmly to a purpose or opinion 145

pertinent: bearing on the matter in hand *90*, 145

peruse: read 17

perverse: turned away from what is right or good 168

pervert: turn away from right or truth; person who has turned from what is normal or natural *135*, 168

pesticide: substance that kills rats, insects, bacteria, etc. 136

pestiferous: infected with or bearing disease; evil 171

pestilential: morally harmful; pertaining to a pestilence 51

petrology: scientific study of rocks 109

petty: trifling *89*

philanthropist: lover of mankind 97

philanthropy: love of mankind 97

philately: collection and study of stamps 97

philharmonic: pertaining to a musical organization 97

philhellenism: support of Greece or the Greeks 97

philippic: bitter denunciation 182

philogyny: love of women 97

philology: study of language 98

philosopher: lover of wisdom 98

phlebotomy: opening of a vein for the purpose of diminishing the supply of blood 111

phobia: fear; dislike 97

photophobia: morbid aversion to light 97

physiology: science dealing with the functions of living things or their organs 109

pianissimo: very soft 217

piano: soft 217

piazza: open square in an Italian town; veranda or porch 224

picador: horseman who irritates the bull with a lance at the beginning of a bullfight 231

picaro: rogue; vagabond 231

piddling: trifling *89*

pièce de résistance: main dish; main item of any collection, series, program, etc. 205

pimento: thick-fleshed pepper used for stuffing olives and as a source of paprika 232

pince-nez: eyeglasses clipped to the nose by a spring 208

pinnacle: highest point *61*

pizza: large, flat pie of bread dough spread with tomato pulp, etc. 223

pizzicato: direction to players of bowed instruments to pluck the strings instead of using the bow 218

plaudit: applause; enthusiastic praise 53

plausible: apparently trustworthy 87

pliable: easily bent or molded; capable of adaptation *144*

plight: unfortunate state 40

plumb: get to the bottom of; ascertain the depth of 64

plutocratic: having great influence because of one's wealth 182

podiatrist: chiropodist 112

podium: dais; low wall serving as a foundation 112

poignant: painfully touching 41

politico: politician 223

pollute: make unclean 78

polyarchy: rule by many 103

polychromatic: showing a variety of colors 103

polygamy: marriage to several mates at the same time 103

polyglot: speaking several languages 104

polygon: closed plane figure having many angles, and hence many sides 104

polymorphic: having various forms 103

polyphonic: having many sounds or voices 104

polysyllabic: having more than three syllables 103

polytechnic: dealing with many arts or sciences 104

polytheism: belief that there is a plurality of gods 103

poncho: large cloth, often waterproof, with a slit for the head 233

ponder: weigh in the mind 85

portfolio: briefcase; position or duties of a cabinet member or minister of state 225

portico: roof supported by columns, forming a porch or a covered walk 221

portly: imposing, especially because of size *41*

posthumous: published after the author's death; occurring after death 75

potpourri: mixture *197*

precipice: cliff 61

precipitous: steep as a precipice; over-hasty 62

précis: brief summary 195

precursor: forerunner 161

predecessor: one who precedes another *161*

predicament: unfortunate state 40, 86

predilection: inclination to like or choose something 85

preeminent: standing out above others 62

prehensile: adapted for seizing 166

prejudice: unreasonable preference or objection 85

premiere: first performance 208

premonition: forewarning 146

premonitory: conveying a forewarning 146

preposterous: senseless 87

prestissimo: at a very rapid pace 216

presto: quick 216

presumptuous: taking undue liberties *91*

pretentious: done to impress others *91*

prim: formal and precise in manner or appearance *90*

prima donna: principal female singer, as in an opera; highstrung, vain, or extremely sensitive person 222

primeval: pertaining to the world's first ages 75

primitive: characteristic of the original state of the world or of man 75

primordial: existing at the very beginning; first in order 75

pristine: in original state; uncorrupted 75

probe: investigation 25

procrustean: cruel or inflexible in enforcing conformity 182

prodigious: enormous 32

profound: very deep 64

progenitor: forefather 65

progeny: children; descendants 65

progressive: going forward to something better 162

projectile: object designed to be shot forward; anything thrown forward 167

propinquity: kinship; nearness of place 80

prosecute: follow to the end or until finished; conduct legal proceedings against 160

protean: exceedingly variable; readily assuming different forms or shapes 183

protégé(e): person under the care and protection of another 192

prow: forward part of a ship 77

proximity: nearness *80*

pseudopod: temporary extension of the protoplasm, as in the ameba, to enable the organism to move and take in food 112

psychology: science of the mind 109

psychopathic: pertaining to mental disease; insane 121

puberty: physical beginning of manhood or womanhood 75

pudgy: short and fat 41

pueblo: Indian village built of adobe and stone 233

puerile: foolish for a grown-up to say or do; childish 75

pungent: sharp in smell or taste; biting 66

purge: cleanse; rid of undesired element or person 79

putrefy: rot *50*

putrid: stinking from decay; extremely bad 67

Pyrrhic: gained at too great a cost 183

qualm: misgiving *39*
queue: line of persons waiting their turn 208

raconteur: person who excels in telling stories, anecdotes, etc. 192
raillery: pleasantry touched with ridicule *54*
raison d'être: reason or justification for existing 208
rancid: unpleasant to smell or taste from being spoiled or stale 67
rank: having a strong, bad odor or taste; extreme 67
rankle: cause inflammation *50*
rapport: relationship characterized by harmony, conformity, or affinity 194
rapprochement: establishment or state of cordial relations; a coming together 201
rapture: state of overwhelming joy *38*
rash: overhasty *62*
rational: able to think clearly; based on reason 87
rationalize: devise excuses for one's actions, desires, failures, etc. 87
ravine: deep, narrow gorge worn by running water 64
raze: demolish 9
rebuff: snub; insult *25*
recuperate: recover health after illness *50*
recur: happen again 161
reek: emit a strong, disagreeable smell; be permeated with 67
reflect: throw back light, heat, sound, etc.; think *88*, 144
reflex: involuntary response to a stimulus 144
refract: bend a ray of light, heat, sound, etc., from a straight course 142
refractory: hard to manage 142
regicide: act of killing (or killer of) a king 136

régime: system of government or rule 201
regimen: set of rules to improve health 51
regressive: disposed to move backward 162
reimburse: indemnify *17*
reinvigorate: give new vigor to *32*
reject: refuse to take 167
rejuvenate: make young again *32*
relevant: bearing upon the matter in hand 90
reluctant: disinclined *60*
remand: send back; recommit 147
remiss: negligent 169
remit: send money due; forgive 169
remorse: regret for wrongdoing *39*
render: deliver; give 25
rendezvous: meeting place; appointment to meet at a fixed time and place 208
renegade: deserter from a religion, party, etc.; traitor 231
repartee: skill of replying quickly, cleverly, and humorously; witty reply 195, *196*
repast: meal 25
repentant: showing regret for wrongdoing *39*
repertoire: list of plays, operas, roles, compositions, etc., that a company or performer is prepared to perform 203
replenish: refill 25
reprehensible: blamable 166
reproof: rebuke *146*
reprove: disapprove or criticize *146*
repugnance: strong dislike *60*
repulsive: offensive *43*
residue: remainder 32
restrict: keep within limits 137
résumé: summary 196
retentive: able to retain or remember 145
reticent: inclined to be silent 10

retinue: group of followers accompanying a distinguished person 145

retire: withdraw from active duty; go to bed 10

retort: reply quickly or sharply in kind; quick, sharp reply 10, 140

retrograde: going backward; becoming worse 163

retrogression: act of going from a better to a worse state 163

retrogressive: disposed to move backward 162

revert: go back 168

revive: bring back to life 139

rift: crack or opening 63

riposte: quick retort or repartee; in fencing, quick return thrust after a parry 196

rogue: tricky, deceitful fellow 231

rotund: rounded-out; full-toned 89

rotunda: round building, especially one with a dome or cupola; large round room 221

rout: state of confusion 197

rueful: pitiable 40

rupture: break; hostility 135

Russophobe: one who dislikes Russia or the Russians 97

salubrious: healthful 51

salutary: beneficial 32

salvo: simultaneous discharge of shots; burst of cheers 225

sangfroid: coolness of mind or composure in difficult circumstances 194

sarcasm: sneering language intended to hurt a person's feelings 55

sardonic: bitterly sarcastic 55

satire: language or writing that exposes follies or abuses by holding them up to ridicule 55

saturnine: gloomy 183

savoir faire: knowledge of just what to do 194

scavenger: animal or person removing refuse, decay, etc. 49

scent: smell; get a suspicion of 67

scent: perfume 67

scherzo: light or playful part of a sonata or symphony 220

score: twenty 25

scrutinize: examine very closely 32

scuffle: fight 17

sebaceous: secreting fatty matter 51

sedate: of settled, quiet disposition 90

seduction: act of leading astray into wrongdoing 159

senile: showing the weakness of age 75

señor: gentleman; Mr. or Sir 230

señora: lady; Mrs. or Madam 230

señorita: young lady; Miss 230

septuagenarian: person in his 70's 74

sequel: something that follows 160

sequence: the following of one thing after another 160

serpentine: winding in and out 89

servile: befitting a slave or servant 64

sforzando: accented 217

sibling: one of two or more children of a family 65

sierra: ridge of mountains with an irregular (saw-toothed) outline 235

siesta: short rest, especially at midday 233

silhouette: outline; shadow 208

simpatico: likable; congenial 223

sinuous: bending in and out 89

siren: dangerous, attractive woman; woman who sings sweetly; apparatus for sounding loud warnings 183

slander: false and defamatory spoken statement 53

slanderous: falsely and maliciously accusing 53

slatternly: untidy 79

sloven: person habitually untidy, dirty, or careless in dress, habits, etc. 79

snub: insult; rebuff 25

sober: not drunk; free from excitement or exaggeration   77

sobriquet: nickname   208

sociology: study of the evolution development, and functioning of human society   109

solo: piece of music for one voice or instrument; anything done without a partner   220

solon: legislator; wise man   183

somniferous: inducing sleep   171

sonata: piece of music (for one or two instruments) having three or four movements in contrasted rhythms but related tonality   220

sophistry: clever but deceptive reasoning   88

soprano: highest singing voice in women and boys   215

sordid: filthy   79

sororicide: act of killing (or killer of) one's own sister   136

sot: drunkard   77

sotto voce: in an undertone; privately   225

souvenir: keepsake   208

specious: apparently reasonable, but not really so   88

speculate: reflect; buy or sell with the hope of profiting by price fluctuations   88

spurn: reject   17

squalid: filthy from neglect   79

staccato: disconnected; with breaks between successive notes   218

staid: of settled, quiet disposition   90

starboard: right-hand side of a ship when one faces forward   78

stentorian: very loud   183

stigma: mark of disgrace   53

stigmatize: brand with a mark of disgrace   54

stipend: salary   17

stricture: adverse criticism   137

stringent: strict   137

stucco: plaster for covering exterior walls of buildings   222

Stygian: dark; gloomy; infernal   184

sublimate: redirect the energy of a person's bad impulses into socially and morally higher channels; purify   62

sublime: uplifting   62

subservient: useful in an inferior capacity; servile   *64*

subvert: undermine   10

succession: the following of one thing after another   *160*

successive: following in order   *160*

suicide: act of killing one's self   136

sullen: ill-humoredly silent   41

sully: soil   79

summit: highest point   *61*

sumptuous: luxurious   *180*

superannuated: retired on a pension; too old for work   76

supersede: force out of use; displace   32

supersensitive: excessively sensitive   *115*

supplant: replace; supersede   *32*

supposition: a guess   *115*

supreme: above all others   *90*

surveillance: close watch   17

survive: remain alive after   139

suture: stitch   25

svelte: slender   42

sweltering: oppessively hot   32

sycophant: parasitic flatterer   43

symbiosis: the living together in mutually helpful association of two dissimilar organisms   110

symmetrical: balanced in arrangement   89

sympathy: a sharing of ("feeling with") another's trouble   120

table d'hôte: describing a complete meal that bears a fixed price   205

tact: sensitive mental perception of what is appropriate on a given occasion   165, *194*

tactful: having or showing tact   165

tactile: pertaining to the sense of touch; able to be touched   165

tangent: touching; line or surface meeting a curved line or surface at one point, but not intersecting it   165

tangential: merely touching   165

tantalize: excite a hope but prevent its fulfillment; tease   184

tarnish: soil or dull   79

technology: industrial science   109

tedium: boredom   193

teetotaler: person who totally abstains from intoxicating beverages   77

telepathy: transference of the thoughts and feelings of one person to another with no apparent communication   120

temerity: insolence; effrontery   31

tempera: method of painting in which the colors are mixed with white of egg or other substances, instead of oil   222

temperate: moderate in eating and drinking   76

tenable: capable of being maintained or defended   88

tenacious: inclined to hold fast   145

tenacity: quality of holding fast   145

tenancy: period of a tenant's temporary holding of real estate   145

tenet: principle or doctrine generally held to be true   145

tenor: adult male voice between baritone and alto   215

tenure: period for which an office or position is held   145–146

tepid: lukewarm   17

terpsichorean: pertaining to dancing   184

terra cotta: kind of hard, brownish-red earthenware, used for vases, statuettes, etc.; dull brownish-red   222

terse: free of unnecessary words   180

tête-à-tête: private conversation between two persons   196

theology: study of religion and religious ideas   109

theory: a supposition supported by considerable evidence   86, 115

therapeutic: curative   51

thespian: pertaining to the drama or acting   184

throes: pangs   41

titanic: of enormous strength, size, or power   184

tonsillectomy: surgical removal of the tonsils   111

toreador: bullfighter, usually mounted   231

torero: bullfighter on foot   231

torrid: sweltering   32

torsion: act of twisting; twisting of a body by two equal and opposite forces   140

torso: trunk or body of a statue without a head, arms, or legs; human trunk   222

tortilla: thin, flat, round corn cake   233

tortuous: full of twists or curves; tricky   140

torture: inflict severe pain upon   141

toupee: wig   206

tour de force: feat of strength or skill   208

toxic: poisonous   51

tracheotomy: surgical operation of cutting into the windpipe   111

tractable: capable of being controlled   10, 144

traduce: expose to contempt or shame by a false report   53, 159

tranquillity: harmony   9

transgress: step beyond the limits; break a law   163

transitory: fleeting; ephemeral   24

travesty: imitation that makes a serious thing seem ridiculous   55

treatise: written account   195

tremolo: rapid repetition of a tone or chord without apparent breaks, to express emotion 218

tribulation: suffering 41

tribute: speech or writing of high praise 52

trio: piece of music for three voices or instruments; three singers or players performing together 220

tripod: utensil, stool, or caldron having three legs 112

truckle: submit servilely to a superior 43

turncoat: apostate *231*

tyrannicide: act of killing (or killer of) a tyrant 136

unfledged: without feathers; immature 72

unflustered: calm 32

unguent: ointment 52

unintentionally: unwittingly *25*

unipod: one-legged support 112

unmanageable: unwieldy *33*

unrestricted: not confined within bounds; open to all 137

unruffled: not agitated 32

unsavory: unpleasant to taste or smell; morally offensive 67

untenable: incapable of being held or defended 146

unwieldy: bulky *33*

unwittingly: inadvertently; by accident 25

vagabond: one who wanders from place to place, having no fixed dwelling *231*

vain: conceited; worthless 91

vainglorious: excessively proud or boastful 91

valet: manservant who attends to the personal needs of his employer 192

vanquish: conquer 141

vaquero: cowboy 231

velocipede: child's tricycle 164

vendetta: feud for blood revenge 224

venerable: worthy of respect because of advanced age, religious association, or historical importance 76

versatile: having many aptitudes 168

verse: line of poetry 168

vertigo: dizziness 168

veteran: person experienced in some occupation; ex-member of the armed forces 76

viaduct: bridge for conducting a road or railroad over a valley, river, etc. 159

vibrato: slightly throbbing or pulsating effect, adding warmth and beauty to the tone 218

victor: winner 141

vignette: a literary sketch; short verbal description 203

vile: unclean; hateful *79*

vilify: speak evil of *53, 159*

virtuoso: one who exhibits great technical skill in an art, especially in playing a musical instrument 223

virulent: extremely poisonous; very bitter 52

virus: disease-causing organism; corruptive force 52

vis-à-vis: face to face; in comparison with; in relation to 209

vivace: spirited 216

vivacious: lively in temper or conduct 139, *181*

vivid: full of life; sharp and clear 139

vivisection: operation on a living animal for scientific investigation 139

vociferous: producing a loud outcry 171

vogue: fashion 206

void: invalid *9*

volition: will 60

voracious: greedy in eating; incapable of being satisfied 139

wager: bet 17

wane: decrease gradually in size 17

wheedle: persuade by pleasing words
42
withdraw: take back; draw back   33
wrangle: haggle; bargain   *24*
wrench: twist violently   *141*
wretched: sunk to a low condition   *63*
writ of mandamus: written order from a
court to enforce the performance of
some public duty   147

xenophobia: aversion to foreigners   97
xenophobic: distrustful of foreigners   97

yore: long ago   76

zany: mildly insane   33
zenith: highest point; point in the heavens
directly overhead   62

Pronunciation Symbols

ə   banana, collide, abut

ˈə, ˌə   humdrum abut

ᵊ   immediately preceding \l\, \n\, \m\, \ŋ\, as in battle, mitten, eaten, and sometimes cap and bells \-ᵊm-\, lock and key \-ᵊŋ-\; immediately following \l\, \m\, \r\, as often in French table, prisme, titre

ər   operation, further, urger

ˈər-
ˈə-r   as in two different pronunciations of hurry \ˈhər-ē, ˈhə-rē\

a   mat, map, mad, gag, snap, patch

ā   day, fade, date, aorta, drape, cape

ä   bother, cot, and, with most American speakers, father, cart

à   father as pronounced by speakers who do not rhyme it with bother

au̇   now, loud, out

b   baby, rib

ch   chin, nature \ˈnā-chər\ (actually, this sound is \t\ + \sh\)

d   did, adder

e   bet, bed, peck

ˈē, ˌē   beat, nosebleed, evenly, easy

ē   easy, mealy

f   fifty, cuff

g   go, big, gift

h   hat, ahead

hw	**wh**ale as pronounced by those who do not have the same pronunciation for both *whale* and *wail*
i	t**i**p, ban**i**sh, act**i**ve
ī	s**i**te, s**i**de, b**uy**, tr**i**pe (actually, this sound is \ä\ + \i\, or \à\ + \i\)
j	**j**ob, **g**em, e**dge**, **j**oin, **j**u**dge** (actually, this sound is \d\ + \zh\)
k	**k**in, **c**oo**k**, a**che**
k̲	German i**ch**, Bu**ch**
l	**l**i**l**y, poo**l**
m	**m**ur**m**ur, di**m**, ny**m**ph
n	**n**o, ow**n**
ⁿ	indicates that a preceding vowel or diphthong is pronounced with the nasal passages open, as in French *un bon vin blanc* \œⁿ-bōⁿ-vaⁿ-bläⁿ\
ŋ	si**ng** \'si**ŋ**\, si**ng**er \'si**ŋ**-ər\, fi**ng**er \'fi**ŋ**-gər\, i**nk** \'i**ŋ**k\
ō	b**o**ne, kn**ow**, b**eau**
ȯ	s**aw**, **a**ll, gn**aw**
œ	French b**oeu**f, German H**ö**lle
œ̄	French f**eu**, German H**öh**le
ȯi	c**oi**n, destr**oy**, s**awi**ng
p	**p**e**pp**er, li**p**
r	**r**ed, ca**r**, **r**a**r**ity
s	**s**our**c**e, le**ss**
sh	with nothing between, as in **sh**y, mi**ss**ion, ma**ch**ine, spe**ci**al (actually, this is a single sound, not two); with a hyphen between, two sounds as in death's-head \'deths-ˌhed\
t	**t**ie, a**tt**ack
th	with nothing between, as in **th**in, e**th**er (actually, this is a single sound, not two); with a hyphen between, two sounds as in knight**h**ood \'nīt-ˌhu̇d\

Pronunciation Symbols 287

th **th**en, ei**th**er, **th**is (actually, this is a single sound, not two)

ü r**u**le, y**ou**th, union \'yün-yən\, few \'fyü\

u̇ p**u**ll, w**oo**d, b**oo**k, curable \'kyu̇r-ə-bəl\

ue German f**ü**llen, h**ü**bsch

u̅e̅ French r**ue**, German f**üh**len

v **v**i**v**id, gi**v**e

w **w**e, a**w**ay; in some words having final \(ˌ)ō\ a variant \ə-w\ oc-
curs before vowels, as in \'fäl-ə-wiŋ\, covered by the variant
\ə(-w)\ at the entry word

y **y**ard, **y**oung, cue \'kyü\, union \'yün-yən\

ʸ indicates that during the articulation of the sound represented by
the preceding character the front of the tongue has substantially
the position it has for the articulation of the first sound of *yard*,
as in French *digne* \dēnʸ\

yü **y**outh, **u**nion, **c**ue, **f**ew, m**u**te

yu̇ c**u**rable, f**u**ry

z **z**one, rai**s**e

zh with nothing between, as in vi**s**ion, a**z**ure \'azh-ər\ (actually, this
is a single sound, not two); with a hyphen between, two sounds
as in ga**zeh**ound \'gāz-ˌhau̇nd\

\ slant line used in pairs to mark the beginning and end of a tran-
scription: \'pen\

' mark preceding a syllable with primary (strongest) stress: \'pen-
mən-ˌship\

ˌ mark preceding a syllable with secondary (next-strongest) stress:
\'pen-mən-ˌship\

- mark of syllable division

( ) indicate that what is symbolized between is present in some utter-
ances but not in others: *factory* \'fak-t(ə-)rē\